EXAMINING
RELIGIONS

Contemporary Moral Issues

Joe Jenkins

HEINEMANN
EDUCATIONAL

Heinemann Educational
a division of Heinemann Educational Books Ltd
Halley Court, Jordan Hill, Oxford OX2 8EJ

OXFORD   LONDON   EDINBURGH
MADRID   ATHENS   BOLOGNA   PARIS
MELBOURNE   SYDNEY   AUCKLAND   SINGAPORE
TOKYO   IBADAN   NAIROBI   HARARE   GABORONE
PORTSMOUTH NH (USA)

First published 1987
91 92 93 94 95   18 17 16 15 14 13 12 11 10 9

British Library Cataloguing in Publication Data

Jenkins, Joe
GCSE religious studies: contemporary moral issues.
1.   Social ethics
I.   Title
170   HM216
ISBN 0 435 30001 6

The Publishers would like to thank the following for permission to reproduce photographs: Mike Abrahams/Age Concern p.89; Mike Abrahams/Network p.83 (top); Amnesty International p.131 (top right); Barnaby's Picture Library pp.46, 60, 62, 186 (top right); Bob Naylor Photography p.167 (bottom right); Bridgeman Art Library p.152; BUAV Cruelty to Animals p.142; Camera Press pp.10 (left), 38, 74, 105 (both), 106, 131 (bottom left), 151, 158, 178, 179, 121; Anita Corbin/Format p.93; Patrick Durand/Sipa Press p.136; Frank Spooner Pictures pp.70 (left), 140, 160, 185; Glasgow Museums and Art Galleries p.110; Mike Goldwater/Network p.131 (top left); Sally and Richard Greenhill pp.58, 131 (bottom right); Kaveh Golestan/Network p.156; Greenpeace pp.82 (top left), 186 (top left); George Hallett p.102; Jeremy Hartley/Oxfam p.186 (middle); Dave Hartman/Afrapix p.146; Harvard College Observatory/Science Photo Library p.6; Frank Herrmann/Sunday Times p.182; H. Kanus/Barnaby's Picture Library p.148; Bedri Kayabal/Camera Press p.7; The Mansell Collection p.63; Mary Evans Picture Library p.26 (left); Martin Mayer/Network pp.40, 54; Joanne O'Brien/Format Photographers Ltd. p.26 (right); Judah Passow/Network p.150; Popperfoto pp.10, 167 (middle and top right); Brenda Price/Format Photographers Ltd. p.49; Rex Features Ltd. pp.70 (right), 131 (middle), 138, 168, 182 (bottom), 186 (bottom right); SCM Press Ltd. p.164; Daniel Simon/Gamma p.83 (bottom); Laurie Sparham/Network pp.118, 169; John Sturrock/Network pp.25 (both), 66, 72, 112; Syndication International Ltd. pp.78, 80, 99; Tate Gallery p 35; Topham Picture Library pp.68, 165, 167 (bottom left), 186 (bottom left); United Nations pp.126, 128; Virago p.84; Val Wilmer/Format Photographers Ltd. pp.44, 92.

The author would like to thank the following people for their help: Nina Bateman, James Hemming, Daniel Leech, Professor Matthew Lipman, John King, John White and Denise O'Hagan.

Cover photographs by: Katalin Arkell/Network (front, top right); Camera Press (front, bottom right); Raissa Page/Format (front, left).

The Publishers would also like to thank the following for their kind permission to reproduce copyright material: Age Concern for the profile of Irene Dyer on p.89; Amnesty International for the cartoon on p.133 and for the logo and 'Letter from a prisoner' on p.134; Animal Aid for the report on p.141 and for the poem 'Just Like Us' on p.142; Band Aid for Bob Geldof's introduction to the Live Aid programme on p.183; BBC for the extract from File on 4 on p.67; British Humanist Association, 13 Prince of Wales Terrace, London W8 5PG (Tel. 01-937 2341) for the extracts from the Humanist Dipper on pp.6, 12, 13, 34, 35, 45, 47, 61, 93 and 97; for the quiz adapted from

the Humanist Dipper on p.15; for the extracts on pp.69, 112 and 113; for the extracts from the Humanist Manifesto 1973 on pp.73 and 159; for the extracts from The British Association General Statement of Policy on pp.102, 117 and 139; and for the article from The Humanist Sept/Oct 1973 on pp.126 and 127. (The British Humanist Association welcomes any enquiries and would be pleased to provide information and teaching material on Humanism to anyone interested); Ras Sam Brown/Leonard E. Barrett for the extract from The Rastafarians on p.59; Campaign Against Arms Trade (CAAT) for the extracts on pp.172 and 173; Catholic Truth Society, 38-40 Eccleston Square, London, SW1V 1PD (Tel. 01-834 4392) for the extracts on pp.36, 45, 72, 80, 81, 93, 100, 115, 118, 130 and 163; Christian Aid for the logo and leaflet on p.184 and for the description of Tondo on p.185; CIO Publishing for the extracts from the Church of England reports on pp.91, 93, 101, 111, 118 and 122; Collins Publishers Ltd. for the article 'Hope and Suffering' by Desmond Tutu on p.147; Health Education Authority for the leaflet on pp.40-41; Daily Express for the article on p.105; Daily Mirror/Syndication Department for the articles on pp.25, 59, 69 and 115; Eyre & Spottiswoode Ltd. for the extracts from The Church of England's Prayer Book on p.61; European Nuclear Disarmament (END) for the logo on p.155; The General Synod of the Church of England Board for Social Responsibility for the extracts on pp.53, 88, 124 and 130; The Green Party for the pamphlet 'Protest and Survive' on pp.160 and 161; Greenpeace for the 'Paradise Lost' article on p.189; Robert Hale Ltd. for the quotations on pp.24 taken from Modern Catholic Dictionary by John Hardon (1980); Help the Aged for the advertisement on p.87; The Controller of Her Majesty's Stationery Office for the DHSS drug leaflet on p.59, for the profile of the Committee of Inquiry on p.100, and for the Home Office statistics on p.104; London Express News and Feature Services for the article on p.105; Longman Group Ltd. for the quotes on pp.82, 120 and 152 from Longman Dictionary of Contemporary English by Della Summers (1978); Lynx for the extract on p.142; Mail Newspapers Plc for the articles on pp.113 and 147; Methodist Board for Social Responsibility for the extracts on pp.24, 43, 45, 47, 51, 55, 58, 95, 97, 120 and 125; Morning Star for the article on p.55; T. Nelson and Sons Ltd. for the quotes from Individual Morality by James Hemming (1969) and for the poem 'Definition' by L. Collinson on p.152; New Internationalist for the extracts on pp.149 and 172; Newsweek International for the extract on p.98; 19 magazine for the two extracts on p.114; Observer Ltd. for the articles on pp.113, 139 and 181; Oxfam for the adaptation from the leaflet Seven Myths about World Hunger on pp.170 and 171; Pan Books Ltd. for the extract North-South: A Programme for Survival (1980) from the report of the Independent Commission on International Development Issues on p.174; Pax Christi for the logo on p.155; Pelican Books Ltd. for the extract on p.177; Penguin Books Ltd. for the extract from Camilo Torres, Revolutionary Priest edited by John Geriffi (1973) on p.149; Quaker Home Service for the extracts on pp.24 and 45; The Rationalist Press Association for the material based on the New Humanist on p.84 and for the extract and poem from Dora Russell's book The Right to be Happy Routledge (1927) on p.85; Sheba Feminist Publishers Ltd. for the extract from Girls are Powerful edited by Susan Hemmings (1982); Sidgwick and Jackson Ltd. for the extract from Is That It? by Bob Geldof on p.182; The Times for items 1-3 on p.10 and for the article on p.65; United Nations for the reports on pp.128, 129, 130, 138, 168, 169; United Press International for the cartoon on p.33; Ed. Victor Ltd. for the extracts from Fragments of Isabella by Isabella Leitner, New English Library (1978) on pp. 78-9; Voluntary Euthanasia Society (EXIT) for the extracts on pp.96 and 97; Warner Bros Music Ltd. for Bob Dylan's song 'With God on our Side' on p.157; World Disarmament Campaign UK for the logo on p.155; Yorkshire Evening Post for the newspaper headlines on p.139.

The Publishers have made every effort to trace copyright holders. However, if any material has been incorrectly acknowledged we would be pleased to correct this at the earliest opportunity.

Design, typesetting and artwork by FD Graphics, Fleet, Hampshire
Illustrations by Gecko Ltd, Bicester, Oxon
Printed and bound in Great Britain
by Butler & Tanner Ltd, Frome and London

CONTENTS

1 INTRODUCTION

We all have different views about what is right and what is wrong. People often disagree with each other about what is right and what is wrong. People have different beliefs and views. Often a person's own particular beliefs will affect his or her view of what is right and what is wrong.

This book aims to do **four** things:

1 to give you some relevant **facts** about some of the important issues and problems facing human beings today,
2 to help you to **understand** these issues and problems,
3 to help you to understand that people have **different views** on these issues and problems and to explain what these views are,
4 to enable you to begin to understand, develop and express **your own views** on these issues and problems.

It can all be rather confusing. How can we ever know that other people's views are the right ones? How can we ever know whether our own views and opinions are the right ones?

One of the best ways of beginning to understand other people's views and our own views on something is to look at the **reasons** they or we give for believing in something.

OFFERING REASONS

We can hold any view we want about something without offering reasons for that view. However, if we refuse to give reasons for our beliefs and views, people are not going to listen to us. Likewise, if somebody else fails to give reasons for their beliefs we are not really likely to take that much notice of them.

To give reasons for our beliefs and opinions is the **key** to greater understanding of ourselves, of others and of the problem or issue under discussion.

It is important to be able to provide and offer reasons for our opinions if we want others to consider them. It is important to be able to offer reasons if we are to persuade ourselves that we hold opinions worth having.

If others are unable to understand why we hold the views we do, they may not listen to us. If we do not understand why **we** hold certain opinions, we are likely to feel rather unsure about **our** opinions.

So we need

a to offer good reasons for our beliefs and opinions,
b to decide whether others are offering good reasons for their beliefs and opinions.

So what are good reasons?
  Generally, good reasons

1 should whenever possible be based on facts,
2 should be relevant,
3 should provide understanding and explain an opinion,
4 should be believable to the listener.

EXERCISE I

When is a reason a good reason?

Look at each of the statements below. For each one decide whether it is
a a good reason,
b a reason but not a good one,
c not a reason.

1 'Gary's homework is written in blue ink. He must have copied mine 'cos I use blue ink.'

2 'I suspect Gary didn't copy my homework. He told me so.'

3 'I suspect Gary didn't copy my homework 'cos his is different from mine.'

4 'Gary must have copied my homework, he can't do the subject anyway.'

5 'I believe in pixies . . . I once saw a photograph of one.'

6 'I believe in pixies . . . when I was young my gran told me they existed.'

7 'I believe in pixies.'

It is important that during your GCSE Religious Studies course you learn how to form your own opinions on the issues and problems of today. You will get more out of the course if you are able to argue your point of view using good reasons. You will begin to understand other people's points of view if you can look closely and carefully at their reaons.

You must also beware of 'jumping to conclusions', and be alert to other people jumping to conclusions. People jump to conclusions when they fail to use reasons to arrive at a conclusion or an opinion.

EXERCISE II

Jumping to conclusions

Here are some examples of reasoning. Decide whether you would classify them as
a good reasoning,
b not so good but possibly all right,
c seems good but possibly unsound,
d poor reasoning.

Explain your choice for each situation below.

1 'My father's been reading in the paper that smoking causes cancer, so he says he's going to give up reading.'

2 'I've been reading that one child out of every five that's born in the world is Chinese. I have three brothers and so I think the next baby in our family will probably look pretty Oriental.'

3 'Whenever I see Jason I ask him what he thinks of Sharon, and he gets really embarrassed. Cor, he hasn't half got a crush on me.'

4 'I once met a French boy who was a brilliant dancer. I'll bet all those Frenchmen are brilliant dancers.'

> ! Whenever you see this symbol in this book think about **good reasons**. It will mean either that you must examine the reasons given or that you must examine your own reasons.

NOTE

The views recorded in this book are not all of the same authority. Official statements, declarations and resolutions of the governing bodies of the Churches have more authority than 'reports' – which may or may not have been accepted by the bodies to which they were presented.

Planet Earth lies in the galaxy called the Milky Way. It is estimated that there are 100 billion galaxies each containing some 10 billion trillion stars and planets (10,000,000,000,000,000,000,000).

'We had the sky up there all speckled with stars and we used to lay on our backs and look up at them and discuss whether they was made or only just happened.'

(Huckleberry Finn)

The Milky Way

The question whether everything was made or 'just happened' is a very important one. Some people believe that the universe exists as it does because of pure accident, others believe that it was made by God. The way we answer the question 'How did we get here?' will affect the way we answer the question 'Why are we here?'

The Bible states that 'In the beginning God created the heavens and the earth' *(Genesis 1: 1)*. It also states that God 'made man in his own image' *(Genesis 1: 27)*. This means that human beings have a special place in creation and have a responsibility to God and to the world.

Some people believe that God does not exist (atheists) and that we are here by pure accident.

'I think the universe is all spots and jumps without unity, without continuity, without coherence or orderliness.'

(Bertrand Russell, philosopher)

However, many people who do not believe in God still think that life has a meaning and purpose. In reply to the question 'What is the purpose of life?' a Humanist would answer:

'We choose our own purposes in life; we choose our own activities. For some people creating a happy family life may be more important than anything else. For others it may be music, playing football, or racing pigeons, sewing or knitting, or swimming or climbing. Humanists hope for fairer societies throughout the world so that more people may choose satisfying ways of life. At present, political oppression and the lack of the basic necessities mean that many people in the world have little freedom of choice.'

(Humanist Dipper)

A famous Humanist called Lord Willis said:

'This life is the only one of which we have any knowledge and it is our job to improve it.'

Some people have a very pessimistic view of life. Thomas Wolfe said:

'Man is born to live, to suffer, to die and what befalls him is a tragic lot.'

Human beings have a lot in common with other forms of life on Earth, especially animals. Sometimes humans are called animals – for instance, here are six statements about human animals.

Human beings are:

- social animals
- thinking animals
- creative animals
- moral animals
- responsible animals
- spiritual animals.

FOR DISCUSSION

▶ Do you think that we 'was made' or 'just happened'?

▶ 'Despite similarities, human beings are generally different from other animals.'

▶ Discuss these three statements:

1 'Man now realizes that he is an accident, that he is a completely futile being.'

! 2 'Even the hairs on your head are all numbered.'

(Jesus)

3 'Man is on his own and this life is all.'

(Harold Blackman, Humanist)

IN GROUPS

Look at these **key questions**, discuss them in groups of three to four, write some notes on your ideas and report back to the class.

▶ How can life be important in such an enormous universe?

▶ Are we merely 'born to die'?

▶ Are we no more than just mixtures of chemicals and gases?

FOR YOUR FOLDERS

▶ Put the following in order of size: galaxy, planet, solar system, Moon, universe, cosmos.

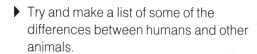

▶ Try and make a list of some of the differences between humans and other animals.

! ▶ Write a paragraph on 'The reason I am here.'

Human suffering: victims of an earthquake in Turkey

3 IS THERE A GOD?

> *'May the force be with you.'*
>
> (Star Wars)

> *'My God, my God, why hast thou forsaken me?'*
>
> (Jesus)

> *'In the beginning God made Heaven and Earth.'*
>
> (Genesis 1)

> *'When you see something big, something infinite, then you are seeing God.'*
>
> (Vincent Van Gogh)

> *'Father of day, Father of night, Father of black and Father of white. Father who moveth the rivers and streams.'*
>
> (Bob Dylan)

> *'God is dead.'*
>
> (Nietzsche)

> *'When I see the glories of the cosmos I can't help but believe that there is a Divine Hand behind it all.'*
>
> (Albert Einstein)

> *'If God did not exist, it would be necessary to invent him.'*
>
> (Voltaire)

Most world religions believe in a God. However, gone are the days when the word 'God' conjures up ideas of an old man with a white beard and kind eyes sitting on some golden throne watching us humans carrying on our business. 'God' means different things to different people.

BASIC CHRISTIAN IDEAS ABOUT GOD

God is:

- perfect
- personal
- creator of the universe
- loving
- the only God
- all-powerful
- unchanging
- infinite
- sustainer of the universe
- holy
- all-knowing
- ever-present.

Some people argue that if there is no God then there is no meaning in life, and life itself is futile. Humanists, however, argue that there is still meaning in life without God and that humans have for too long blamed God for the world's problems rather than facing up to them and being responsible for them themselves.

People who believe in God are called **theists**.

People who do not believe in a God are called **atheists**.

People who are not sure whether God exists are called **agnostics**.

People who believe in more than one God are called **polytheists**.

8

DOES GOD EXIST?

Here are some ideas which might help you.

Reasons why God might exist	Reasons why God might not exist
1 There is so much order, design, beauty and purpose in the world, it must have come from some designer. Look at the complexity of life, of nature. It must have been designed.	1 If there is a God why is there so much suffering in the world? Wars, poverty, disease, floods, earthquakes, the threat of nuclear destruction, etc.
2 Everything has a cause. The world, the universe, must have begun from something. God was this creator.	2 I need proof. I need to see God. Where is he? What is the point of believing in something which I can't see and others can't see either?
3 Throughout history, so many have experienced God – felt God – that they can't all be talking nonsense.	3 People made God. They invented God to give them some comfort and security in a harsh huge universe and in a world full of death, darkness and disease.
4 We will never prove God exists (or evil does not exist), but everything in the world points to the possibility of Design and Purpose.	4 The universe was not created, it has always been. It had no beginning.
5 Humans are different from all other animals – they have art, music, culture, morality. This is all the result of some Divine Purpose for them.	5 If there is a God, then why doesn't he help us? He never answers my prayers or stops wars and things.
6 There are many things that as humans we can't see . . . atoms, love, electricity, hope, dreams, time, etc. . . . yet we know they exist. So to say I don't believe in a God because I don't see him is foolish.	6 Science has proved the Bible to be wrong about many things. The role of God in our world has been reduced stage by stage with the advance of science.

TO DEBATE

! The motion is 'This house believes that God does not exist.' Using the arguments in the table, organize a class debate and take a vote before and after.

FOR YOUR FOLDERS

▶ Without using the arguments listed, make a list of
  a why some people believe in God,
  b why some people don't believe in God.

▶ Look at the quotes. Write a sentence explaining what each one is trying to say.

FOR DISCUSSION

! ▶ Does it really matter if God exists or not?

Here are five news items from *The Times*, 7 August 1986.

SYDNEY DELUGE

SIX PEOPLE were killed in Sydney, Australia, when the city was hit by the worst storms recorded there.

MAN FACES SIX MURDER CHARGES

A MAN aged 23 who faces three murder charges, including two in Stockwell, South London, appeared in court yesterday, accused of murdering a further three old people and attempting to murder a fourth.

Man of fifty-four on rape charge

A FATHER of two girls was accused at Horseferry Road Magistrates' Court yesterday of raping a girl aged eight at a South London church.

RAIL DISASTER

(DELHI)—AT LEAST 43 people were killed and 35 injured when an express collided with a goods train in the Indian state of Bihar.

Hiroshima remembers devastation

THE names of almost 5,000 victims of the Hiroshima nuclear blast who died over the past year were added to the memorial roll yesterday as the city marked its devastation 41 years ago.

A natural evil: volcano erupting

- why do such things happen?
- why is our world so full of evil and suffering?

For people who believe in God (theists) the problem of evil and suffering poses some serious questions. Why does God allow evil? Why doesn't God do something about it?

KEY IDEA

If God is all-powerful he must be able to prevent evil.

If God is all-loving he must be willing to prevent evil.

But if God is both able and willing to prevent evil, then why does evil exist?

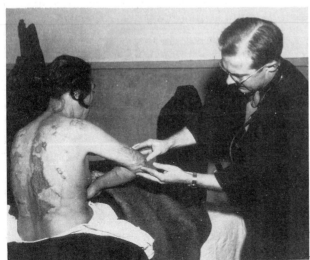

A moral evil: a Hiroshima survivor

There are, roughly speaking, two types of evil.

Moral evil	Natural evil
e.g.	e.g.
stealing	earthquakes
lying	flooding
killing	volcanoes
rape	disease
war	tornadoes

Some people have argued that because the first human beings (Adam and Eve) disobeyed God, all evil is a punishment. However, why, for example,

1 do young babies die of terrible diseases?
2 did hundreds of innocent children die in the Hiroshima bomb in 1945?
3 do evil people frequently do well in life while others suffer?

THINGS TO FIND OUT

▶ Look at a daily newspaper. Make a list of
a the moral evil,
b the natural evil reported there.

FOR DISCUSSION

! 'God can't exist – look at all the suffering in the world.' In groups of four to five discuss this statement.

FOR YOUR FOLDERS

▶ Make notes on some of the main ideas that came out of your discussion.

JANE: Why did God allow 6 million Jews to be killed by the Nazis?

JOHN: I believe that when God made us, he gave us freedom to choose between right and wrong. The Nazis, through ignorance and prejudice, chose to do wrong.

JANE: Why, then, didn't God make us free always to do right, rather than cause all this suffering?

JOHN: God didn't cause this suffering, human beings caused it.

JANE: OK. So why didn't God make us free to do right?

JOHN: Because if we always did right we wouldn't be free. We'd be just like unthinking machines.

JANE: But didn't God know when he made us that all these terrible things would happen?

JOHN: Perhaps he did. But God gave us the choice not to make them happen!

JANE: OK. So the Nazis chose evil. But you still have not explained why things like floods and diseases occur.

JOHN: Many types of natural evil could be destroyed if we put our minds to it, like famine or disease.

JANE: But what about earthquakes or volcanoes or death itself?

JOHN: This is the way the world has been made – it is all part of the balance of life. As for death – well, many Christians believe that Jesus's death has given us life.

JANE: Try telling that to a mother whose child has just died of starvation!

JOHN: Yes, I agree. But the idea of a perfect world seems incredibly ridiculous.

JANE: Why not . . . it sounds all right to me!

JOHN: For a start, without death we would be over-populated and people of 90 would be young.

JANE: OK.

JOHN: Also, suffering helps us to grow in life and learn. Imagine a world without pain. I could jump off the Post Office Tower head first and survive. I could light a fire to cook my dinner but I wouldn't burn my fingers if I put them in the fire. It'd be ridiculous.

5 HUMANISM OUTLINED

Humanists believe that:

- if human problems are to be solved at all, they will only be solved by human beings
- life should be as satisfying as possible for every individual
- human beings have evolved from simpler forms of life through natural processes taking millions of years
- people can more than ever today influence, for better or worse, the future of life on this planet
- because human beings have evolved together, all have equal rights without discrimination by race, sex or age.

Humanists do not believe:

- in a God or gods. Many describe themselves as agnostic (*a-gnostic* = 'not knowing', i.e. a person who does not claim to know). They say nobody can really know whether there is a supernatural power or not. All live their lives as atheists (*a-theist* = 'without God')
- in life after death. But they *do* believe that the effect of a person's life can be felt long after she or he has died
- that there is a supernatural power to guide us or help us.

Humanists would agree with these statements which are sometimes referred to as the *golden rule* of human behaviour:

Confucius	The treatment which you would not have for yourself do not mete out to other people.
Buddha	Hurt not others with that which pains yourself.
Jain scriptures	The essence of right conduct is not to injure anyone.
Jewish Talmud	What is harmful to yourself do not do to your fellow men. That is the whole of the law and the remainder is but commentary.
Jesus	Always treat others as you would like them to treat you.

HUMANIST MORALITY

Humanists do not believe in a God-given code of behaviour

Morality is about how people should treat one another. Humanists believe that human experience of life and of one another is an adequate guide as to how to behave.

They use their own reason, and try to think out all the possible consequences of their actions. The main questions they ask themselves are: 'Will it make someone feel better (happier, more loved)?' and 'Will it hurt anyone?'

Humanists have a great regard for sincerity, fairness and compassion. They try to behave responsibly and thoughtfully, rejecting the temptation to exploit or cheat anyone.

They respect and care for older people – whether parents, neighbours, the homeless and disabled or others. But they reserve the right to criticize dishonesty, unkindness and unreasonableness.

Humanists think that moral decisions involving sex should not be put in a separate category. The same principles should apply as in all other matters – not hurting anyone, being responsible, thoughtful and sincere.

WHAT ARE HUMANIST VALUES AND PRINCIPLES?

Humanists value **people** and their **happiness**. They value our human powers of **reasoning** and **imagining**, and they value **love**. These qualities are fundamental because they make us distinctively human.

Humanists try always to give reasons for the values they live by, such as

- **fairness** and **justice**, because they regard each person as valuable and entitled to a happy and satisfying life
- **tolerance**, because they accept people's right to hold differing views and opinions, so long as they do not make others suffer
- **sincerity** and **talking** and **listening**, because understanding of one another is important. Only if feelings are expressed sincerely can people learn how to help each other and to appreciate points of view different from their own
- **curiosity** and **creativity**, because they lead us to extend our understanding and enjoyment of the world

- **courage**, because in order to live fully, we need the heart to face difficulties, and to stand up for what we believe to be right
- **feeling**, because it is not only having the right ideas but also the capacity to feel with sensitivity and passion that makes life rich for ourselves and others
- **independence**, because they believe that there is no Infallible Authority. We have to work things out for ourselves as intelligent human beings
- **freedom** – as much as possible for each, so long as it does not interfere with other people's freedom, happiness and security
- **confidence,** based on the development of our own powers, so that we can set about making the world a better place
- **cooperation**, because it is by participating together to achieve things that human progress is made
- **concern for the world and for the future** because we are united with all life through evolution so that we must accept responsibility for the future of Planet Earth, its life and its peoples.

WHAT DO HUMANISTS ACTUALLY DO?

Some **play an active part in local humanist groups** which hold discussions, social events and conferences. Many are active in their local areas in such things as getting more attractive Registry Offices for people who don't want to marry in church; trying to get better nursery school provision; making surveys of parents' attitudes to religion in schools; giving practical help in providing hostels for young people in difficulties, and raising money for projects in developing countries overseas.

Some of them **work in campaigns**. For example, to ensure a humane and responsible approach to abortion; for a free Family Planning service; for people not to be punished because they are homosexuals; for civil liberties and freedom of expression, especially in books, films, plays and TV programmes.

Some **work for bodies** such as:

- The Independent Adoption Society – for people who do not practise a religion who wish to adopt children;
- The Humanist Housing Association – housing for elderly people.

Humanists **support and join organizations** such as Shelter, Friends of the Earth, The Conservation Society, Oxfam, Age Concern, the National Council for Civil Liberties, Amnesty International, the British Pregnancy Advisory Service, the Howard League for Penal Reform, the World Disarmament Campaign and CND.

Some **work as individuals** in marriage guidance counselling; as prison and hospital visitors; as local councillors; as social workers, teachers, nurses and doctors; as magistrates; as officiants (the person in charge) at funerals where no hymns or prayers are included.

(Humanist Dipper)

FOR DISCUSSION

▶ Humanists think it unfair when a religious person assumes that 'the unbeliever has no moral standards'. Why might Humanists think this?

! ▶ Is it easier to face life, and to make decisions throughout it, if you believe in God, or if you don't believe in a God?

FOR YOUR FOLDERS

! ▶ If you had a million pounds to support a team of research workers, describe what you would like them to investigate. Give reasons for your choice.

▶ Think back over your life. Pick out an incident in which you remember someone behaving with particular thoughtfulness and consideration. Write about it.

Christianity is the world's largest religion. There are many different Christian groups. Although they share some common beliefs, their expressions of these beliefs can seem very different. Also their views on certain issues can vary tremendously, so we must be careful about saying 'Christians believe . . .' because one Christian might have very different views on something from another Christian.

At the centre of a Christian's faith is Jesus of Nazareth who lived in Palestine (now called Israel) about 2,000 years ago. Each Christian remembers his life, his teachings and his death.

It is not easy to define exactly what ordinary Christians believe and think about their religion. In general, however, it is possible to say they hold the following beliefs:

- there is a God who created the world. They pray to him as 'Our Father in Heaven'. They believe that God has the whole world in his care; that God is perfect, loving, all-powerful, infinite, holy, all-knowing and ever-present

- God gave the world his only son, Jesus Christ, who saved the world from sin

- God has made his will known to humans by a holy book called the Bible

- by dying on the cross, Jesus gave human beings eternal life

- the spirit of God helps and guides people

- the teachings of Jesus, as laid out in the New Testament, show human beings what God requires of them and as far as possible must be followed

- God has given human beings the freedom to choose between good and evil but humans have often chosen evil which separates them from God. Jesus's death and resurrection has brought humanity closer to God.

THE APOSTLE'S CREED

I believe in God, the Father almighty,
creator of heaven and earth.

I believe in Jesus Christ, his only Son, our Lord.
He was conceived by the power of the Holy Spirit
and was born of the Virgin Mary.
He suffered under Pontius Pilate,
was crucified, died, and was buried.
He descended to the dead.
On the third day he rose again.
He ascended into heaven,
and is seated at the right hand of the Father.
He will come again to judge the living and the dead.

I believe in Holy Spirit,
the Holy Catholic Church,
the communion of saints,
the forgiveness of sins,
the resurrection of the body
and the life everlasting.

KEY IDEA

The way people look at the world and the things they believe about the world **affect** the way they behave in the world. Because Christians believe that God exists, that life has purpose, and that Jesus was God's son, their whole view of the problems and issues in the world today is affected.

FOR YOUR FOLDERS

▶ Write an article of about 150 words on 'The major beliefs of Christianity'.

????????? QUIZ ?????????

WHAT DO YOU BELIEVE?

Christians and Humanists share many ideas and ideals. Individual Christians differ from each other, as do individual Humanists. The 'typical' Christian, however, differs from the 'typical' Humanists (or follower of other values). These questions are designed to bring out some of these differences. When you have answered each question, use the checklist to see whether your answer is a Christian (C) or Humanist (H) view, or neither (N).

1 Are you
  a atheist?
  b agnostic?
  c a believer in God?

2 Which do you think is the *basic* reason why human lives are important?
  a they are given by God?
  b they are valuable for what they do in society?
  c they are valuable individually, as human beings?

3 Do you think it is important to
  a do what the state (or a political party) tells you?
  b use your reason and obey authority if reasonably based?
  c follow the teaching of Jesus, Muhammad, or some other prophet?

4 Do you believe in
  a reincarnation?
  b eternal life after death?
  c death as the end of life; but that people's influences live on?

5 Do you think the Bible is
  a inspired by God?
  b irrelevant?
  c interesting in parts but not to be taken as literally true?

6 Do you
  a act in an honest and very outspoken way?
  b behave sincerely but try to avoid hurting people?
  c say what you think people want to hear?

7 Which do you believe is the most important?
  a happiness for all, now and in the future?
  b one's relationship to God?
  c preserving this world for the future?

8 Do you think
  a that the question 'Where did the universe come from?' is correctly answered by 'God created it'?
  b that the answer 'God created it' invites the question 'But where did God come from?'

9 Do you believe that
  a it is impossible to know whether there is a God or not?
  b the evidence seems to be against there being a God?
  c there is an all-powerful God?

10 Do you believe that
  a God is the giver and taker of life?
  b people who wish to die should be helped to die with peace and dignity?

CHECKLIST

Question	a	b	c
1	H	N	C
2	C	H	N
3	N	H	C
4	N	C	H
5	C	N	H
6	H	C	N
7	H	C	H/C
8	C	H	
9	N	H	C
10	C	H	

(adapted from the Humanist Dipper)

7 CHRISTIAN ETHICS

THE OLD TESTAMENT

The Old Testament stresses that human beings have a duty to follow the commands of God. This obedience to the law is very important.

> 'It is no trifle; it is your life.'
>
> (Moses, in *Deuteronomy* 32: 46)

Through the teachings of the Old Testament the people learnt what God required of them.

> 'You shall be holy, because I am holy.'
>
> (*Leviticus* 20: 26)

Throughout the Old Testament there are rules and laws on every aspect of life.

KEY IDEA

The Old Testament stresses that to love God one must love one's neighbour. The Laws apply to everyone and are designed to protect the helpless.

Some important teachings

> 'Love your neighbour as yourself.'
>
> (*Leviticus* 19: 18)

> 'Let justice roll down like waters.'
>
> (*Amos* 5: 24)

> 'An eye for an eye, a tooth for a tooth.'
>
> (*Leviticus* 24: 20)

The Ten Commandments (Decalogue)

1　I am the Lord your God.
2　You shall have no other gods before me.
3　You shall not blaspheme.
4　Keep the sabbath holy.
5　Honour your parents.
6　You shall not kill.
7　You shall not commit adultery.
8　You shall not steal.
9　You shall not lie.
10　Do not desire what is not yours.

> (*Deuteronomy* 5:6–21)

THE NEW TESTAMENT

At the centre of Christian ethics is the idea of concern for all people. Christians calls this concern 'love'. Christian love is called 'agape' (from a Greek word). It is not sexual or romantic love but rather an attitude of caring for all people no matter who they are or what they are like. It is the kind of love shown in the Parable of the Good Samaritan (*Luke 10: 25ff.*).

KEY IDEA

Christian ethics centre on the idea of love (concern and respect) for all human beings.

The Gospels are full of incidents showing Jesus's concern and love for other people. His teachings, too, illustrate this.

> 'Always treat others as you would like them to treat you.'
>
> (*The Golden Rule, Matthew 7: 12*)

Jesus's teachings differ from the Old Testament in that they do not consist of a set of rules or laws to be followed. Instead Jesus was concerned that people change their inner thoughts. He believed that thoughts and feelings matter as much as actual conduct or action. An example of this was when he condemned not only murder but the anger that may be behind it:

'Everyone who is angry with his brother shall be liable to judgement.'

(Matthew 5:22)

St Paul summed up the teachings of the New Testament when he said that all the commandments of the Old Testament are contained in the one rule:

' "Love your neighbour as yourself." Love cannot wrong a neighbour; therefore the whole law is summed up in love.'

(Romans 13: 9–10)

BIBLICAL TEACHINGS AS A GUIDE

The teachings in the Bible can act as a **guide** for Christians in the modern world. Obviously, some of the great problems and issues that face us today are specifically modern problems, and so no direct reference can be found to them in the Bible, e.g. nuclear weapons, conservation, genetic engineering, unemployment and drug abuse. However, the teachings are often **guidelines** and so can be **applied** to present-day problems.

FOR YOUR FOLDERS

▶ **Situation 1** Certain members of a class begin bullying a new boy.
▶ **Situation 2** As you walk through a deserted street at night you see a man groaning on the floor. He has obviously been beaten up.
▶ **Situation 3** You have a new music centre and have been playing it loudly. Your neighbour asks you to turn it down.
▶ **Situation 4** A classmate falsely accuses you of stealing her bike. She later apologizes.
▶ **Situation 5** You find yourself thinking nasty things about somebody.

1 Now match these five situations up with five New Testament teachings that can be applied to them.
▶ **A** 'Judge not and you shall not be judged.'
(Matthew 7: 1)
▶ **B** 'Love your enemies.'
(Matthew 5: 44)
▶ **C** 'Do to others what you would have them do to you.'
(Matthew 7: 12)
▶ **D** 'Do not set yourself against the man who wrongs you.'
(Matthew 5:39)
▶ **E** The Parable of the Good Samaritan
(Luke 10: 25–37)

2 Can you match any of these teachings to the following problems and issues?
- racism
- soccer violence
- world poverty
- international relations
- unfaithfulness in marriage
- capital punishment.

From the moment we are born we begin learning. At first we learn most things from our parent(s) but as we grow so do our influences. These are our major influences:

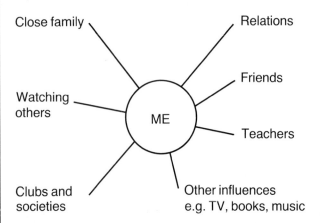

The way we learn about the correct way to behave in our own society, and the habits, customs, language and manners of our society is called **socialization**. We also slowly learn what is right and what is wrong, what is good and what is bad.

Some of the ways we begin to discover what is right and what is wrong are:

- by **consequence** – if you do this, such and such a thing will happen
- by **example** – watching how others behave
- by **experience** – if you do something yourself you find out what happens
- by **emotions** – e.g. do this to please your mother.
- by **following rules**.

Morality is concerned with what is right and wrong. As human beings we are able to think about what we do and say. Because we are able to think, we are also able to decide or choose what we think is the right way and what we think is the wrong way to behave.

- a **moral** act – an act considered to be right
- an **immoral** act – an act considered to be wrong
- an **amoral** act – an act that shows no understanding of right or wrong
- a **non-moral act** – an act not concerned with right or wrong
- a **non-moral** judgement – a view or opinion that is nothing to do with right or wrong.

Sometimes we get confused by language. Can you see the difference between Statements A and Statements B?

Task A
Write a sentence on the differences between these statements.

Statements A	Statements B
'It is right to help the poor.'	'He got ten out of ten right.'
'Martin Luther King was a good man.'	'This apple is good.'
'It is bad to tell lies.'	'The school team are bad.'
'It is wrong to steal.'	'You are wrong – they will win the cup.'

JUDGEMENTS

Our sense of what is right and what is wrong depends upon many things – upbringing, parental attitudes, friends, what type of environment we have grown up in and live in now, and so on. Morality is therefore very complicated. What we consider to be right, somebody else might see as wrong. In the end we have to come to our own decisions about how we live and how we look at the way others live. We all have the ability to make moral judgements.

Task B
Look at the following situations. How would you judge them?

! Try and give reasons for your opinion of each
• situation.

1. killing animals for meat,
2. bombing an enemy's city during wartime,
3. making abortion illegal,
4. refusing to give a fully qualified black person a job,
5. bullying younger children.

IN GROUPS

▶ In groups of four to five discuss the following.

CONSEQUENCES

We are usually able to work out the consequences of our actions. As children we often learn about consequences by quite hard experience but as we grow up we are more able to see the possible results of our actions. Let us have a look at some consequences.

Consequences I

You have a Saturday morning job in a shop. A good friend asks if she can buy a magazine. As you get it for her, you notice her putting a bar of chocolate from the counter into her pocket.

Do you tell her to put it back?
Do you tell the owner of the shop?
Do you ignore her?
Do you tell her parents?

What are the consequences of all these?

Consequences II

There is a film on at the pictures that you want to see with your friends. However, you know your parents do not want you to see this particular film. You also have no money.

Do you ask your mother for the money?
Do you tell her what it's for?
Do you pretend it's for something else?
Do you tell your friends that your parents won't let you go or tell them you have no money?
Do you try and borrow the money from a friend?
Do you try and get the money another way?

What are the consequences of all these?

▶ Now report back your findings to the rest of the class.

Consequences I

Consequences II

9 SOME ETHICAL THEORIES

Although it might seem easy to decide what is right and wrong in some situations, in others it is not so simple. Every situation is different and, as a result, the way you approach a situation and decide what is the right course of action may be different every time. Many of the problems we face as individuals or as a community are very complicated and it is not always easy to know the right way to react to them.

Thinkers have tried to solve this difficulty in two ways.

1   Morality as **a system of rules**. This is when people have a system of moral laws that they hold and then apply them to a given situation. (These people are called **deontologists**.)

2   Morality as **a set of goals**. This is when people do not apply rules to a situation, but rather decide on what end result they want and follow the actions that reach this result. (These people are called **consequentialists**.)

A CASE

You have two Jews hiding upstairs from the Nazis. The Gestapo ask you if you know of any Jews being hidden.

What would you do:

1   if you were a deontologist who has a rule 'I will never lie'?

2   if you were a deontologist who has a rule 'All people should be respected'?

3   if you were a consequentialist who believed that it is wrong to persecute people?

4   if you were a consequentialist who believed that Nazism was evil?

Over the ages certain theories have been developed about the best way to make ethical decisions in life. Ethics can be simply defined as the 'science of behaviour'.

HEDONISM

Epicurus was a Greek thinker born in 342 BC. He wrote over 300 works and believed that everybody strives after pleasure which is happiness, the main end of human life. He wrote: 'Pleasure is the beginning and end of living happily.' Epicurus did not just mean physical pleasure but pleasures of the mind and soul as well. Indeed, he believed that excessive physical pleasures lead to pain and become nothing like pleasures. He believed that true pleasure and happiness lay in 'freedom of the body from pain, and of the soul from confusion'.
A Hedonist believes that the 'good' is pleasant or whatever is pleasant is good.

ETHICAL EGOISM

This theory does not refer to 'big-heads' or selfish, egoistic people. It is a theory stating that a person's one and only basic duty is to obtain for themself the greatest possible balance of good over evil. Ideally, if everybody's own personal advantage did not hurt anyone else then the world would be a good place. However, often in practice when we do something to help ourselves we might hurt someone else.

UTILITARIANISM

This system was devised by two eighteenth-century British thinkers, Jeremy Bentham and John Stuart Mill. They were both actively involved in improving prisons and the law in Britain. The utilitarian slogan is 'the greatest good of the greatest number'. All our actions and rules are to be decided upon by finding out which of them produces the greatest amount of good for the greatest number of people.

SITUATION ETHICS

In 1966 an American professor called Joseph Fletcher wrote a very important book called *Situation Ethics*. Fletcher believed that when we are faced with a decision about what is the right thing to do then we should not apply any rules but act on the basis of love. There is no absolutely right or wrong way to decide what to do; rather we have to work each particular situation out and then respond in a loving way.

FOR DISCUSSION

A On the Wilderness trail in the pioneering days in America many people lost their lives to the Indians. On one occasion a woman had a crying baby which threatened to give her party's hiding position away. She strangled the baby with her two hands to stop its crying – and all twenty people escaped.

B Your house is burning down. Inside are two people: your aged father who is in a wheelchair and a doctor who has discovered a cure for one of the world's greatest diseases, and who still carries the formula in his head. There is only time to save one. Whom do you save?

▶ Discuss these two situations.

▶ How would followers of the four theories you've looked at respond to these situations?

FOR YOUR FOLDERS

▶ Write a sentence on hedonism, utilitarianism, situation ethics and ethical egoism.

We all think we can judge fairness pretty well. We recognize at once what is not fair and can usually give a quick answer to the question 'Why not?'

Fair means honest and just, giving the same chances and treatment to everyone, according to the rules if there are any.

Life would be fair if we all had an equal chance; if everyone had enough to eat and clean water to drink; if everyone were treated equally regardless of their colour, sex, or religion; if everyone could say what they wanted; if everyone could vote freely.

These are some examples of things that are fair. They are **human rights** and are due to every single one of us just because we are human. Human rights should automatically belong to everybody.

But life isn't fair, and many people are denied these rights. In some countries children starve to death; only the wealthy can go to school; people are treated differently because of the colour of their skin; people are tortured and imprisoned for saying what they think; there are no elections.

There are many more examples of unfairness. Being fair is not always easy. It means more than fair-sharing, and sometimes what is fair to one

person may not be fair for another. It becomes more complicated when we consider people's **freedoms** and their **rights**. Freedoms and rights are quite different from each other. Having a party and riding a bicycle are freedoms – they are things we are lucky enough to enjoy. They are not rights – things we should all have. But both freedoms and rights involve fair treatment and responsibility.

In the same way, having rights involves having **responsibilities.** We may say what we like, but we shouldn't insult people. Having rights means being fair to others. It is our responsibility.

Being fair to others is often difficult. It is made more difficult by the great **inequalities** that exist. It is becoming more and more urgent that we achieve greater fairness in the world. When unfairness and suffering get worse, so, often, does violence and even war. The world needs to try and find a balance between rights and responsibilities. If there is no such balance people and nations will not trust and tolerate each other. To **tolerate** someone means to accept and understand them. It is sometimes difficult to be tolerant when something seems unfair.

FOR YOUR FOLDERS

Look at the following list of human rights and responsibilities. The rights and responsibilities are muddled up.

- A name and identity of our own
- To show respect to other people of other countries
- A country to belong to
- Food, shelter, warmth
- To be educated and develop new skills
- To buy and own things
- To treat other people as individuals, not as things or just part of a group
- To have the protection of the law
- Not to steal people's things
- To share our things with needy people
- To meet together to share new ideas
- To be safe from violence and fear
- To be helped when we are old or ill
- To protect other people from unfair treatment
- To listen to others

- To always try and find out what the truth is
- To respect other people's religious beliefs
- To be able to vote
- To always be friendly and helpful to everyone
- To treat animals kindly

Divide your page into two columns headed 'Rights' and 'Responsibilities'. Put each of the above statements in its correct column. Use the drawings to help you.

! ▶ Make a list of fairness and unfairness that you can think of. You can include things in your life as well as about people in general.

▶ In two columns write down 'My needs' and 'My wants'.

▶ Write a sentence about each of the following: human rights, freedom, rights, responsibilities, inequalities, tolerance.

Some examples of fairness, freedom, rights and responsibilities

ORIGINS

Money can be anything that is accepted as a medium of exchange, e.g. cattle among the tribes of Africa; shells in some Pacific islands. The most common forms of money are coins and banknotes. Stamped coins, as opposed to a mere standard of weight of metal, came into use in Asia Minor about 2,600 years ago. Coins first appeared in Britain in about 760 AD. Money is only valuable for what it can buy. Today other kinds of money have evolved, e.g. cheques, credit cards.

HOW PEOPLE OBTAIN MONEY

- by working • if unemployed, from the DHSS
- by investing money • by stealing • by borrowing
- by gambling • from pensions.

GAMBLING

To gamble is defined as 'to play cards or other games for money, risk money . . . to take the risk that something will go well'.

A CATHOLIC VIEWPOINT

'The Catholic Church has never condemned gambling outright, in spite of the evident abuses to which it generally gives rise. Yet gambling may become a sin, even a serious sin, when it goes to excess that would destroy personal honesty, or expose a person to loss so great as to jeopardize society and, above all, their family dependants.'

(modern Catholic dictionary)

A METHODIST VIEWPOINT

'Gambling appeals to chance and therefore cannot be reconciled with faith in God. Because we belong to one another, we must live by love and mutual obligation. Gambling disregards moral responsibility and neighbourly concern.'

(Methodist Conference, 1981)

USURY

Usury means the practice of lending money to be paid back at a large rate of interest. This was regarded as being one of the Seven Deadly Sins in the medieval Church.

Necessities – e.g. shelter, water, food
Luxuries – e.g. household gadgets, leisure.

THINGS TO DO

▶ As a family of four you have a weekly income of £150. Work out how you would spend this money (include bills, mortgage or rent, food, repairs, clothes and rates, for example). How much, if any, is left over for luxuries?

▶ Now do the same for youself – your weekly income and your expenditure.

TALKING POINTS

- 'People not profit.'
- 'Servant not master.'
- 'You can't take it with you.'
- 'Money doesn't talk, it swears.'
  (Bob Dylan)
- 'Remember that time is money.'
  (Benjamin Franklin)
- 'Wine maketh merry: but money answereth all things.'
  (Ecclesiastes)
- 'He looked up and saw the rich people dropping their gifts into the chest of the temple treasury; and he noticed a poor widow putting in two tiny coins.'
  (Luke 21: 1–2)

- 'God shows his contempt for wealth by the kind of person he selects to receive it.'
  (Austin O'Malley, 1858–1932)
- 'Money can't buy me love.'
  (The Beatles)
- 'Money gives me pleasure all the time.'
  (Hilaire Belloc)
- 'The love of money is the root of all evil.'
  (I Tim. 6: 6–10)
- 'You cannot serve God and money.'
  (Matthew 6: 24)
- 'Good master, what must I do to win eternal life?' . . . and he said, 'Go sell everything you have and give to the poor, and you will have riches in heaven.'
  (Mark 10: 17–21)

Living in poverty

Affluent living

FOR YOUR FOLDERS

▶ Write a sentence about the two photos. Why might the woman in the left photo have a different view of money from the people in the right photo?

▶ '5% of the population own 40% of the nation's wealth and 50% of the population own 4% of the nation's wealth.'

(Inland Revenue)

! In your opinion, is this unfair or just a fact of life?

▶ From the Talking Points, write a paragraph on the Biblical attitudes to money.

▶ Answer the following questions.
How much does Dr Wilmot earn every year, according to the report in the *Daily Mirror*, 12 April 1985? Why does he earn so much? Does he deserve this salary, do you think?
Write a paragraph on a religious view of gambling.

£2,000 A DAY OVERTIME!

BY ROBERT HEAD

COMPUTER ace Dr Rob Wilmot earns £2,000 a day when he works overtime.

It is part of an amazing deal thrashed out between 40-year-old Dr Wilmot and the Standard Telephone and Cables giant.

The firms pays Dr Wilmot £80,000 a year for his part-time services plus £2,000 for every extra day's work he does.

Dr Wilmot also collected a golden handshake of nearly £191,000 last year when STC took over the ICL computer firm where he was chairman.

A spokesman for STC said last night: "We are more than happy with the time he puts into STC." He explained that the £80,000 agreement involved Dr Wilmot doing "well over a normal working week a month."

But that is peanuts compared with what two directors of the BSR electronics firm earn.

Their latest report shows that directors Bryan Christopher and Neal Stewart, both working for the company in Hong Kong, collected £526,000 each last year.

(*Daily Mirror*, 12 April 1985)

12 THE FAMILY

WHAT IS THE 'FAMILY'?

- a husband and wife with children
- a biologically related group
- parents, children, etc., living in a household
- the group that someone grows up in.

The family is our basic social unit. It is the smallest and most common group in our society. It is found in every country and in every age through history.

Sociologists (people who study society and social behaviour) often distinguish between two types of family:

- the **nuclear family**, where husband and wife live alone with their children, and no close relatives live in the household or in the neighbourhood
- the **extended family**, which consists of several generations possibly living in the same house and having relatives living in the neighbourhood.

Every family is different. The picture of the 'ideal family' in advertising differs a great deal from most people's experiences of the family.

The organization and characteristics of the family may vary enormously.

- **monogamy** – in some countries the law states that a person may have only one partner in marriage

- **polyandry** – in some societies a woman can have more than one husband
- **polygamy** – where there are two or more husbands or wives
- **kibuttzim** – communes where families and single people all choose to live together. Each person has a specific job, and babies and children are put into nurseries and communal homes. Most *kibbutzim* are in Israel
- **single parent families** – either a man or woman, for a variety of reasons, looks after the child or children
- **arranged marriages** – in some countries marriages are arranged by the parents
- **the elderly** – in some societies the old remain as the head of the family
- **reversed roles** – sometimes the woman goes out to work and the man brings up the children
- **step-parents** – children may be related not by blood but by a re-marriage.

WHAT DOES A FAMILY DO?

- it plays an important part in controlling sexual behaviour
- it is a responsible basis for having and rearing children

An extended Victorian family

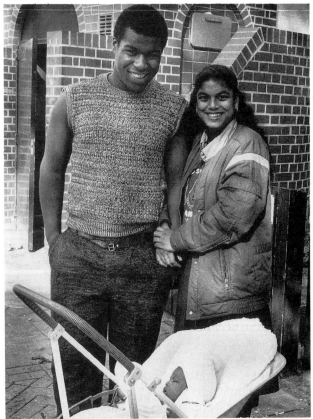

A modern nuclear family

- it teaches us an acceptable way to behave, and the customs and traditions of our society (called socialization)
- it allows wealth and property to be passed on to a new generation
- it forms the group in which most humans spend most of their time
- it provides a base for the care of its dependants (e.g. the aged, the sick and the handicapped)
- it gives husband and wife certain economic rights and responsibilities.

FAMILY LIFE AND THE BIBLE

In the Old Testament there are specific references to family duty and loyalty:

'Honour your father and your mother.'

(Fifth Commandment, Exodus 20: 12)

'Listen to your father who gave you life, and do not despise your mother when she is old.'

(Proverbs 23: 22)

In the New Testament we read in Luke's gospel that Jesus was a dutiful son to his parents, although once they lost him when he went to the Temple (*Luke 2*). When he was older he was very concerned about his mother, Mary, a widow. At his death he asked his best friend to look after Mary when he was gone (*John 19*).

Jesus taught that human beings, as well as giving love, need to receive it. In terms of the family, it means that all the relationships (parent–child, brother–sister, etc.) should be loving, loyal, caring, and respectful – treating people as individuals in their own right.

A HUMANIST VIEWPOINT

'The living and lively family nest is the basis of future mental and moral health within society.'

(**James Hemming,** *Individual Morality*)

Hemming outlines five important aspects of family life:

1 freedom of children from being made neurotic by their parents
2 a warm relationship between children and parents
3 a loving relationship between the parents
4 a closely knit and supportive family unit
5 understanding and consistency in discipline.

THE MODERN FAMILY

Although some families in our society are happy and closely knit, many are not. Indeed, even so-called 'happy families' have their problems. Today, there are even more pressures on family life, and tension in the family can be caused by such things as unemployment, changing roles, money worries and alcohol abuse.

FOR YOUR FOLDERS

- Make a list of some causes of tension in the family.
- Write down the names of members of your 'nuclear family' and 'extended family'.
- Write a paragraph about the way that the family has changed in our society over the last century.
- ! Explain why many people regard the family as being so important. What do you think?

THINGS TO DO

- At home, try to work out your family tree. (Your parents and your grandparents may be able to help you.)

FOR DISCUSSION

- 'If men and women are to live the same lives, the family must be abolished.'

(Plato, *c.* 300 BC)

IN GROUPS

- In pairs (do this with a friend), discuss the following:
  1 arguments in my home,
  2 my parents don't understand me,
  3 I'll bring my kids up differently,
  4 James Hemming's five points and my family.

13 SINGLE PARENT FAMILIES

In 1985 there were almost 200,000 children living with their fathers alone and about 900,000 with their mothers. Over 5% of all families in Britain in 1985 were single parent families. These figures have doubled since 1961. The single parent is usually without a partner for one of the following reasons:

- he or she has divorced or separated – the majority of single parents are in this group
- one of the spouses has died
- he or she has been deserted
- she has made a deliberate choice. Some mothers do not want to (or cannot) marry the father of their child.

John lives with his daughter, Annie, who is nine. Here are John's thoughts on his family.

'I've always got on with children. Having a younger brother by 13 years has helped me. One of the finest things I've noticed is the way that people, especially women, have encouraged and supported me. Strange really, because a lot of women do exactly the same thing and get no support or thanks at all. What they do is taken for granted. Women are expected to do it, but without support and encouragement they can find it quite devastating. Generally, most men don't fully appreciate what a demanding job it is bringing up children.

For many people the initial stages of becoming a single parent can be a difficult time. Often it is caused by the traumas of divorce or the grief of bereavement. This can be a tremendous strain. Sometimes, however, a child can feel a great sense of relief when he or she becomes part of a single parent family, after perhaps years of parental strife, arguments and marital breakdown.

John and Annie

Our society all too often stereotypes the abilities of men and women. I've had no problems with cooking, cleaning, washing and looking after our home. The only 'skill' I had to learn was how to iron. As for sewing, I still can't do it, and probably never will. Generally, however, supposedly 'feminine skills' are no problem to me.

Annie is a well-balanced and popular child. She's got lots of friends and is a very happy girl. I've given her a lot of room to express all her thoughts and feelings. Sometimes, quite naturally, she misses her mum. I let her cry and talk about what she's feeling. There's no point in hiding things from kids. I've always been honest and straightforward about our split-up and she sees her mum regularly.

There is something very wrong with the way our society is structured. Most people lead such private lives behind closed doors. Many people hardly ever come into contact with children and this is not good. It amazes me to think that often the first time a woman (or a man for that matter) holds a baby in her arms is in the maternity hospital – her own child.

Schools are at fault, too. All the students, not just the few young women who do child care, should learn about babies and young children. For goodness sake, it is often only a matter of months after leaving school that some young women start having children of their own. Yet we expect people to bring up a happy, well-balanced new generation.

Bringing a child up on your own is not always easy. Sometimes it'd be good to have another adult to share your experiences with.

However, it's got many advantages. You really get to know your child well. You can bring them up the way you want. You can give them all your love and all your time. The relationship can become very deep and loving. The child is not subject to a couple of warring parents. I'm lucky, it's been a joy bringing up Annie.'

FOR DISCUSSION

▶ 'Generally, most men don't fully appreciate what a demanding job it is bringing up children.' What do you think are the advantages and disadvantages of being a single parent, after reading John's story?

▶ Boys should be taught child care and home economics at school.

FOR YOUR FOLDERS

▶ Can you write down some of the reasons why there are more and more single parent families?

▶ 'Gingerbread' is a group that tries to help single parents. Can you think of some of the ways it can help?

TALKING POINT

'It amazes me to think that often the first time a woman (or a man for that matter) holds a baby in her arms is in the maternity hospital – her own child.'

Outside of our family, perhaps the most important influence on our lives is the friendships we make. Unlike our own families, we can pick and choose our own friends. They might influence the way we dress, think about life, the music we listen to, the interests we have and even the way we speak. Indeed, friends can greatly influence and even change our opinions, our attitudes and our beliefs about life.

In theory, any of the 55 million people living in Britain and indeed people living elsewhere could be our friends. In practice, most of our friends come from the area where we live and most of these will be around our age. We might meet and make friends in a variety of ways.

- our neighbours
- our church
- through introductions
- through work or school
- whilst on holiday
- through clubs or groups
- at discos/dances
- in clubs
- at evening classes.

WHAT ATTRACTS US TO SOME PEOPLE?

Some of the factors that go into making us friendly with people might include:

- appearance
- sense of humour
- common interests
- different interests
- somebody's nature (similar or opposite to ourselves)
- when we admire somebody
- characteristics
- being thrown together in a situation and getting to know somebody.

'No man is an island' (John Donne). Human beings are generally sociable – we need other people's company. Friendships help us to share our experiences with others, learn from others, feel wanted, help our self-confidence, and so on. Our friends sometimes change as our interests and our situations change. Sometimes a friendship may be for a short time. Sometimes a friendship can be for life. Many of the friends you have now may no longer be your friends in, say, five years' time. Sometimes our best friends can be from the opposite sex. (This is called platonic love.)

It is possible to love our friends in the same way as we love members of our family. In the New Testament Jesus's close friends are his disciples, and in particular Peter. Jesus said to his disciples,

'This is my commandment, that you love one another as I have loved you. Greater love has no man than this, that a man lay down his life for his friends. You are my friends if you do what I command you.'

(John 15: 12–14)

This is the ultimate type of friendship – to be willing to sacrifice one's own life for a friend.

Jesus also said, 'You shall love your neighbour as yourself,' (*Mark 12: 31*). Christians believe that we should try to love and respect all people and not *just* people who are closest to us.

IN GROUPS

'One rotten fish plus one fresh fish equals two rotten fish.'
(Old Maori saying)

'The name of a friend is common, but faith in friendship is rare.'
(Phaedrus)

▶ What do these sayings mean?

! ▶ Do you agree with them?

FOR YOUR FOLDERS

▶ Make a list of the 10 qualities you consider to be most important in friendship.

▶ What did Jesus mean in *John 15*? Can you think of examples of people who have actually lived out this teaching?

????????? QUIZ ?????????

HOW DO YOU RATE AS A FRIEND?

1 If you quarrel with a friend, are you the first to make it up?
- a Yes
- b No
- c Sometimes

2 If your friend bores you by continually going on about the same thing, do you politely try to change the subject?
- a Yes
- b No
- c No, tell them to shut up

3 Do you gossip to others about your friends?
- a Yes
- b No, never
- c Only sometimes

4 Do you sometimes tell your friend little white lies?
- a Yes
- b No
- c Sometimes

5 Do you keep the secrets that your friend tells you?
- a Yes
- b No
- c Not always

6 If you borrow an LP from your friend and accidently scratch it would you
- a Tell your friend?
- b Keep quiet?
- c Offer to buy another one?

7 How much do you listen to your friend when they tell you their problems?
- a A lot
- b Not much
- c Occasionally

8 Your friend likes to show off in front of the opposite sex. You get embarrassed. Do you
- a Walk away?
- b Tell them to shut up?
- c Explain in private that you are embarrassed?

HOW TO SCORE

Below 6 is poor.
6–8 is fair.
8–10 is good.
10–12 is very good.
12–16 is excellent.
ADD UP YOUR TOTAL.

	c 2		c 1		c 1		c 1			
	b 0		b 0		b 0		b 0			
8	a 1	**7**	a 2	**6**	a 2	**5**	a 2			
	c 1		c 1		c 0		c 1			
	b 2		b 2		b 1		b 0			
4	a 0	**3**	a 0	**2**	a 2	**1**	a 2			

31

15 LOVE

If we look at this week's Top Thirty we can be sure that many of the songs will be about love. Ever since men and women have written songs and poems, one of the most popular themes has been love. One hit song by Howard Jones was called 'What Is Love?' and this question has been asked many times.

The word 'love' means many different things. Some of the main types of love are:

- warm affection or liking something, e.g. 'I love the Welsh mountains' (called *storge* by the Greeks)
- sexual affection, passion or desire (called *eros* by the Greeks)
- love of friends (called *philos* by the Greeks)
- love of family
- Christian love (called *agape* by the Greeks), which includes things like charity, tolerance and respect towards all people.

Love is a two-way process. We both receive love and give love. People who find it difficult to love have not always received love in the first place.

KEY IDEA

True happiness does not consist in just receiving love. Rather it is a balance of the receiving and the giving of love.

Young people sometimes get very confused by the emotions connected with love. Often at school relationships between boys and girls can cause problems. We can 'fall in love' with somebody who we 'fancy' and usually this means we are physically attracted to them. Sometimes we can fall in love with somebody and find out later that we don't even like them. Sometimes we can 'fall out of love' as quickly as we fall in love. Occasionally we find ourselves falling in love with somebody who we did not fancy or find attractive at first. Sometimes we fancy someone but are too shy to let them know – this is painful and is called 'unrequited love'.

Love is different from lust. Lust is defined as an 'animal desire for sex'. In conversation today the word 'sex' is usually taken to mean the physical act of sex relations between a couple. The word 'love' is usually taken to mean the whole personal relationship between a couple, including sex. Thus 'love' covers a far wider area than 'sex'.

A young couple 'in love'

What is love? Is it just a sort of chemical reaction in the body when two people meet? Many people think it is more than this and one of the finest definitions of love was written nearly 2,000 years ago by St Paul:

'Love is patient; love is kind and envies no one. Love is never boastful nor conceited, nor rude; never selfish, not quick to take offence. Love keeps no score of wrongs; does not gloat over other men's sins, but delights in the truth. There is nothing love cannot face; there is no limit to its faith, its hope and its endurance. Love will never come to an end.'

(I Corinthians 13:4–8)

Humanists believe that love is very important and is one quality that makes us distinctively human.

THINGS TO FIND OUT

▶ Look at this week's Top Thirty. Make a list of all the songs that are about love.

▶ Are any of them about lust? (List them.)

FOR YOUR FOLDERS

▶ What do *eros* and *agape* mean?

▶ What is unrequited love?

▶ What is the difference between love and lust?

▶ List some of the qualities of love that St Paul mentions.

▶ Write a letter to a problem page about some problematic aspect of love. Try to think up a reply, offering advice.

THINGS TO DO

! ▶ Look through magazines and newspapers. What impressions do you think they try to give of love? Are they always realistic?

love is...

. . . going to a Halloween party with her

FOR DISCUSSION

▶ 'Love is a fanclub with only two fans
Love is what happens when the music stops
Love is you and love is me
Love is a prison and love is free
Love's what's there when you're away from me
Love is . . .'

(from 'Love Is . . .' by Adrian Henri)

Most healthy human beings have the ability to reproduce. Unlike some other less complex forms of life, we do this sexually – involving the male and female of our species. Without this ability to reproduce there would be no biological survival. The sexual drive is one of the strongest drives known to us – at its biological level it is the desire to reproduce. However, human beings are different from other animals in that our sex drive is linked to our emotional and psychological needs as well.

We live in what is often called a 'permissive society'. This means that in general people are open-minded about sex. Often we like to think that sex, with all its problems, is a new thing and that our particular generation 'discovered' it. However, history tells us another story. Demosthenes, a Greek statesman (about 350 BC), said about ancient Greece:

'We keep prostitutes for pleasure, we keep mistresses for the day to day needs of the body.'

In 50 AD the Roman historian Juvenal wrote about the Emperor Claudius's wife Messalina that at night she would creep out of the palace and spend the night working in a brothel to fulfil her sexual desire:

'There she stood with nipples bare . . . here she graciously received all-comers, asking from each his fee.'

Generally in the ancient world sexual immorality was common. A man could easily divorce his wife and women were usually treated like things rather than like human beings. Prostitution, concubines and brothels were commonplace.

KEY QUESTION

Is it wrong for people to have sexual intercourse outside of marriage?

It has been said that in earlier generations sex outside marriage was not as common as it is today because of three fears:

1 fear of detection
2 fear of infection
3 fear of conception.

Sex outside marriage, which means pre-marital (before marriage) and extra-marital (during marriage), has now become more common, possibly because of the following reasons:

- virginity is not considered to be so important
- contraceptive devices have improved
- education about contraception has improved
- abortions are easier to obtain
- sexual permissiveness is often encouraged in the media
- fewer people follow the teachings of the church
- medical facilities have improved.

However, the results have been very serious:

- sexually transmitted diseases are increasing
- more children are being born out of wedlock
- emotionally immature young people are sexually active
- divorce rates have risen
- there is now a risk of contracting AIDS.

CHRISTIANITY AND SEX OUTSIDE MARRIAGE

Christians generally would say that sex outside marriage is wrong not just because it leads to the problems listed above but because Jesus spoke out against it. However, some Christians would agree that sexual intercourse between a couple who love one another and intend to create a life together is morally acceptable.

The New Testament frequently discusses sexual matters. Fornication and adultery are condemned over 30 times. Basically, Christianity teaches that:

- **sex is a beautiful gift from God demanding responsibility, commitment and total love**
- **it is always wrong to use a person as a thing**
- **sexual intercourse is very special (it can create new life)**
- **sex is the most beautiful expression of a deep, loving, life-long union between two people.**

HUMANISTS ANSWER SOME QUESTIONS ABOUT SEX

Do Humanists believe in sleeping around?
No they don't. Because casual sexual relationships all too often show lack of concern and lead to people getting hurt. Humanists believe that love is something we share with one another, sometimes with passion, but always with responsibility and caring. Love for one another and respect for one another go together.

If you don't think sex before marriage is wrong, what about illegitimate babies?

Happiness and love and security are especially vital, because babies will grow into unique, valuable individual people. Babies are created by their **parents**. This is why moral decisions involving sex may be difficult, in case an unplanned pregnancy should result. Efficient methods of contraception have made it possible for people to explore life deeply with another person without necessarily being tied to them forever. Babies should only be started when you are sure you can give them a loving and secure upbringing.

Is sex education important?

Indeed it is. Children's questions should be answered honestly all the time, and particularly those about sex, since it can be a very wonderful part of our lives. Nowadays biased ideas about sex are directed at school leavers from many sources – but decisions involving sex should be made (as should decisions not involving sex) from a standpoint of factual knowledge, and not in the darkness of ignorance. Therefore Humanists think you should learn about your own bodies and about sex, love, pregnancy, contraception, abortion, venereal disease and psychology.

(Humanist Dipper)

Rodin's 'Kiss'

FOR YOUR FOLDERS

▸ Write down what the following mean: permissive society, pre-marital sex, extra-marital sex, life-long union.

▸ Write a paragraph on each of the following: the Christian view of sex; the Humanist view of sex.

! ▸ Write down some of your own thoughts on sex outside marriage.

! ▸ Write down what you think the 'three fears' are about.

FOR DISCUSSION

▸ 'If [the unmarried] cannot control themselves they should marry. Better be married than burn with vain desire' (*I Corinthians 7: 9*). Discuss this statement of St Paul's.

▸ Discuss some of the reasons why sex outside marriage is apparently more common these days than for earlier generations.

IN GROUPS

In groups of two to three (be with your friends) do the following task.

▸ Imagine that you had to plan a sex education programme for people of your own age. There are 10 sessions of 45 minutes to organize. Discuss what topics you would like to be covered. Take 20 minutes to do this. Then write down on a piece of paper your suggestions and fold the paper before handing it to the teacher, who will arrange a class discussion.

> **Contraception** – 'various methods by which a couple can avoid an unwanted pregnancy.'

WHY IS CONTRACEPTION USED TODAY?

- a couple may decide not to have children
- a family may already be large enough
- it helps people to plan their future
- it enables couples to enjoy sex without worrying about pregnancy
- it helps to control the population
- in cases of pre-marital sex, it can prevent unwanted pregnancy.

METHODS OF CONTRACEPTION

- **Natural Family Planning (NFP)**
  NFP refers to the woman becoming aware of her own fertile and infertile cycles by recording the natural signals of her body (e.g. the temperature method, the Billings (or 'ovulation') method and the sympothermal method). Many Roman Catholics prefer these methods.
  Is it safe?
  The World Health Organization puts the sympothermal method in the top three methods of birth control.

  (Catholic Truth Society)

- **Rhythm method**
  Some days during the menstrual cycle a woman is not fertile – so a couple can have sex during those days. But they need to work out the 'safe' days very carefully indeed – the woman will have to take her temperature regularly – and this has to be done every month as the cycle is different every time.
  Is it safe?
  This method is not safe at all, as it is so easy to make a mistake.

- **Withdrawal method**
  The man withdraws his penis before his sperm are released, so that none of them enter the woman's vagina.
  Is it safe?
  No, because the man may not withdraw his penis in time. Also, sperm can be released at any time while the couple are having sex.

- **The Pill**
  The Pill is now taken by about 55 million women worldwide. It works by altering the hormone balance of the woman's body, so that she does not become fertile.
  Is it safe?
  As a method of contraception, it is the safest. There may be side-effects in that other parts of the body such as the breasts, or body hair may be affected. Women taking the Pill may also suffer from depression. The long-term effects are not known.

- **The vault cap and diaphragm**

  These are both rubber domes on a flexible ring.
  The diaphragm is wider and flatter. Both are
  smeared with contraceptive jelly and slipped into
  the woman's vagina. The cap fits over the mouth
  of the cervix. The diaphragm fits right across the
  vagina. Both must be fitted by a doctor and
  checked regularly or they will not work. They
  must be left in place for at least six hours after the
  couple have had sex.

  Are they safe?

  Both are reliable so long as they are fitted
  properly and used correctly.

- **The sheath or condom**

  This is the method a man can use. He pulls the
  sheath on to his erect penis and leaves it there
  until his sperm have been released. It's safer if
  the woman puts contraceptive cream in her
  vagina as well.

  Is it safe?

  Again, it is safe if correctly used. More and more
  people are using the sheath now because it is the
  best available protection against infection by the
  AIDS virus.

- **The IUD (inter-uterine device) or coil**

  This is made of plastic or metal and has a small
  piece of copper wire attached to it. It is fitted
  inside the woman's womb by a doctor. No one is
  sure how it works, but it is thought to prevent a
  fertilized egg from attaching itself to the wall of
  the womb, where it can begin to grow into a foetus.

  Is it safe?

  The IUD is a reliable way of preventing pregnancy.
  Side-effects may be heavy or prolonged periods,
  or cramp-like pains. Occasionally the woman may
  expel it from her body.

THREE VIEWS ON CONTRACEPTION

1. **Humanists regard sex as one of the greatest
   pleasures of life, not just the means of
   reproduction. If contraception helps a
   relationship, then it is a good thing.**
2. **The Catholic Church teaches that the primary
   purpose of sexual intercourse is the begetting of
   children. Intercourse is a sin unless the
   procreation of children is intended, or at least
   not hindered, because children are a gift from
   God. In the papal encyclical *Humanae Vitae*
   (1968) all artificial forms of contraception are
   condemned.**
3. **The Anglican view on contraception is that a
   couple may practise forms of contraception that
   are acceptable to both partners.**

FOR YOUR FOLDERS

- ▶ List some contraceptives that are
  available for (a) men and (b) women.

- ▶ What contraceptives can be unsafe?

- ▶ Write a paragraph about some of the
  foolish things that Jill says in the cartoon.

- ▶ Write a paragraph about the following
  statement: 'No one has the right to
  create a life thoughtlessly.'

- ▶ In 1984 the Pope said:
  'Only natural forms of birth control do
  not offend the moral order established
  by God.'
  - a What do you think he means by
    'natural birth control'?
  - b How would he argue that 'unnatural'
    forms of birth control would offend
    'the moral order established by God'?

FOR DISCUSSION

- ▶ 'The availability of contraception makes
  society less moral than it used to be.'
- ▶ 'Sex is a function primarily for having children.'
- ▶ 'The method of contraception is not just up to
  the woman.'

It is illegal for a man to have sexual intercourse with a girl under the age of 16. However, many girls under 16 go to a doctor or clinic for contraceptive advice. This puts many doctors in a difficult position. In 1974 the Department of Health and Social Security (DHSS) issued advice to doctors saying that to give girls under 16 contraceptives was not in any way criminal if they acted with 'professional responsibility'. They should do all in their power to persuade the girl to tell her parents. However, if doctors were told to make sure that the girl's parents knew, then many girls would risk pregnancy or sexually transmitted diseases rather than go to the doctor.

Mrs Victoria Gillick, a Cambridgeshire housewife with five daughters, was determined that none of her daughters should be able to get birth control advice whilst they were still under 16 without her knowing. She won a High Court Ruling which declared that

> '*no doctor or other professional person employed by the Area Health Authority might give contraception advice, or abortion advice or treatment to any child below the age of sixteen without the prior knowledge and consent of the child's parent or guardian*'.

Many people agreed with Mrs Gillick and the High Court's decision that parents should know if their daughter has been given contraception. However, many people disagreed.

In 1985 the DHSS appealed against this ruling to the House of Lords. The case was heard before five Law Lords and by a slender majority of three votes to two the High Court judgment was overturned and the appeal from the DHSS upheld. The statements made by the five judges are very important and will be discussed for many years to come.

Mrs Victoria Gillick

Lord Fraser pointed out that the parents' right to control the child existed not for the benefit of the parent but for the child. He also said:

> '*It is notorious that children of both sexes are often reluctant to confide in their parents about sexual matters . . . and to abandon the principle of confidentiality for contraceptive advice to girls under sixteen might cause some not to seek professional advice at all, thus exposing them to the immediate risk of pregnancy and sexually transmitted diseases.*'

A doctor could give contraceptive advice and treatment to girls under 16 without the consent or even knowledge of her parents provided that he was satisfied that:

1   The girl would understand his advice.

2   The doctor could not persuade her to tell her parents or allow him to inform them.

3   She was likely to have sexual intercourse with or without contraceptive treatment.

4   Unless she received contraceptive treatment her health would suffer.

5   Her best interests required him to give her contraceptive advice, without parental consent.

Lord Brandon voted in favour of the High Court judgment. He argued that because it was unlawful for a man to have sexual intercourse with a girl under 16, any person who promoted, encouraged, or helped this act would be breaking the law. Lord Templeman was concerned about the rights of parents and whether a girl under 16 was mature enough to make a balanced judgement.

TWO VIEWS ON THE HOUSE OF LORDS JUDGEMENT

'Catholic moral teaching does not permit the use of artificial means of contraception. This applies irrespective of age . . . it is tragic that our young people should be subjected to so many influences which contribute to sexual permissiveness and a lowering of moral standards.'

(Cardinal Basil Hume)

'In most families parents will know what their children are doing: but it is the minority we work with where relations have almost broken down. The new ruling will be most helpful in that doctors will have room to make a judgement. A very vulnerable group will at last have somewhere to turn.'

(The Church of England Children's Society)

FOR YOUR FOLDERS

▶ Explain in your own words:

  a   what the DHSS advice was to doctors;

  b   who Victoria Gillick is;

  c   what the High Court Ruling was;

  d   what the House of Lords judgment was;

  e   why Lord Fraser, Lord Brandon and Lord Templeman voted the way they did;

  f   the Catholic and Church of England responses.

▶ Try and write a paragraph for each of the following:

  a   Why some people believe that girls under 16 should have confidentiality as regards contraceptive advice or treatment.

  b   Why some people argue that parents should have the right to know.

! ▶ Explain your own opinions on this matter. (Bear in mind that one day you may have a daughter of your own.)

FOR DISCUSSION

▶ 'Girls under 16 are not mature enough to make reasonable decisions.'

▶ 'The Gillick viewpoint would mean more teenage pregnancies.'

▶ 'The last people to talk to about sex are one's parents.'

'AIDS stands for "Acquired Immune Deficiency Syndrome". It is a condition which develops when the body's defences are not working properly. As a result, people are more likely to get illnesses which the body would normally be able to fight off easily. These illnesses can be serious or fatal. At the moment there is no treatment which can cure AIDS.

AIDS is caused by a virus called HIV which gets into the blood and destroys the white blood cells leaving the body wide open to attack from other infections. Anyone who has the HIV virus could pass the virus on to someone else.'

(Health Education Authority leaflet)

Since 1981 tens of thousands of cases of AIDS have been reported worldwide and the numbers are increasing fast. The main groups at risk are:

* practising homosexual and bisexual men
* drug users who share injection equipment
* haemophiliacs and others who have received blood products
* sexual partners of all these people
* babies born to infected people.

But the infection is now spreading among heterosexual people, since it can be passed on by sexual intercourse. In 1987 the Government put aside £20 million to educate people about the danger of AIDS.

The Terrence Higgins Trust, named after the first person to die from AIDS in Britain, offers the public a wide variety of services concerning AIDS. These include help and support for people with AIDS, their families and friends; health education for those at risk; and support for medical research into AIDS.

At first it was thought that only homosexuals could contract or pass on AIDS, but it is now accepted that AIDS can affect the whole community. Some people have called AIDS 'God's wrath' on homosexuals and other people who have contracted the disease through sexual relations. However, most Christians strongly disagree with this, and in September 1986 the World Council of Churches Executive Committee stated:

'AIDS is heartbreaking and challenges the Churches to break their own hearts, to repent of inactivity and of rigid moralizing. Since AIDS cuts across race, class, gender, age, sexual orientation and sexual expression, it challenges our fears. [The Churches] must work against the real danger that AIDS will be used as an excuse for discrimination and oppression and work to ensure the protection of the human rights of persons affected directly or indirectly by AIDS.'

How can you reduce your risk of getting the virus?

'A lot of work is being done to develop a vaccine to protect people from the virus, but it is unlikely that one will be available in the near future.

We are all being alerted to the danger of AIDS

Here is some advice to help you reduce your risk of getting the virus.

- The fewer sexual partners you have, the less risk you have of coming into contact with someone who has the virus.

- The fewer partners your partner has, the less risk of you getting the virus.

- The way you have sex also affects the risk. But of course, you will only catch the virus if you have sex with an infected partner. If you are unsure of your partner, remember that some ways of having sex are much more risky than others.

  Anal intercourse (when the penis enters the rectum, or back passage) is *particularly risky*. This may be because the walls of the rectum are much more delicate and more likely to tear than those of the vagina, making it easier for the virus to pass from one person to another.

  Vaginal intercourse (when the penis enters the woman's vagina) is also risky.

  Oral sex is where one partner stimulates the other's genitals with their mouth or tongue. Oral sex carries some risk because there is always a chance that the virus could pass from the man's semen into the other person's body.

  Any practice that breaks the skin or draws blood, either inside the vagina or anus or on the skin, could increase the risk of getting the virus.

Can the HIV virus be passed on in other ways?

Women who have the virus can pass it on to their baby during pregnancy (through the placenta), at birth or through their breast milk.

Normal everyday contact with an infected person is perfectly safe. The virus is not passed on through touching or shaking hands, or through saliva or tears.

You cannot catch the virus by touching objects used by an infected person: cups, cutlery, glasses, food, clothes, towels, toilet seats and door knobs. Swimming pools are also safe.

- Safer sex. Using a condom (a sheath, or rubber), during sex will reduce the risk of getting the virus and other sexually transmitted diseases too.

- Avoid sharing any device that punctures the skin, unless it has been properly sterilized.

- For drug misusers, the easiest way to avoid the risk of getting the virus is not to inject drugs. But if you do inject, always use your own set of works. Never share with anybody, no matter how well they may seem to you.

- To prevent infected blood from entering your bloodstream, it's best not to share razors or toothbrushes (because many people's gums bleed when they brush their teeth).

- Until more is known about AIDS, women who have the HIV virus should avoid becoming pregnant. If a woman who has the virus gets pregnant, she is more likely to go on to develop AIDS herself. And she may pass the virus on to her baby.'

(Health Education Authority)

THINGS TO DO

▶ Read the extract 'How can you reduce your risk of getting the virus?' Discuss it seriously with a friend. It is very important.

▶ Look up the biblical reference *John 9: 1–3*. What does this tell us about Jesus's view of the relationship between suffering and sin?

FOR DISCUSSION

▶ 'Celibacy, chastity, virginity and faithfulness are no longer old-fashioned virtues. They are back and here to stay because of AIDS.'

▶ Why might many practising Catholics find themselves in a dilemma as regards the use of a condom?

▶ 'People must become "sexually honest" with their partners.'

▶ 'AIDS does not discriminate.' Would you agree?

FOR YOUR FOLDERS

▶ Write two short articles of about 100 words each, entitled 'AIDS: the facts' and 'The problems facing an AIDS victim and their family'.

▶ Write a paragraph explaining in your own words the World Council of Churches' statement.

> **Celibacy** – 'the state of being unmarried, especially as the result of a religious promise'.

In 1139 celibacy among practising priests was made law in the Catholic Church. In the early Church many of the leaders were married but the Church in 1139 felt that the celibate priest is more free to devote himself fully to the work of the Church. However, over the last 20 years the idea of celibacy among priests has become a controversial issue in the Catholic Church. In 1966 the National Association for Pastoral Renewal (NAPR) was formed to work for, among other things, optional celibacy. Hans Kung, a Swiss Catholic thinker, said: 'There will be no rest about this matter in the Catholic Church until celibacy is again – as it was originally – left to the free decision of the individual.' However, successive Popes have ruled that celibacy among priests must remain. They argue that celibacy enables a priest to dedicate himself entirely to his ministry. During the Second Vatican Council (1962–5) the idea of priestly celibacy was confirmed.

> *'To the unmarried and the widows I say that it is well for them to remain single as I do.'*
>
> *(I Corinthians 7: 8)*

> **Chastity** – 'the state of being sexually pure'.

To refrain from having sexual relations (sexual abstinence) for personal reasons is known as 'chastity'. People decide to be chaste for a number of reasons:

- to practise self-control
- to concentrate all their energies in other directions
- to practise birth control
- to dedicate themselves to some religious ideal
- as an experiment within a relationship.

In monasteries (communities of monks) and convents (communities of nuns), men and women make three vows – poverty, chastity and obedience.

> **Virginity** – 'the state of being a virgin (one without sexual experience)'.

IS BEING A VIRGIN IMPORTANT?

The most important thing about virginity is for a girl or boy to be sure in their own mind why they do or do not wish to have sexual intercourse.

WHY ARE THERE DIFFERENT VALUES?

Many factors will play their part in making up a person's mind about virginity (their society, its values, their friends, families, etc.). In some countries in the past a father could kill his daughter if she lost her virginity before marriage. It is important to be sure in your own mind what you want to do and to realize that having sexual intercourse is something that should not be undertaken lightly.

IS THERE A DIFFERENCE BETWEEN MEN AND WOMEN WHERE VIRGINITY IS CONCERNED?

There is much hypocrisy here. Men may be called 'Casanova', 'Don Juan' or 'a bit of a lad' if they have a lot of different sexual partners. But if women do, they may be called names like 'tart', 'slut', 'whore'. There is no history of men being punished for loss of virginity. And until contraception was widely available, many women chose to remain virgins rather than risk unwanted pregnancy. The attitude that it is more acceptable for men to be sexually active is still common. In reality, both men and women are capable of feeling jealous if their partner has already 'slept around'. Or both may consider that a marriage is more likely to work if the partners are sexually experienced.

WHY DO PEOPLE CHOOSE TO REMAIN VIRGINS?

There may be a number of reasons.

- They may refrain from sexual intercourse because their partner does not feel that the time is right for sexual intercourse. In this way they are respecting the rights of the individual.

- They may be nervous, insecure, or unsure about sexual intercourse and its implications.

- They may wish to remain virgins so that they can make a gift to the one they really love.

- They may be deeply religious and follow the teachings of their Church. For instance, 'Every sexual act must be within the framework of marriage' (Catholic teaching in the encyclical 'Casti Conubii'); 'The Christian affirms abstinence from sexual intercourse outside the marriage bond' (Methodist Conference, 1981). In these cases they will remain virgins until they marry.

FOR DISCUSSION

▶ What do you think about the following two statements? Compare and discuss them.

a 'It's a good idea to have sex before marriage so that you'll be able to be experienced when you meet your marriage partner.'

! b 'If you sleep around you soon lose the wonder and mystery of sex, which should only be shared with your loved one.'

FOR YOUR FOLDERS

▶ Explain the following words: celibacy, chastity, virginity.

▶ There are about 1½ million individuals committed to celibacy in the Catholic Church and about 2,000 men in religious orders in the Church of England. Why do you think these people have chosen this path? Try and write down at least **two** reasons.

▶ Make a list of some of the dangers of 'sleeping around'.

▶ Dear Marje,
I am 15 and a virgin. I have been going out with this 18-year-old boy for six months. We have quite heavy petting sessions but he wants me to have sex with him. I have told him 'No' – but he's threatened to finish with me if I don't go to bed with him. I love him but don't want to lose my virginity. Help me, please.
Yours sincerely,
Confused

Write a letter back to 'Confused', giving her some advice.

The word 'homosexuality' was first coined by a Swiss doctor, K. M. Benkert, in 1869. Greek 'homo' has been added to Latin 'sex' to indicate an attraction of sexual preference for the same sex. Female homosexuality is also described as 'Lesbianism', taking its name from the island of Lesbos, where the Greek poet Sappho once lived in a female community. Evidence suggests that the incidence of homosexuality among adult men and women is about five per cent. There has been much debate among scientists about the causes of homosexuality but, because of the complexity of human sexual drives, no conclusion has yet been reached. However, it is generally agreed that homosexuality is not a matter of choice. The traditional Christian teaching has been that homosexual people must remain physically inactive, or celibate, on the grounds that the only form of proper sexual behaviour is between married men and women.

THE BIBLE AND HOMOSEXUALITY

There can be no doubt that homosexuality is not a modern phenomenon. In the book of Leviticus, written over 3,000 years ago, we can find references to homosexuality, e.g. 'You shall not lie with a man as with a woman' (*Leviticus 18: 22*). Also, in *Genesis 19* we can read the story of the destruction of Sodom and Gomorrah, supposedly destroyed because of their 'wicked ways', including homosexuality. Some experts have questioned this, saying it was destroyed not just because of homosexual practices, but for other reasons as well. However, it is clear that the writers of the Old Testament condemned homosexuality.

In the New Testament we also find references to homosexuality:

> '. . . no fornicator or idolater, none who are guilty either of adultery or of homosexual perversion . . . will possess the kingdom of God'.
>
> (I Corinthians 6: 9–10)

Jesus made no specific reference to homosexuality during his teaching and ministry. In his book *Christian Attitudes to Homosexuality* Peter Coleman writes: 'Jesus would presumably have regarded it as one of the types of sexual sin for which forgiveness and repentance were more appropriate than punishment.'

A homosexual relationship can be loving and caring

HOMOSEXUALITY AND THE LAW

Sexual relations between females have never been against the law except in the case of members of the armed services. Executions for male homosexual acts continued into the eighteenth century. Though the death penalty was removed in most European countries in the nineteenth century, it was still very severely punished by long terms in prisons. Fear of prosecution probably caused many suicides. However, by the middle of the twentieth century many states had adopted a more tolerant attitude.

During and immediately after the Second World War, there was a rapid increase in the number of homosexual offences known to the police. As a result, the Wolfenden Committee was set up to look at homosexuality. In 1967 the Sexual Offences Act removed the threat of prosecution from consenting adults (over 21) who share homosexual practices in private.

THE HUMANIST ATTITUDE TO HOMOSEXUALITY

About five in every 100 people are primarily homosexual, yet male homosexuality was against the law until quite recently, and many men were sent to prison for homosexual activity. Humanists, however, regarded it as nobody else's business if two adults of the same sex chose to give each other sexual pleasure. So Humanists, in cooperation with some progressive religious people, campaigned for the law against homosexuality to be changed, and eventually it was changed in 1967.

FOR DISCUSSION

▶ Read the following statements in class. Discuss what you think they mean, and whether you are in agreement with them.

'In sacred Scripture they [homosexuals] are condemned . . . this does not permit us to conclude that all those who suffer from homosexuality are personally responsible for it, but it does point to the fact that homosexual acts are disordered and can in no case be approved of.'
(Roman Catholic *Declaration on Sexual Ethics*, 1975)

'It is the nature and quality of a relationship that matters; one must not judge it by its outward appearance but by its inner worth . . . an act that expresses true affection between two individuals – does not seem to us to be sinful by reason alone of the fact that it is homosexual.'
(A Quaker essay, *Towards a Quaker View of Sex*, 1963)

'For homosexual men and women, permanent relationships characterized by love can be an appropriate and Christian way of expressing their sexuality.'
(A Methodist report, 1979)

'Homosexuality in this culture is a stigma label. To be called a "homosexual" is to be degraded, denounced, devalued, or treated as different. It is the knowledge of the cost of being publicly recognized as a homosexual that leads many people to conceal their sexual identity.'
(K. Plummer, *The Making of the Modern Homosexual*, Century Hutchinson, 1981)

'Love, security, happiness are the important things. If two people of the same sex behave towards one another in a loving and considerate way, and if their relationship brings them security, joy and contentment, then Humanists would wish them well.'
(Humanist Dipper)

'We believe that fear or hatred of homosexuals is a social evil, similar to anti-semitism, racism, slavery, and with the same evil consequences. It harms both the victimized individuals, and the society which tolerates it.'
(The Campaign for Reason, *Towards a Charter of Homosexual Rights*, 1978)

FOR YOUR FOLDERS

▶ After reading this section try and write an article (about 200 words) about some aspect of homosexuality.

! ▶ Which of the statements you have discussed do you agree with most? Give reasons for your answer.

In 1984 in Britain there were 396,000 marriages. Almost half of these took place in a Register Office and many were second marriages. In our society people are only allowed one partner (**monogamy**). In some societies it is acceptable to have more than one partner (**polygamy**).

WHY MARRY?

The main reasons are:

- to commit yourself to the person you love for a lifetime
- to bring up children in a secure and loving home
- to control and direct the sex instinct
- for friendship and companionship through life.

THE MARRIAGE VOWS

These can be found in the Book of Common Prayer.

> 'I take thee to be my wedded husband (or wife)
> to have and to hold
> from this day forward
> for better and worse
> for richer and poorer
> in sickness and in health
> to love and to cherish
> till death us do part
> according to God's holy law
> and thereto I give thee my troth [promise].'

Both partners make this promise. Then the ring is placed on the third finger of the woman's hand (often men have a ring too). Then the man and the woman say separately:

> 'With this ring I thee wed;
> with my body I thee honour and all my worldly goods with thee I share
> in the name of the Father, the son and the Holy Spirit.'

THE CHURCH OF ENGLAND WEDDING CEREMONY

The vicar or minister begins by explaining the Church's view of marriage – it is a gift of God, blessed by Christ, and is a symbol of Christ's relationship with the Church. He then advises that marriage should not be approached rashly, without

Just over half the marriages in Britain take place in a church

thought or to satisfy lust, but with respect, consideration and seriousness. The core of the ceremony is in four parts:

1. 'Is there any impediment to marriage?' If any reason is known why the marriage should not take place, it must be stated at this point.
2. 'Wilt thou have?' The question is asked of the bridegroom first and then the bride. They reply 'I will'.
3. The vows (when rings are exchanged). The couple promise to love, comfort, honour and keep themselves for each other. The promise (vow) to 'serve and obey' is only used if the bride requests it.
4. 'Those whom God hath joined together let no man put asunder.' With this declaration from the vicar or minister the couple are now married and the register can be signed.

The bride's father (or close relative) stands with the bride at the altar steps until he has completed his role – that of giving his daughter's hand in marriage to the bridegroom. The best man (a friend or relative of the bridegroom) completes his role by handing over the ring(s) which are blessed by the minister. After the ceremony the bridal party move to the vestry. Here the marriage register is signed by the bride, the groom, and two witnesses (often the best man and chief bridesmaid).

IN THE REGISTER OFFICE

The law requires that two statements must be repeated in turn by the bridge and groom:

1 *'I do solemnly declare that I know not of any lawful impediment why I (say full names), may not be joined in matrimony to (say full names).'*

2 *'I call upon these persons here present to witness that I (say full names) do take thee (say full names) to be my lawful wedded wife/husband.'*

When a marriage takes place in a register office these vows are made in front of the Superintendent Registrar of the district. The register is then signed.

A HUMANIST VIEW

In this country, marriage has always been basically a civil contract. Up to the sixteenth century a couple who wished to marry needed only to make a declaration in front of witnesses outside the church door – like the "handfasting" ceremony which was legal until quite recently in Scotland. (Nowadays the couple who marry in church are not legally married until they have signed the register in front of witnesses.)

If Humanists wish to marry they usually do so in a Register Office, and celebrate as they wish afterwards. (About half of all marriages now take place in Register Offices, some of which go to a great deal of trouble to make their premises fittingly attractive and welcoming.)

(Humanist Dipper)

A METHODIST VIEWPOINT

'Christian marriage has a twofold purpose – fellowship and parenthood. Permanence in the union is an essential condition. It both expresses and develops not only constancy in affection, but also spiritual qualities of trust, faithfulness, mutual consideration, reverence and love.'

(Methodist Conference, 1980)

IN GROUPS

▶ In groups of six, with each person taking a part, write a short play about the following situation.

Kevin and Michelle are not churchgoers and they are planning their wedding. They would like to have a ceremony in a register office but Michelle's parents are keen churchgoers and would like them to marry in church. Kevin's mother, too, wants a church wedding but his father doesn't mind either way. Act out the discussion that might take place.

FOR DISCUSSION

▶ Marriage is still popular although it is frequently attacked. What are the reasons for its popularity and for the attacks on it?

▶ Discuss the meaning of the marriage vows.

FOR YOUR FOLDERS

▶ In your own words, describe why people marry.

▶ Explain in your own words what the marriage vows mean.

▶ According to Methodists, what qualities should a Christian marriage express?

! Can you think of any other qualities that should be included?

SOME IMPORTANT BIBLICAL TEACHINGS ON MARRIAGE

'In the beginning, at the creation, God made them male and female. For this reason a man shall leave his father and mother and be made one with his wife and the two shall become one flesh. It follows that they are no longer two individuals: they are one flesh. What God has joined together, man must not separate.'

(Jesus, in *Mark 10: 5–9*)

'The husband must give the wife what is due to her, and the wife equally must give the husband his due. The wife cannot claim her body as her own; it is her husband's. Equally the husband cannot claim his body as his own; it is his wife's.'

(St Paul, in *I Corinthians 7: 3–5*)

A ROMAN CATHOLIC VIEW

When Pope John Paul II made his pastoral visit to Britain in 1982, he spoke about marriage. He presented this vision of married life:

'A man and a woman pledge themselves to one another in an unbreakable alliance of total mutual self-giving. A total union of love. Love that is not a passing emotion or temporary infatuation, but a responsible and free decision to bind oneself completely, "in good times and in bad", to one's partner. It is the gift of oneself to the other. It is a love to be proclaimed before the eyes of the whole world.'

MARRIAGE IS NOT ALWAYS EASY

An organization that tries to help married couples is the **National Marriage Guidance Council**. It believes that:

1 marriage needs responsibility and unselfish love
2 happy family life is the basis of society
3 marriage is a partnership for life
4 family planning can help a marriage
5 a happy and loving sex life will help a marriage.

THE HUMANIST VIEW OF MARRIAGE

Humanists believe that marriage is a valuable institution in that it raises children and gives society stability. They believe that marriages have to be worked at and that too often newspapers, television, magazines and society in general romanticize about marriage, making it out to be the end result of a beautiful romance. It is no such thing, say Humanists. It is the beginning of a relationship. Marriage partners should be tolerant, kind and respectful towards each other. They should be sympathetic to each other, listen to the other's problems and concerns and try to take an interest in their partner. Sex is not the most important part of marriage – it is only one aspect of what should be a deep, well-developed, caring relationship.

SOME PROBLEMS WITHIN MARRIAGE

'It was OK until the baby came. Now I never see her – we never go out together.'

(Paul, aged 24)

'Since John got laid off it's been terrible. He's home all day and has lost the will to go out at all. He's under my feet – just moping about.'

(Erica, aged 35)

'We argue like hell, about money mainly. She spends money like water.'

(Lloyd, aged 23)

'I was married at nineteen. I'd never known anyone else except Richard. One day I met this lovely bloke at the keep-fit club. He's kind, charming, gentle . . . everything that Richard was until we got married. I think I would like to have an affair with him.'

(Stephanie, aged 22)

'I never see Gordon. He doesn't get home from work till eight and every weekend he leaves me and the kids and plays golf.'

(Cheryl, aged 30)

'Marriage is the beginning of a relationship'

FOR DISCUSSION

▶ In groups of four to five discuss the five cases of Paul, Erica, Lloyd, Stephanie and Cheryl. How would you try to help these people?

▶ 'Marriage is out of date.' Do you agree?

FOR YOUR FOLDERS

▶ Write a paragraph on the Christian view of marriage.

▶ What qualities would a Humanist try and bring to their own marriage?

▶ Make a list of the problems married couples face.

THINGS TO DO

▶ Ask two or three couples you know what they think 'makes for a successful marriage'.

!▶ In pairs, decide on an order of importance for the following qualities in making a marriage successful:

1 Having children
2 Sexual compatibility
3 Love, affection
4 Mutual trust (no secrets)
5 Understanding and discussing things together
6 Comradeship – doing things together
7 Good temper
8 Sense of humour
9 Financial security – no debts
10 Being considerate (give and take).

Britain has the highest divorce rate in Western Europe, though the percentage is still lower than in the United States.

There are many pressures on marriage in our society.

- **finance** – unemployment, inflation and the high cost of living
- **lack of communication** – due to work, hobbies, children, couples do not have time to discuss things together
- **lack of companionship** – your marriage partner ought to be your best friend. But sometimes money worries, work, leisure activities and time factors separate the partners from one another
- **false hopes** – people become disillusioned when the realities of married life do not come up to their expectations
- **human nature** – everybody changes. The person you marry at 21 may be a different person at 30
- **children** – children can make or break a marriage. Sometimes they can bring couples much closer together and sometimes they can increase tensions in a home.

DIVORCE AND THE LAW

In 1857 a man could obtain a divorce if he could prove that his wife had been unfaithful. In 1878 a women could obtain a separation if the man had been cruel. By 1937 desertion and insanity were grounds for divorce as well. In 1966 a Church of England report called *Putting Asunder* stated that divorce should be allowed for the breakdown of a marriage, which included the idea of unreasonable behaviour. This brought about the 1969 Divorce Act. Some people felt that this Act made divorce too easy. In fact, many marriages had broken down before the 1969 Act, but they just had not been legally dissolved.

THE BIBLE AND DIVORCE

'Suppose a man marries a woman and later decides that he doesn't want her because he finds that she is guilty of some shameful conduct. So he writes out divorce papers, gives them to her, and sends her away from his home.'

(Old Testament, Deuteronomy 24: 1)

'Man must not separate . . . what God has joined together.'

(Jesus, in *Mark* 10: 9)

'Moses permitted you to divorce your wives because your hearts were hard. But it was not this way from the beginning. I tell you that anyone who divorces his wife, except for marital unfaithfulness, and marries another woman, commits adultery.'

(Jesus, in *Matthew* 19: 8–9)

THREE SOLUTIONS

If a couple find it impossible to live together there are three main solutions.

1 **Desertion** – One partner simply leaves the other to live elsewhere.
2 **Judicial** – The courts grant a separation, meaning the couple are not allowed in any way to interfere in each other's lives. After five years one partner can apply for divorce without the consent of the other.
3 **Divorce** – The marriage is officially declared by the courts to be at an end. After two years of living apart, and if both partners are willing, they may apply for a divorce.

A CATHOLIC VIEW OF DIVORCE

The Catholic Church teaches that a marriage between two baptized couples is a *sacrament* (a sacred ceremony) and cannot be dissolved. However, if the marriage involves one partner who is not baptized then the marriage can be dissolved under serious circumstances. (i.e. if one partner converts to Catholicism but the other 'refuses to live peacefully with the new convert') (Code of Canon Law). Also, a marriage between two partners who are baptized can be dissolved if there is a just reason (Canon 1142), e.g. impotence or the inability to assume the obligations of marriage.

The Catholic Church also can *annul* a marriage. An *annulment* is 'a declaration that the marriage bond did not exist' whereas a *dissolution* is the breaking of a bond that did exist. A marriage can be annulled if there is:

- *a lack of consent* (e.g. somebody has been forced into marriage)
- *a lack of judgement* (e.g. if somebody marries without being fully aware of what marriage entails)
- *an inability to carry out the duties of marriage* (e.g. somebody might be mentally very ill)
- *a lack of intention* (e.g. if one of the partners intends at the time of the marriage not to have children).

◇

A QUAKER VIEW OF DIVORCE

There is a diversity of views on divorce by Quakers but most would agree with the Quaker report, *The Marriage Relationship*, of 1949:

'No couple, marrying with any deep conviction of permanence, would willingly give up the struggle to overcome their difficulties and seek a way of escape. But where the difficulties involved in a marriage are, of their very nature, serving to drive a couple further apart in bitterness of mind and heart, or where they reduce them to an empty and conventional semblance of living together, then there can be little reason for keeping within the bonds of legal marriage two people between whom no spiritual marriage exists. Broken marriages are always a calamity, but particularly so if there are children, since they need above all a stable home and the love and care of both parents.'

WHAT HAPPENS WHEN YOU SMOKE?

Tobacco is made up of some 300 chemicals, 40 of which are known poisons. When you smoke, these chemicals enter the bloodstream:

- nicotine – a very powerful drug which makes the heart beat faster
- tar – which contains a number of substances which can cause cancer
- irritants – which damage the fine hairs which keep the lungs clear, producing smoker's cough
- carbon monoxide – a deadly gas which affects the blood's ability to carry oxygen round the body.

SOCIAL EFFECTS

- money – cigarettes are very expensive. Money spent on cigarettes can't be spent on other things
- pollution – non-smokers are forced to smoke because of smokers. They become 'secondary smokers'. A recent report says that non-smoking wives who live with smoking husbands have a 50% increase in the risk of lung cancer
- Health Service – smoking costs the NHS about £180 million a year. Cigarette smoking is responsible for 50,000 premature deaths a year and thousands of serious illnesses
- the third world – it takes one acre of trees to dry and cure tobacco. The long-term effects of growing tobacco are deforestation, erosion of soil and loss of land fertility. In some Third World countries land is given up to produce tobacco crops for export, and because of this the local population may go hungry.

SMOKING AND APPEARANCE

SMOKING AND HEALTH

Smoking contributes to and causes many illnesses and diseases.

- **bronchitis** – smoking causes 75% of deaths from chronic bronchitis which kills over 30,000 people a year
- **emphysema** – this is a disease of the lung, affecting breathing
- **heart disease** – nicotine increases the heart-rate and so wears down the heart. Smoking causes 25% of deaths from heart disease
- **cancer** – 90% of deaths from lung cancer are caused by smoking
- **other problems** – smokers are less fit than non-smokers, and are more likely to get colds, flu and other infections. Smoking can damage unborn babies, and can cause problems like blood clots and stomach ulcers.

WHY DO PEOPLE SMOKE?

- from habit
- to relax
- for pleasure
- to conform
- because of advertizing.

PROFILE OF A SMOKER

Name: MARCUS JONES
Age: 15

INTERVIEWER: How much do you smoke?
MARCUS: About ten fags a day.
INTERVIEWER: How much does this cost you?
MARCUS: Nearly a fiver a week.
INTERVIEWER: When did you begin smoking?
MARCUS: I had my first fag when I was
                about nine – I felt really sick. I
                started smoking regularly
                when I was about 13.
INTERVIEWER: Do many of your mates smoke?
MARCUS: Yeah, about half of 'em, but a
                few are trying to give up.
INTERVIEWER: And you, are you going to give up?
MARCUS: Perhaps when I'm older.
INTERVIEWER: Why did you start smoking?
MARCUS: My mum and step-dad
                smoked. I started pinching
                their fags. I feel a bit
                rebellious smoking, I suppose.
INTERVIEWER: What do you mean?
MARCUS: Well, it's not the thing to do
                these days, is it? So it feels
                different to be called a smoker.

CHRISTIANITY AND SMOKING

Smoking was unknown during biblical times.
However, we can apply some teachings of the Bible.

'Love your neighbour as yourself.'

(Jesus, in *Matthew 22: 39*)

'Your body is a temple of the Holy Spirit.'

(*I Corinthians 6: 19*)

A CHRISTIAN VIEWPOINT

**'Christians hold that life is a gift from God and
consequently place a high value on its
preservation. The Christian ideal has been to
refuse to expose life to actions or circumstances
which carry with them high risks of harm . . . It has
been shown that smoking renders the individual
prone to illness and to premature death. It can
therefore be argued that it is a denial of the
goodness of created existence.'**

(Church of England briefing)

FOR YOUR FOLDERS

▶ Look at the biblical quotes. Write a
  paragraph on their relevance to
  smoking. (Think of 'social effects' and
  'smoking and health'.)

▶ In order, write down which of the
  following you find the most frightening:
  a On average, each cigarette takes
     5½ minutes off your life.
  b An average smoker loses about 5
     years of their life.
  c Only 6% of people diagnosed as
     having lung cancer survive.
  d Cigarette smoking kills. On
     average, it kills 1,000 people
     prematurely a week.
  e 25% of heart attacks are caused by
     smoking.

▶ Design an anti-smoking poster, using
  one of these statistics as a slogan.

THINGS TO DO

▶ Interview someone who is a smoker. Either
  tape-record or make a report of the
  interview. Ask the same sort of questions as
  in 'Profile of a smoker'.

▶ List as many sporting events as you can that
  are sponsored by tobacco companies.

FOR DISCUSSION

▶ 'The Health Service should refuse to treat
  smokers.'

▶ 'The government earns millions by taxing
  cigarettes, yet it tells us to stop smoking.
  How hypocritical can you get?'

WHAT IS ALCOHOL?

Alcohol is a chemical, a drug, an element, a fuel, a poison, a preservative and a solvent.

The alcoholic content of
beer and cider is 4–7%
wine is 10–12%
spirits is 40–55%
fortified wine (e.g. port, sherry) is 15–22%

WHY DO PEOPLE DRINK ALCOHOL?

- to celebrate
- to be sociable
- to relax
- to feel adult
- for medicinal purposes
- in religious ceremonies

HOW DOES ALCOHOL AFFECT THE BODY?

- **the heart** – It increases blood pressure and heart rate
- **the nervous system** – It acts as a depressant
- **the liver** – It passes through the liver and in large amounts causes disease of the liver
- **the stomach** – Small amounts help digestion; large amounts cause vomiting
- **the skin** – It makes you feel warm but really your body is losing heat
- **the brain** – It affects the way you speak, act and think.

Research in America has shown that societies which have a low rate of alcoholism exhibit the following characteristics:

- the children are exposed to alcohol early in life
- parents drink moderately
- alcohol is often taken with food
- wine and beer are drunk at home
- drinking is not seen as good or bad
- drinking is not seen as being 'grown up'
- abstinence is socially acceptable
- people socialize without alcohol.

THE COST OF A DRINK

- **personal** – Sometimes people who drink too much become loud and aggressive and say things they later regret
- **death** – 9,000 people in the UK died in 1984 because of alcohol abuse
- **loss of production** – Absenteeism, accidents, etc., caused by alcohol
- **health costs** – Alcohol abuse costs the country's medical services millions of pounds every year.

Crime
In a survey of prisoners:

- 41% claimed to have been drinking before committing the offence
- 50% of murderers had been drinking at the time of the offence.

Drinking causes such things as soccer violence, sexual crimes, vandalism and assault.

Drinking and driving
The major cause of death in people aged 18–25 is road accidents as a result of drinking.

Family conflicts
Drink can cause family rows, tensions, divorce, child and wife battering and poverty.

People drink alcohol to be sociable and relax

KEY IDEA

Alcohol if abused is extremely dangerous for individuals and society. Some Christians never drink alcohol (Salvation Army members, Methodists, Pentecostalists) and believe that the government should do more to reduce alcohol abuse. Other Christians believe that alcohol used moderately and responsibly is the best approach. In the New Testament Jesus is depicted as drinking wine.

A METHODIST VIEW

'**Alcohol can give pleasure and cause harm. It is used in celebration, socialization and relaxation; it can be enjoyed for its taste. It is also a significant factor in a range of personal and social problems, and can lead to accident, illness and death . . . All Methodists (should) consider seriously the claims of total abstinence, and make a personal commitment either to total abstinence or to responsible drinking.'**

(Through a Glass Darkly, Responsible Attitudes to Alcohol, 1987)

'IGNORANT DRINKING IS THE BIG KILLER'
London campaign alerts public to risks of alcohol

A CAMPAIGN was launched in London yesterday to alert the public to the risks of alcohol – dangers which the government is keeping "mum" about, claimed the organizers.

"Many people are drinking more than their safe limit simply because they do not know how much is too much, and nobody is telling them," said the organizers of Drinkwise London.

At least 26% of men and 4% of women drink more than the generally accepted safe level and 6% of men and 1% of women drink "seriously damaging amounts of alcohol," they added.

Alcohol consumption has doubled in the last 30 years in Britain and drink now figures in 40% of all road accidents, 33% of all domestic accidents and 30% of deaths by drowning. A third of all child abuse is also linked to regular heavy drinking.

More than 1,000 young people died in 1984 as a result of drinking alcohol compared with 235 from drug abuse, said the organizers.

(Morning Star, 29 September 1986)

FOR DISCUSSION

▶ Comment on the American research about low rates of alcoholism.

▶ 'Without alcohol our society would to go pieces.'

▶ Some people describe getting drunk as having a 'good time'. What leads them to such a view? In what sense could getting drunk be described as having a 'bad time'?

▶ What is your opinion about total abstention or moderate drinking as the best Christian approach?

FOR YOUR FOLDERS

▶ Earlier this century there was total prohibition in America. Write an article for a magazine pretending that you believe that we should now have total prohibition in Britain because of the personal and social cost of alcohol.

THINGS TO DO

▶ Make a list of:
  a all the ads on TV in one week about alcohol,
  b the images these ads try to create,
  c the types of drink advertized,
  d the time of night the ads are on.

27 DRUGS I

At some time in our lives, we almost all use drugs of one sort or another. A drug is any substance which alters the chemistry of our bodies and, consequently, affects the natural balance of our minds and emotions. Drugs which can be prescribed by a doctor include substances such as penicillin which are intended to cure infections, and sleeping pills, tranquillizers and anti-depressants intended to help us relax and cope with the stress and tensions of everyday life. Cigarettes and alcohol, which we can 'prescribe' for ourselves, have a similar function.

People turn to illegal drugs for much the same reasons. Adolescence can be a particularly difficult period. We may be under conflicting pressures from parents, school and friends, and many difficult choices may have to be made. It can also be a time of frustration and boredom. As a result, young people are always vulnerable to the offer of something which may be 'fun' or 'make them feel better'. But they often don't know about the risks involved, or how easily a serious drug problem can develop from a light-hearted experiment.

DRUGS WHICH CAN BE DANGEROUS

Drug	What it looks like	How it's used	What it does	Risks
Amphetamines (Speed)	A white powder or brown powder, may be in pill or capsule form	Usually sniffed or injected	Makes people lively, giggly, over-alert; depression and difficulty with sleep may follow	Heavy use can produce feelings of persecution
Cannabis (Pot, Dope, Hash, Grass)	Hard brown resinous material or herbal mixture	Smoked in a reefer or pipe, sometimes with tobacco	Users may seem drunk and talkative	Risks of accidents when intoxicated
Cocaine (Coke)	A white powder	Usually sniffed, can be injected or smoked	Similar effects to amphetamines	More likely to lead to dependence
Heroin (Skag, Smack)	A white or speckled brown powder	Usually heated on silver paper and fumes inhaled; can be sniffed or injected	Alertness at first, then drowsiness and drunken appearance	Overdose can cause unconsciousness; regular, frequent use leads to dependence; giving up then causes withdrawal symptoms like bad 'flu
Magic Mushrooms	Mushrooms, found growing wild in the UK	Eaten fresh or dried	Similar to cannabis	Mainly from eating other poisonous mushrooms by mistake
Other Opiodes (Dikes, 118s)	May include red or white tablets or ampoules	Swallowed or injected	Same as heroin	Same as heroin
LSD (Acid)	Tiny coloured tablets; micro spots on blotting paper; small absorbent stamps	Taken by mouth	Glazed eyes and sometimes over-excitement	Heavy use can cause bad confusion and ideas of persecution
Tranquillizers	Prescribed tablets and capsules, taken illegally for kicks	Taken by mouth	Similar to alcohol, effect increased when taken with alcohol	May lead to dependence; withdrawal symptoms can include attacks of extreme fear

56

WHAT ARE THE DANGERS OF ILLEGAL DRUG TAKING?

The main dangers are:

- having an accident while under their influence
- some drugs may depress or stop breathing
- accidental overdose can lead to unconsciousness or even death
- regular use can lead to addiction or dependence

Drugs can also have nasty side-effects:

- they can bring on confusion and frightening hallucinations
- they can cause unbalanced emotions or more serious mental disorders
- first time heroin users are sometimes violently sick
- regular users may become constipated and girls can miss their periods
- later still, there may be more serious mental and physical effects
- If a drug user starts to inject, infections leading to sores, abscesses, jaundice, blood poisoning and even the AIDS virus may follow.

OTHERS PROBLEMS CAUSED BY DRUG ABUSE

Personal problems

- relationships may become strained, especially with friends and family
- rather than helping you to face up to life, drugs may simply become one more problem in addition to the ones you already have.

Legal problems

- by taking illegal drugs you are risking heavy fines or even imprisonment
- if you are arrested the result may be a police record, difficulty finding a job later, and other embarrassments.

Money problems

- it costs money to take drugs – they are expensive. A heavy user may end up spending all their money on 'feeding the habit'.

HOW ABUSING DRUGS CAN HARM SOCIETY

- a heavy user will find it difficult to contribute to society
- there is a connection between drug addiction and crime.

HOW ABUSING DRUGS CAN HURT OTHER PEOPLE

- family life can be affected
- relationships can be ruined
- medical resources have to be used to cope with drug abusers, at the expense of other people who need them
- a baby born to a drug-addicted mother will become an addict
- sometimes drug abuse leads to crimes of violence
- the use of drugs during pregnancy can threaten the baby's life
- many drug traffickers are involved in other forms of crime. By buying drugs, the user may be indirectly financing major crimes.

FOR YOUR FOLDERS

▶ Explain the following words: addiction/dependence, speed, dope, smack, dikes, acid, overdose.

▶ Write a short article entitled 'Why some kids say "yes" '.

▶ Design a poster on the theme 'The dangers of drug abuse'.

▶ John Stuart Mill, a nineteenth-century philosopher, wrote in an essay entitled *On Liberty* in which he argued that a person should be free to do whatever they want so long at it does not harm anyone else. Write an essay about whether drug abuse is entirely a matter for the individual.

▶ Write a letter to a friend who has told you that they have been offered drugs. Try and explain the dangers that they will face by accepting these drugs.

A CHRISTIAN APPROACH

Most Christian churches believe that to abuse the body and the mind with drugs is wrong. However, as well as condemning drug abuse, the churches would agree that many drug addicts and people with drug-related problems need care and help. Also, the question, 'Why do some people in our society resort to drugs?' needs to be seriously considered. One biblical reference that might be applied to drug abuse could be the following:

> *'Do you not know that you are God's temple and that God's spirit dwells within you? If anyone destroys God's temple, God will destroy him. For God's temple is holy and that temple you are.'*
>
> *(I Corinthians 3: 16, 17)*

This declaration by the Methodist Church in 1974 sums up the attitude of many modern Christian churches to drug abuse:

> *'Several guidelines help the Christian to determine his personal attitude to the non-medical use of drugs. Obviously he must face the serious scientific evidence about the harmful effect of drugs. His faith teaches him to use all things, including his money, responsibly. He seeks to meet problems and stresses by following Christ's teaching and living by his power. To Christ he offers the undiminished vigour of his body and mind. He loves his neighbour and therefore examines the probable effect of his behaviour, habits and example on that neighbour. He accepts his part in the responsibility of the Church in the work of education and rehabilitation.'*

THE RASTAFARIANS

Many Rastafarians use 'ganja' (marijuana) as part of their religious ritual, and as an aid to meditation. The Rastafarians say that God who created all things made the herb for human use and will cite *Genesis 1: 12* as their proof:

> *'And the earth brought forth grass, and herb . . . and God saw that it was good.'*

Ganja is part of Rastafarian culture

A leading Rastafarian has this to say of ganja:

> *'Concerning ganja and the amount of publicity it has received of late, it becomes imperative that I should impart some knowledge on it regarding its history and usage among the Rastafarians. We know that in the wars of the Crusades, the Moslems were using a form of Hashish from which they get the name Assassin. This same Hashish was used religiously. In Jamaica, we do not make full use of Hashish in that form; what we use is ganja. The Rastafarian sees ganja as part of his religious observance. He sees ganja as the smoother of mental imbalances and as a meditatory influence. Ganja is really used to bring forth a peaceful and complacent aspect within man. We do not believe in the excessive use of ganja. It cannot be used to excess. In that case it would be bad for man. But in truth, ganja used moderately is not bad. We do not find ganja as a mental depressor, ganja sharpens your wit, and keeps you intellectually balanced. It is not a drug; it is not an aphrodisiac either. We smoke it, we drink it, we even eat it sometimes. We do not find it a poison. I have been smoking ganja since I was 18 years of age. I am now 50, and I have never been to a doctor for any ganja related ailments.'*

> *(Taped interview with Ras Sam Brown, 1975, from The Rastafarians by Leonard E. Barrett, Heinemann, 1977)*

There are thousands of Rastafarians living in Britain. Many of them do not smoke cigarettes or drink alcohol. However, by smoking 'ganja' they often come into conflict with British law. In the DHSS briefing *Drug Misuse* (1985), the Institute for the Study of Drug Dependence has this to say about the long-term use of marijuana:

'There is no conclusive evidence that long-term cannabis use causes lasting damage to physical or mental health. This may be because the kinds of study needed to detect slow-to-develop and infrequent outcomes have not been done. However – like tobacco smoke – frequently inhaled cannabis smoke probably causes bronchitis and other respiratory disorders, and may cause lung cancer.

People who use cannabis are more likely to try other drugs. Likewise people who smoke tobacco or drink are more likely to try cannabis. In neither case is there any evidence that using one drug actually causes people to use another. Cannabis does not seem to produce physical dependence, though regular users can come to feel a psychological need for the drug's effects or may rely on it as a "social lubricant".

The effects of cannabis may cause special risks for people with existing lung, respiratory, or heart disorders and heavy use in persons with disturbed personalities can precipitate a temporary psychiatric disorder.'

GATEWAY TO HELL
Runcie's drug warning
By PAUL SMITH

DRUG-TAKING isn't a short cut to heaven but a path to hell, the Archbishop of Canterbury warned yesterday.

Dr Robert Runcie said the drugs menace was one of the greatest challenges facing Britain's youth.

He told a church congregation in London: 'You can, I believe, help those who are tempted and who imagine they are taking an exciting short-cut to heaven, to realize that they will in fact be treading a frightening path to the gateway of hell.'

The Archbishop, who was addressing a service of the National Council YMCAs, said a Parliamentary report had highlighted the drugs epidemic in America, and he feared that the problem in Britain was set to get much worse.

He said: 'None of us has done enough to combat this abuse.'

(*Daily Mirror*, 3 June 1985)

TALKING POINTS

- 'It's my own body, I can do what I like with it.'

- 'Drugs harm others more than they harm you.'

- Discuss these Home Office statistics about drug-related deaths in the UK:
  Smoking:
    100,000 per year in the UK, 1984
  Alcohol:
    9,000 per year in the UK, 1984
  Other Drugs:
    235 per year in the UK, 1984

- 'The more teachers and governments talk about drugs the worse it's going to get.'

- 'To legalize cannabis is the thin end of the wedge.'

FOR YOUR FOLDERS

▸ Write a few sentences on the Christian view of drugs.

▸ Write down three reasons why a Methodist is against drug abuse.

▸ What are some of the views of Ras Sam Brown on ganja?

▸ Why do you think Dr Runcie thinks drugs are evil?

! ▸ What are your views on the legalization of cannabis (marijuana)?

29 DEATH

In 1983, 659,000 people died. Half of the deaths were caused by diseases of the heart and of the blood circulation system. One quarter of the deaths were caused by cancer (152,000 deaths). Road accidents accounted for nearly 3% of deaths.

The Greek thinker Socrates said 'All men are mortal', meaning that we all have to die someday. In the Old Testament it says 'The days of our years are three score years and ten' (Psalm 90). This statement is roughly correct today – men on average live to about 70 and women to 74. About 1,000 people in Britain reach their 100th birthday each year.

Every year we see thousands of 'deaths' on TV. Some are real and some are fictional. In our newspapers we read about people dying. Death always seems to be happening to other people, not to ourselves. Death is a 'taboo' subject – people don't like to talk about it. We try to pretend it doesn't exist. We put people in 'homes for the dying' or in hidden wards or geriatric hospitals. So when somebody close to us dies we often don't know how to cope.

Experts tell us that the emotions of the bereaved develop in stages:

1 shock
2 guilt
3 idealization of the deceased.

Other feelings occur, too:

1 denial
2 anger
3 bargaining ('I'd do anything to have them back')
4 depression
5 acceptance.

ADVICE

Sometimes the bereaved suffer alone. This is usually because people say 'I don't know what to say to him . . . what can you say?' People are afraid to speak because they don't know how to react to death or how to respond to somebody else's grief. It is very important, say psychiatrists,

- to make yourself available to the grieving person
- to give them your time
- to let them talk
- to listen quietly to them
- to let them cry
- to try and help them to see that guilt is a natural part of the grieving process
- perhaps to write them a letter
- not to assume they have somebody else to talk to.

Most people feel a need for some kind of religious ceremony when someone dies. Although it is possible to have a disposal of the body without one, most people opt for a church service.

'Most people feel a need for some kind of religious ceremony when someone dies'

BURIAL OF THE DEAD

Here are some extracts from the Church of England's service first published in 1662:

'Man that is born of a woman hath but a short time to live, and is full of misery. He cometh up, and is cut down, like a flower; he fleeth as it were a shadow, and never continueth in one stay.'

'In the midst of life we are in death; of whom may we seek for succour but of thee, Oh Lord.'

'For as much as it have pleased Almighty God of his great mercy to take unto himself the soul of our brother here departed, we therefore commit his body to the ground; earth to earth, dust to dust, in sure and certain hope of the Resurrection to eternal life . . .'

A HUMANIST VIEWPOINT

'Humanists accept death as natural and inevitable and are not afraid of talking about death, dying and funerals. They don't wait until the event happens and accept the traditional religious ritual. They like to sort out the kind of funeral service they would prefer. (There is no law that requires that only a registered person may officiate at a funeral.)

Often, a Humanist friend will compose a short 'life-story' to be read at the crematorium; many people choose their favourite poems or pieces of music. Humanist groups often receive requests to conduct a non-religious funeral for someone. The British Humanist Association's booklet on non-religious funerals includes these words: 'A Humanist funeral is a leave-taking – but it is more than that. It should be a celebration of the good life and personality that have been.'

Many Humanists donate their bodies for medical or teaching purposes; their eyes so that blind people may be offered a corneal graft; their kidneys . . . because they do not believe that bodies are sacred, but are ours to use and dispose of as we will.'

(Humanist Dipper)

CREMATION

More and more people today opt for cremation. The service is similar to the service for burial of the dead. The whole service may take place in a crematorium – consisting of a chapel and the ovens in which the dead body is burned. The ashes of the deceased are placed in an urn. Either this is buried or the ashes are scattered on the grounds of the crematorium. Ashes may also, with official approval, be scattered elsewhere. Some people have them scattered in places that were special to the deceased (mountains, the sea or even a football ground).

TALKING POINTS

'Any man's death diminishes me, because I am involved in mankind; and therefore never send to know for whom the bell tolls; it tolls for thee.'

(John Donne)

FOR DISCUSSION

▶ Why do you think so many people prefer a Christian burial?

▶ In what ways can a priest help the bereaved?

▶ Why is cremation becoming more popular, do you think?

FOR YOUR FOLDERS

▶ Write a letter to a close friend who has just lost a relative.

▶ Look through the Christian service for burial of the dead. List some of the ideas and beliefs mentioned.

Early societies: When people buried their dead they placed objects like simple tools, ornaments and clothes near the corpse. Often they would paint the body with red ochre (red representing blood which symbolizes life) and tie the body in the foetal position. All these things suggest that from the dawn of history people have believed in immortality (everlasting life).

The Ancient Egyptians: The Egyptians built great tombs, or pyramids, for their pharaohs. The corpse would be embalmed to stop it decaying and items such as food, clothing, furniture and weapons would be buried with the body ready for the next life.

The Tibetan Book of the Dead: Written thousands of years ago, this explains in great detail the journey of the soul after death.

Judaism: The Jews in the Old Testament believed in a place called 'Sheol' meaning 'pit' or 'grave' which everyone went to, never to return. However, about 350 BC the Jewish priests began talking about Paradise (for the good) and Gehenna (for the bad).

'The Egyptians built great tombs, or pyramids, for their pharaohs'

Hinduism: Hindus believe that human beings have a soul ('atman') which, after death, is reborn in another body. This is called reincarnation. The type of life you are reborn into depends on how well you lived this life.

Christianity: Christians have always said that the body and soul are part of the one whole person. This has led them to develop the idea of the 'resurrection of the body'. The main idea is that our essential personalities will be reconstituted (reconstructed); after death you will be recognizable as 'you'. Some Christians, especially Roman Catholics, believe that the soul goes to Purgatory first, where it will atone for its sins before returning to God. Some Christians believe in a place of torture and fire (hell), but today many Christians reject this, believing that a loving God will not allow anyone to suffer in hell.

Humanists: Humanists believe that humans have developed from earlier animals and are similar in many ways to other animals. They do not see this as taking away from human dignity. They believe that we do not have to live for ever to be worth something – that we earn our worth by rejecting 'superstitious' ideas (like immortality), by learning to think rationally and by working for an end to human suffering. Many Humanists think that beliefs in immortality represent people's fears of death.

Spiritualists: Spiritualists believe it is possible to communicate with 'the other side'. They believe in the existence of ghosts and spirits which are the spirits of those who have died.

Near-death experiences: In the 1970s Dr Raymond Moody in America began investigating people's experiences after they had 'died' and then been revived. Many of them spoke of bright lights, meeting 'dead' friends or family, and a feeling of approaching some sort of barrier.

SURVEY

In 1983 an RE teacher conducted a survey among 200 fourth-year pupils at Helston School, Cornwall.

The pupils were asked, 'Which, if any, of the following do you believe in?', and given 10 categories. Some of them believed in more than one type of life after death. Here are the results:

- God 68%
- The Devil 46%
- Heaven 30%
- Hell 16%
- Some sort of life after death 70%
- Reincarnation 61%
- Ghosts 53%
- Contacting the dead 40%
- Death is the end 30%
- Resurrection of the body 22%

Reincarnation

More people in the Western countries are beginning to believe in reincarnation. Some of them point to three interesting areas. First, *déjà-vu* ('already seen' in French) – the feeling of 'having been here before'. Secondly, the lines of the palm – perhaps marking out our past and present lives. Thirdly, 'hypnotic regression' – when people under hypnosis speak with great detail and clarity about a 'past life'.

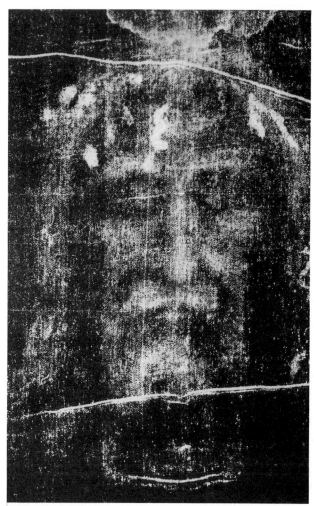

Many people believe that the famous Turin Shroud is proof of the resurrection of Jesus

THINGS TO DO

▶ Conduct a survey like the one above.

FOR DISCUSSION

▶ Discuss the results of your survey.
▶ If a small child asks you about death what should you tell them?
▶ 'The belief in immortality is nothing more than a foolish wish.'

FOR YOUR FOLDERS

▶ Explain the words: Paradise, Gehenna, atman, resurrection, spriritualism, hypnotic regression.

▶ Write an article of around 150 words on 'Beliefs about life after death'.

! ▶ Write a paragraph on 'My own view about immortality'.

! ▶ Look at the photo of the Turin Shroud. Why do you think it is important to many people?

31 **SUICIDE**

FACTFILE

- suicide accounts for less than 1% of total deaths in Britain every year
- suicide rates went up by 20% between 1975 and 1985
- men, on average, are twice as likely to commit suicide as women
- the suicide rate among alcoholics is 80 times greater than for the rest of the population
- up to 1961 it was a criminal offence to commit suicide or attempt to do so
- in 1961 the Suicide Act was passed but it still remains a criminal act, punishable by up to 14 years' imprisonment, to aid or advise suicide
- attempted suicides are probably running at about 200,000 a year
- every day throughout the world at least 1,100 people commit suicide (one every 80 seconds).

CAUSES

There are many reasons why people commit suicide. Here are some of them:

- bereavement (the death of a loved one)
- insecurity (stemming from childhood)
- loneliness
- losing faith in the future
- threat of nuclear war (in 1985 a man killed himself and his family after seeing *Threads*, a film about nuclear war)
- loss of self-confidence
- deep depression caused by mental illness
- an attempted suicide can be a 'cry for help'
- old age
- disease (terminal illness or a long drawn out illness)
- pressures at work
- money worries
- drink and drug problems
- self-sacrifice
- to avoid capture (in war, e.g. in 73 AD, 960 Jews committed suicide at Masada rather than surrender to the Romans).

CHRISTIAN ATTITUDES

In some cultures, people believed it was perfectly honourable to take one's own life (e.g. 'hari-kiri' in Japan'). However, Christians have always believed that all life is sacred and ultimately belongs to God.

Therefore they believe that people have no right to kill themselves, any more than they have the right to kill others.

In the past, the Church insisted that if you committed suicide you would not have eternal life. Today, however, the Church has a more compassionate attitude, accepting that people are often under great pressure and often commit suicide when their minds are not stable.

Christians try to work for a better community and society, believing that only a caring environment will help people to live happier and more fulfilled lives.

What the Bible says

'Every man's life is in his [God's] power.'
(Job 12:10)

'Love your neighbour as you love yourself.'
(Mark 12:31)

'I have the strength to face all conditions by the power that God gives me.'
(I Corinthians 10:13)

THE SAMARITANS

In 1953 Chad Varah, a Church of England priest, was appalled to discover that three suicides were taking place every day in London. He installed a telephone in his church and publicized the fact that anyone thinking of committing suicide could telephone him and talk to him. This was the start of the 'Samaritans'. Today there are 174 centres and over 20,000 carefully selected and trained volunteers offering a 365-day 24-hour service (Christmas is their busiest time). They speak to two and a quarter of a million callers every year.

The Samaritans:

- are not all Christians
- must not 'preach' if they are Christians
- must be good listeners, sympathetic and caring.

EXIT

This is a society which is willing to help people to put an end to their lives, where the people concerned have repeatedly and strongly expressed the desire to commit suicide. Usually these are people dying of an incurable illness.

A HUMANIST VIEW

'The humanist sees it as a fundamental human right to be able to choose to die.

'Here again it is only comparatively recently that the law of this country has been reformed so as to allow suicide. Until 1961 suicide was illegal – though, of course, it was only *unsuccessful* suicide attempts that offenders could be punished for! (Except, that is, for the 'punishment' of not being given a Christian funeral).

'It is still against the law to help someone else to commit suicide – and, indeed, it is obvious why this should be so. However, humanists think that one kind of suicide help should be allowed – and that is the kind known as 'euthanasia' (mercy killing), in the case of incurable illness'.

(B. Smoker, *Humanism*, Ward Lock Educational, 1973)

TALKING POINTS

• 'We are all responsible for those around us. Sometimes we simply need someone to talk to. The Samaritans are always there and they have time to listen.'

(John, Samaritan volunteer)

• 'The man who, in a fit of melancholy, kills himself today would have wished to live had he waited a week.'

(Voltaire)

• 'He who saves a man against his will as good as murders him.'

(Horace, 1 BC)

• 'The question is whether suicide is the way out or the way in.'

(Emerson, 1839)

FOR DISCUSSION

▶ Suicide has been called 'that most selfish of acts'. Do you agree?

▶ Discuss reasons why the attitude of some churches towards suicide has changed over the last few years?

! ▶ People have the right to die, and to be helped in certain circumstances to take their own life.'

FOR YOUR FOLDERS

▶ Write a piece on 'The causes of suicide'.

▶ List some of the qualities you think a Samaritan volunteer should have.

! ▶ Which talking point do you most agree with? Give reasons for your answer.

KEY WORDS

A. Prejudice a feeling and attitude we have about certain types of people before we have had personal experiences of them. A 'pre-judgement'. Once our prejudices are established we build up **stereotypes**, which are crude mental pictures of the appearance and character of the groups we dislike.

B. Discrimination Prejudice is an attitude, usually of dislike, that we have towards certain people. As long as these feelings and attitudes remain inside as thoughts, no one is hurt but ourselves. However, when we act positively against the things we don't like we are **discriminating**.

FOR YOUR FOLDERS

▶ Copy our Key Words **A** and **B**. Explain what you think is the difference between them.

▶ 'We believe that blacks are taking over our country.'
'White European race is the superior race and always will be.'
What are your views on these opinions?

▶ Read the following account of racism as recorded for the radio. Write two paragraphs:
a on examples of prejudice in the extract.
b on examples of discrimination in the extract.

! ▶ From reading the extract, what do you consider to be one main cause of racist attacks?

▶ Look at the photo below. Explain in your own words what is happening.

This National Front demonstration is a good example of racial prejudice and discrimination

EXTRACT FROM *FILE ON 4*

The following material is extracted from *File on 4*, first transmitted on BBC radio on 25 February 1981, in which Janet Cohen interviewed residents of the East End of London.

Cohen: Racial tension is no stranger to the East End of London. Traditionally, it's played host to generations of immigrants, with an uneasy mixture of hospitality and hostility. The mosque in Brick Lane, East One, came to the Muslims third-hand. First it was a Huguenot church and then a synagogue. When in the thirties the British Union of Fascists held rallies here, they found support as well as opposition. Today's violence takes place against a background of rising unemployment. In some boroughs, one person in seven is out of a job. A report published today claims that blacks are more likely than whites to lose their jobs in the economic recession, but skinheads on the streets don't see it this way. Their heads shaved, their trousers cropped six inches above the ankle, their faces pinched in the cold, they feel the blacks are stealing their jobs. As for violence against the ethnic communities:

1st skinhead: Do I condone it? Yes. They've got no right to be here.

Cohen: That families should have bricks thrown through the window, airgun pellets, that kind of thing?

1st skinhead: Well, only blacks like, and Jews, yeh. White European race, right, is the superior race and always will be.

Cohen: Is it really fair that families should be intimidated, after all, they are people?

1st skinhead: Yes, course it is. They're not people, they're parasites, they're just poncing off us.

2nd skinhead: I've just come out of prison myself, if I may say so, I just come out after doing 15 months.

Cohen: For doing what?

2nd skinhead: Smashing a Pakistani up. I just stabbed him.

Cohen: Really?

2nd skinhead: In a pub.

Cohen: Why?

2nd skinhead: I don't know. I was just drunk and I just stabbed him through the back.

3rd skinhead: The fact is, right, ordinary people don't like 'em moving in around the East London environment round there, right, and they want 'em out.

Cohen: But is it fair to attack their families?

All skinheads: Yes, it is.

3rd skinhead: It's the only way isn't it, I mean the Government ain't doing nothing are they, nobody's doing anything, are they?

1st skinhead: It takes ten years for a bill to get through Parliament, right, and nothing happens, right, so if you give them like a good dig and all that like, it might just send a couple of them home; you know what I mean. They might think, oh, you know like, we've had enough like, we're going to get home. So we're doing our little bit.

Cohen: What's your badge, by the way?

3rd skinhead: Can't you see? (Laughter)

Cohen: I don't know what it is.

3rd skinhead: SS. Yeh. Nazi badge.

1st skinhead: Nazi sympathizer.

Cohen: What does that stand for?

3rd skinhead: That means that I like what the Nazis did.

4th skinhead: We're proud to be Nazis. We're not no party or nothing. I'm proud to be a Nazi.

3rd skinhead: We're just kids off the street, you know what I mean.

4th skinhead: We believe that the blacks are taking over our country, the Yids are taking over our country.

Cohen: So how much violence do you think there is around here, then, towards . . .

All skinheads: There's a lot more, there's a lot more, there should be a lot anyway. There is, there is a lot going around.

FOR DISCUSSION

▶ **In groups four to five discuss the views expressed in the above extract.**

▶ **'I detest your views, but I am prepared to die for your right to express them.'**

(Voltaire)

67

Psychologists tell us that three factors are very important in the formation of prejudice.

1. **Grouping** People seem to need to belong to groups, probably for security. Sometimes groups have special 'in' customs and types of behaviour. Common groups among young people include those that belong to 'sub-cultures', e.g. mods, rockers, punks and heavy metal freaks. The important thing about any group, however, is that outsiders are excluded. Often the 'in-group' feels superior to, and secure against, the 'out-group'.

2. **Scapegoating** The idea of a 'scapegoat' originated in many early religions. The book of *Leviticus (14:20)* records how Aaron, the priest, recited all the sins of the tribe over a goat's head. The goat was then sent away to lose itself in the wilderness. The idea was that evil could be transferred. In modern society too we often blame somebody else if something goes wrong. Somehow it makes the situation easier if we can accuse a group we already dislike, no matter how innocent they are. In Nazi Germany, for instance, the Nazis blamed the Jews for unemployment and inflation. Although the Jews were not the real cause, 6 million of them died in the Nazi death camps.

3. **Fear** Fear is a part of prejudice. We have in-groups because basically we are afraid. We find scapegoats because we are afraid. Often fear arises out of ignorance – we are frightened of things we don't fully understand.

A small child has no prejudices. Often our prejudices are formed by our environment; by our parents and friends; by TV, magazines and by our general culture.

Racial prejudice has three basic elements:

1. **Colour prejudice** Some people are prejudiced against other human beings just because of the colour of their skin.

2. **Ethnic prejudice** Some people have a dislike or fear of the cultural and social attitudes of groups different from theirs. This type of prejudice was, and still is, often directed against the Jewish nation (called **Anti-Semitism**) amongst others.

3. **Xenophobia** Some people simply say they don't like 'foreigners'. This is usually born out of ignorance and fear. It is rather strange because millions of the 'British race' come from foreign stock (e.g. French or German).

A CHRISTIAN VIEW

'Every human being created in the image of God is a person for whom Christ died. Racism, which is the use of a person's racial origin to determine a person's value, is an assault on Christ's values, and a rejection of his sacrifice.'

(World Council of Churches, 1980)

Prejudice against groups of people can lead to discrimination which in turn can lead to violence, injustice, exploitation, a divided society and, as in Nazi Germany, to possible **genocide** (the killing of a whole race of people). Many groups of professional people have tried to work out ways of ridding our society of prejudice and discrimination. In 1985 the Swann Report stressed that schools have a vital role to play.

The Jews were victims of genocide, the most extreme example of racial prejudice

A HUMANIST VIEW

'Humanists believe that prejudice is caused by ignorance and fear. Racism robs people of their humanity, both the perpetrator of racism and the victim of racism. Racism is a denial of human dignity.'

School shake-up call in drive to stamp out classroom colour bar

By NICK WOOD, Education Correspondent

TRADITIONAL teaching methods must be changed to stamp out racial prejudice in Britain's schools, the controversial Swann Report urged yesterday.

The report called for a major shake-up in the way subjects are taught and said: "Multi-cultural understanding has to permeate all aspects of a school's work.

"Britain is a multi-racial and multi-cultural society and all pupils, including whites, must be taught to understand what this means."

It said that RE lessons should cover all the main world religions, not just Christianity, and that children should be taught to understand the "plurality of faiths in modern Britain."

Lord Swann, 65-year-old former chairman of the BBC and head of the committee which produced the report said there was "enormous frustration and disenchantment" with our society among many of the 2½ million British-born people from ethnic minorities.

He said they suffered from widespread prejudice and discrimination for which the education service was partly to blame.

The report calls for an end to traditional lessons putting our own country's culture and values first.

The report calls for:–

A NATIONAL effort by exam boards, curriculum experts, and local and national inspectors to devise multi-cultural exams and syllabuses.

AN END to teaching subjects like history and geography from a purely British standpoint.

SCRAPPING of textbooks giving a "stereotyped" view of black people and POLICY statements outlawing racism and backing the multi-cultural approach.

QUOTE
'ASIANS rarely have sons and daughters who are going to be bright GCE candidates. It isn't the fault of the education system and it isn't the fault of Western civilization – it's inherent in life.'
Teacher

QUOTE
'TEACHERS expect very little of coloured children.'
Student

'Most of my friends who have got jobs are white.'
West Indian

QUOTE
'WHEN I was a junior I never bothered about colour, but since I came to this school I have encountered a lot of racial prejudice. I realized that my colour was making them horrible to me.'
Indian Girl

(*Daily Mirror*, 1985)

FOR YOUR FOLDERS

▶ Explain in a sentence the following: in-groups, scapegoats, ethnic prejudice, xenophobia, genocide.

▶ List some of the groups in our society who are all too often 'scapegoats'.

▶ Write a sentence on why Christians should not be racially prejudiced and a sentence on why Humanists should not be racially prejudiced.

▶ Read the *Daily Mirror* newspaper article. Use it to produce a short account of the main ideas of the Swann Report, including some of its recommendations.

! ▶ How do you think racial prejudice develops and what do you think can be done to eliminate it?

▶ What do you think of the quotes from the *Daily Mirror*?

THINGS TO DO

▶ Look in your school library. Can you find any books there that 'stereotype' black people and their cultures?

FOR DISCUSSION

▶ 'Prejudice is a great time-saver; you can make up your mind without bothering with facts.'

▶ 'If I knew what my prejudices were I wouldn't have them.'
(W. H. Auden, poet)

CASE HISTORY I

A young Pakistani woman, born in Britain, describes some of the conflicts of coming from a strict Muslim family and attending a mainly white British school.

'There were a number of things that caused me anxiety at school which I never mentioned to my parents. There were also a number of happy events I wanted, but was reluctant, to share. I had won the long jump at an area sports day at school which meant going on to the large stadium in my home town to take part in the inter-schools sports events. I had to have my legs uncovered and would be wearing shorts. So I took part in the event, without telling my parents, feeling inside that I was doing wrong by uncovering my legs in front of so many people. I wanted my parents to be proud of me, but asking them and getting a refusal was too big a risk to take.

In retrospect I feel that much of my anxiety during those childhood years must have been unfounded. My parents had bought me the sportswear and therefore knew I was wearing them, so why the guilt feelings on my part? All I can say now is that at that young age I must have picked up the general social values expressed at home and applied them to myself and the school situation. I do not blame my parents as being the cause of my anxiety. I didn't communicate what I felt was wrong to them, so how were they to know? Because they were so loving and caring with regard to everything else, I didn't feel they were being nasty. It must have been that security at home which helped me to cope with any contradictions which arose because of cultural differences. So, therefore, I remember my childhood as basically happily dotted here and there with a little confusion. But it must be like that for most children, Asian or not, to a greater or lesser degree.

Sade, a famous British singer

One of Britain's leading comedians, Lenny Henry

*The contradictions and conflicts over the years did increase. The adolescent years were filled with moments of having to sit back and analyze my situation **vis-à-vis** my family, my religion and the social mores of the wider society and what I would do. Now, being 23, having been through university, and being in full-time employment, away from home, I feel thankful that I was exposed to two cultures at the same time. It has been a painful path to tread, at times, but it has resulted in a keen awareness and respect for the differences and more important, the similarities, between human beings regardless of colour, race or religion. I feel a special bond of love and respect for my parents who despite not understanding me during my adolescent years especially, gave me examples of human strength, love and tolerance. It can't have been an easy time for them. I was experiencing the conflict, they were watching it, not always understanding it, often not being able to help even when they wanted to.'*

CASE HISTORY II

Chris Mullard was born in Britain in 1944. He is British and he is black. He describes how as a child he was taught to be ashamed of his colour.

*'In an extremely **subtle** way school taught me to consider the colour of my skin as ugly. My teachers never mentioned my colour. Instead they mentioned the customs of black people in far-off lands, Britain's former role in civilizing the natives, making them acceptable to the white man and in turn to themselves. They made me learn **nationalist** songs, recite poetry **enraptured** with the glories of the Empire; they taught me British **etiquette**, how to be nice to everybody and how to **doff** my hat to my superiors. But I took a back row seat whenever **dignitaries** visited the school because I was not white and I was told numerous stories about wicked black people who were responsible for all the troubles in the world. As a teenager I emerged believing that black was wrong, white was right. Whenever asked about my colour, I explained that it was only **superficial**. It was no more than a heavy sun tan which I got from frequent holidays in the Caribbean.'*

FOR YOUR FOLDERS

▶ Write a précis (a précis is a shortened account of something, mentioning the main points) of the young Pakistani woman's early experiences.

▶ Briefly explain why Chris Mullard experienced anxiety at school.

! ▶ Can you think of other problems that might be caused by being 'exposed to two cultures'?

▶ What racial problems do you think Sade and Lenny Henry may have had in Britain?

THINGS TO DO

▶ Try and find out about some of the beliefs and customs of Hindus and Muslims and Sikhs. Go to the school library or ask your RS teacher for help.

▶ In groups of three or four try to work out some of the problems faced by:
a immigrants to Britain coming from other cultures;
b being born in Britain and having parents who were immigrants;
c being black and living in Britain.

FOR DISCUSSION

▶ Discuss your findings.

When immigrants from the New Commonwealth started to arrive in Britain in the 1950s there were no laws to protect them against discrimination. However, in the 1960s it became obvious that something was needed to guarantee the basic rights of the newcomers and their children.

There have been three Race Relations Acts: 1965, 1968 and 1976. The 1976 Act attempts to remedy the weaknesses from which the earlier laws suffered. It also set up the **Commission for Racial Equality** which has a general duty to work for the ending of discrimination in Britain, and to promote equality of opportunity and good relations between people of different racial groups.

THE 1976 ACT

The law provides for equality of opportunity in the following areas:

- employment – 'It is unlawful for an employer to discriminate in relation to employment.'
- housing
- education
- goods services and facilities.

It is also against the law to publish or, in a public place, use language which is threatening, abusive or insulting and which is likely to stir up hatred against any racial group in Britain.

The Commission for Racial Equality (CRE) employs over 200 people who work towards the elimination of discrimination and to promote equality of opportunity and good relations between different racial groups.

Some people argue that the law is not the right way of dealing with racial discrimination. They say that there is no law which can make people treat their neighbours fairly.

ROMAN CATHOLIC TEACHING

*'The Church's teaching on this matter is clear and straightforward. Every human being is made in the image of God. We are all brothers, and neighbours, of each other. There is no special merit in being good to members of your own family, your blood relations. To be good to people of your own religion, or nation, is to be expected, though behaviour often falls short of this expectation – the parable tell us how a priest passed by the man who had been robbed and beaten up in the street, and took no notice of him, though he had every duty to help him; it was a stranger, of another place and people, who helped the robbers' victim. The message is quite explicit: the stranger was the one who was the neighbour. And to love your neighbour as yourself is one of the two great, fundamental commandments. Charity, for the Christian, does not begin at home or end at home. Charity lies in what you **do** or allow to be done – not in how you think.*

Racism is not the only kind of division, or form of selfishness, hindering human brotherhood. But in our time it is a particularly important one.'

(Catholic Truth Society)

'There is no law which can make people treat their neighbours fairly.

A HUMANIST VIEW

'We deplore racial, religious, ethnic, or class antagonisms. Although we believe in cultural diversity and encourage racial and ethnic pride, we reject separations which promote alienation, and set people and groups against each other.'

(Humanist Manifesto II, 1973)

THE NEW TESTAMENT AND RACE RELATIONS

In the book of Ezra (Old Testament) we find the Jews to be very wary of people who were not Jews (Gentiles).

> *'Separate yourselves from the peoples of the land and from foreign wives.'*
>
> *(Ezra 10: 10)*

However, later the Book of Ruth is written as a protest against this, showing how King David was a descendant of a mixed marriage.

In the New Testament we find that Jesus and St Paul worked for equality and good race relations. However, many Jews refused to have any contact with Gentiles. In this famous parable Jesus tries to break down some barriers.

The Parable of the Good Samaritan

'25On one occasion an expert in the law stood up to test Jesus. "Teacher," he asked, "what must I do to inherit eternal life?"

26"What is written in the Law?" he replied, "How do you read it?"

27He answered: " 'Love the Lord your God with all your heart, with all your soul, with all your strength and with all your mind'; and, 'Love your neighbour as yourself.' "

28"You have answered correctly," Jesus replied. "Do this and you will live."

29But he wanted to justify himself, so he asked Jesus, "And who is my neighbour?"

30In reply Jesus said: "A man was going down from Jerusalem to Jericho, when he fell into the hands of robbers. They stripped him of his clothes, beat him and went away, leaving him half dead. 31A priest happened to be going down the same road, and when he saw the man, he passed by on the other side. 32So too, a Levite, when he came to the place and saw him, passed by on the other side. 33But a Samaritan, as he travelled, came where the man was; and when he saw him, he took pity on him. 34He went to him and bandaged his wounds, pouring on oil and wine. Then he put the man on his own donkey, brought him to an inn and took care of him. 35The next day he took out two silver coins and gave them to the innkeeper. 'Look after him,' he said, 'and when I return, I will reimburse you for any extra expense you may have.'

36"Which of these three do you think was a neighbour to the man who fell into the hands of robbers?"

37The expert in the law replied, "The one who had mercy on him."

Jesus told him, "Go and do likewise." '

(Luke 10)

FOR YOUR FOLDERS

▶ What is the Race Relations Act?

▶ Explain briefly the work of the Commission for Racial Equality.

▶ Write a paragraph on the Catholic and the Humanist views of race relations.

▶ The Parable of the Good Samaritan concerns race relations. The Jews despised the Romans and the Samaritans. Explain in your own words:
  a how Jesus tried to show people why their prejudices were wrong in the story;
  b how the Parable of the Good Samaritan is more than just a story about helping people.

! ▶ Try to explain:
  a why the law is not sufficient in itself to stop discrimination,
  b why Humanists reject 'separations' – and say what you think.

Martin Luther King was born in Atlanta, Georgia, on 15 January 1929, in the heart of the American south. From an early age he was aware that black people were not treated as equal citizens in America. Four million Africans had been torn from their homes and shipped to America to work as slaves. Even though slavery had been abolished by Abraham Lincoln in 1869, most blacks still lived in poverty in the richest nation on earth. They earned half of white people's wages; many could not vote; they lived in ghettos and they were segregated (separated) in public places. Some whites (like a secret society called the Ku Klux Klan) wanted slavery reintroduced and used violence against black people.

Martin Luther King was a Christian. He became a doctor of theology and in 1954 a Baptist minister in Montgomery, Alabama. He believed that the only way to achieve equality was by non-violent and peaceful forms of protest. Not all blacks agreed with him. The Black Power movement (led by Malcolm X) believed that equality would only be achieved by violence.

In Montgomery black people could only sit at the back of buses and even the old had to give up their seats if a white person asked them. Martin Luther King organized a 'bus boycott', (when black people refused to use the buses until they were desegregated). This movement became known as the Civil Rights movement and in 1960 Martin Luther King became its leader. In 1956 the government passed a law making it illegal to segregate people on buses.

Martin Luther King campaigned endlessly. In 1957 he spoke to a crowd of 40,000 in Washington at a 'freedom march'. He organized various forms of peaceful protest. Often the police reacted with violence. In 1960 he led a march of a quarter of a million people in Washington demanding that black people be given the vote.

Throughout his life Martin Luther King was confronted by violence. His home was bombed, he was stabbed, his family received death threats but he kept to his Christian belief that violence and hatred could only be conquered by love and forgiveness. In 1964 he was awarded the Nobel Peace Prize, and in 1965 equal voting rights were given to black people.

In 1967 America became involved in the Vietnam War. Over 400,000 Americans were fighting in the war and thousands of Vietnamese civilians had

Martin Luther King preaching

died. In a Christmas Eve speech in 1967, Martin Luther King said: 'Man is a child of God, made in his image . . . until men see this everywhere . . . we will be fighting wars.'

In 1968 a white man called James Earl Ray shot Martin Luther King dead in Memphis. The world was stunned. He was only 39. His wife Coretta later wrote: 'The killers of the dream could end his mortal existence with a single bullet but not all the bullets in all the arsenals in the world can affect his death.'

> *'I have a dream that my four little children will one day live in a nation where they will not be judged by the colour of their skin, but by the sort of persons they are. I have a dream that one day . . . all God's children, black men, white men, Jews and Gentiles, Protestants and Catholics, will be able to join hands and sing in the words of the black people's old song, Free at last, free at last, thank God Almighty, we are free at last!'*

FOR DISCUSSION

▶ In pairs, discuss what would be said if Martin Luther King met Malcolm X.

▶ Conduct an interview between the two.

THINGS TO DO

▶ Tape the interview. It will need an introduction about what it was like to be black in America before 1970.

FOR YOUR FOLDERS

▶ What do the following words mean? How do they fit into the story of Martin Luther King?
slavery, Ku Klux Klan, Black Power movement, bus boycott, Civil Rights movement, segregation, Nobel Peace Prize, Vietnam.

▶ Copy down the three statements from the following list that you think say most about the piece you have read.
1   Martin Luther King was a troublemaker.
2   Malcolm X was right.
3   Non-violence is the best solution.
4   Martin Luther King was a brave man.
5   Black people were treated as if they had no dignity.
6   Because of the way he died, all Martin Luther King's beliefs were proved wrong.

▶ Write a diary of events plotting Martin Luther King's life.

▶ Write down a list of some of Martin Luther King's beliefs.

▶ What did Coretta King mean about her husband's death?

▶ Why do you think the Rock star Stevie Wonder has campaigned for 15 January to become a national holiday in the USA?

▶ Jesus said, 'No prophet is recognized in his own country' *(Luke 4: 24)*. How might this be interpreted in the light of Martin Luther King's life?

▶ Why do you think Christians regard Martin Luther King's life as being so inspirational?

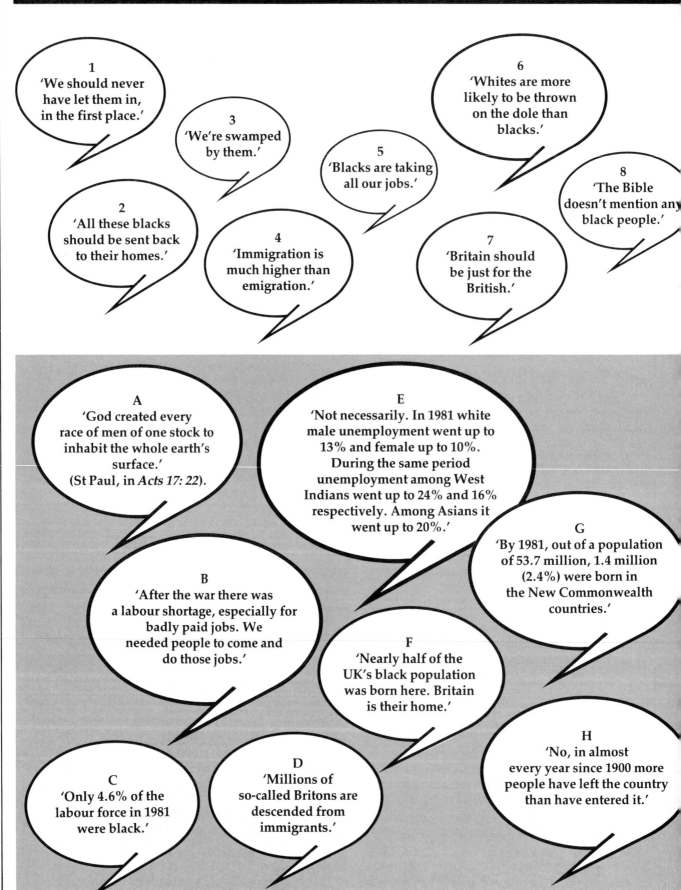

1
'We should never have let them in, in the first place.'

2
'All these blacks should be sent back to their homes.'

3
'We're swamped by them.'

4
'Immigration is much higher than emigration.'

5
'Blacks are taking all our jobs.'

6
'Whites are more likely to be thrown on the dole than blacks.'

7
'Britain should be just for the British.'

8
'The Bible doesn't mention any black people.'

A
'God created every race of men of one stock to inhabit the whole earth's surface.' (St Paul, in *Acts 17: 22*).

B
'After the war there was a labour shortage, especially for badly paid jobs. We needed people to come and do those jobs.'

C
'Only 4.6% of the labour force in 1981 were black.'

D
'Millions of so-called Britons are descended from immigrants.'

E
'Not necessarily. In 1981 white male unemployment went up to 13% and female up to 10%. During the same period unemployment among West Indians went up to 24% and 16% respectively. Among Asians it went up to 20%.'

F
'Nearly half of the UK's black population was born here. Britain is their home.'

G
'By 1981, out of a population of 53.7 million, 1.4 million (2.4%) were born in the New Commonwealth countries.'

H
'No, in almost every year since 1900 more people have left the country than have entered it.'

9
'When in Rome, do as the Romans do. They should leave their culture at home.'

10
'Jesus makes no reference to race relations.'

11
'Some people are less equal than others. It says so in the Bible.'

I
'In *Acts 8: 26–40*, we hear of Philip meeting an Ethiopian black man who becomes converted to Christianity.'

J
'A multicultural society is varied, interesting and exciting, full of different life-styles, customs, beliefs, foods, clothes, types of music and attitudes. It gives society so much more.'

K
'In *Luke 17: 11–19* Jesus makes the point that of the 10 lepers who were cleansed the only one who gave thanks to God was a hated Samaritan. Jesus did not distinguish between people on the grounds of race.'

FOR YOUR FOLDERS

▶ Read through the statements marked 1 to 11. Now try and match these with the statements marked A to K. Here is an example:

11		A
'Some people are less equal than others. It says so in the Bible.'	=	'God created every race of men of one stock to inhabit the whole earth's surface.'

(Acts 17: 22)

▶ The 'Old Commonwealth' countries are Australia, Canada and New Zealand. The 'New Commonwealth' countries are the others which Britain used to rule or still rules today and are members of the British Commonwealth of Nations. Try and list some of the 'New Commonwealth' countries. Here are some to start you off: Hong Kong, Kenya, Jamaica . . .

▶ How is this section trying to make you 'think again'?

▶ Why do you think it is important that people think again?

FOR DISCUSSION

▶ In groups of four to five discuss statements 1 to 11 and A to K. Are you surprised by them?

(The figures are taken from *Britain's Black Population*, by the Runnymede Trust and the Radical Statistics Race Group, 1980, Gower Publishing Co. The writers of the book use the word 'black' as a convenient term to include everyone whose skin is black, brown, yellow, or mixed.)

In the 1930s the Nazis under Adolf Hitler embarked on a programme that was planned to rid the world of all Jews and all 'Jewish blood'. It was called 'The *Final Solution* to the Jewish Problem'. The Nazis began to use the Jews as scapegoats for the problems that faced Germany. By 1945, over six million Jews had died, most of them in the gas chambers of concentration camps like Belsen, Dachau, Treblinka and Auschwitz among others. The 'Final Solution' was one of the worst examples of racism that the world has ever seen. It is impossible for us to begin to imagine the amount of human suffering involved. After the war the Jews called it 'The Holocaust'.

On 28 May 1944 Isabella (aged 17), her four sisters, mother and brother were herded, together with other Jews from the Hungarian town of Kisvárda, into cattle trucks. Their destination was Auschwitz. Her mother and youngest sister, Potyo, died almost immediately. Somehow she and her three sisters survived the Holocaust, mainly because of each other. Here are some extracts from her remarkable and moving book:

'Kisvárda was just a little town. It's where I began, where I yearned to be away from. I didn't think I could take a large enough breath there. I cannot count the times I was called a 'dirty Jew' while strolling down Main Street, Hungary. Sneaky whispers: 'Dirty Jew'. No, 'Smelly Jew' – that's what I heard even more often. Anti-Semitism, ever since I can remember, was the crude reality. It was always present in the fabric of life. It was probably so everywhere, we thought, but surely so in Hungary – most certainly in Kisvárda . . .

We were afraid. Our neighbours, we knew, would be Hitler's willing accomplices when the bell would toll. And the bell tolled.

On Monday morning, 29 May 1944, the ghetto was evacuated. Jews, thousands upon thousands of Jews – every shape and form, every age, with every ailment, those whose Aryan blood was not Aryan enough, those who had changed their religion oh, so long ago –

In 1944 Isabella and her family were rounded up in Kisvárda

dragged themselves down the main street toward the railroad station for what the Germans called 'deportation'. Upon their backs, bundles and backpacks – the compulsory '50 kilos of your best clothing and food' (which the Germans could later confiscate in one simple operation).

And the Hungarian townspeople, the gentiles – they were there too. They stood lining the streets, many of them smiling, some hiding their smiles. Not a tear. Not a goodbye. They were the good people, the happy people. They were the Aryans.

'We are rid of them, those smelly Jews', their faces read. 'The town is ours!'

Main Street, Hungary.

Soon we are packed into the cattle cars . . . cars with barred windows, with planks of wood on the bars, so that no air can enter or escape . . . 75 to a car . . . no toilets . . . no doctors . . . no medication.

The Arrival

We have arrived. We have arrived where? Where are we?

Young men in striped prison suits are rushing about, emptying the cattle cars. 'Out! Out! Everybody out! Fast! Fast!

The Germans were always in such a hurry. Death was always urgent with them – Jewish death. The earth had to be cleansed of Jews. We already knew that. We just didn't know that sharing the planet for another minute was more than this super-race could live with. The air for them was befouled by Jewish breath, and they must have fresh air.

The men in the prison suits were part of the Sonderkommandos, the people whose assignment was death, who filled the ovens with the bodies of human beings, Jews who were stripped naked, given soap, and led into the showers, showers of death, the gas chambers.

Isabella completes her book with a chapter on the birth of her second son, Richard, in 1962.

'We have another son, Mama. We have named him Richard. He is like nothing else on the face of the earth. He looks like Uncle Joe and Aunt Sara, like all our cousins, like all of our family.

He looks like nobody else.

He is the sound of your soul. He is the voice of the six million. He is Richard.

Mama, I make this vow to you: I will teach my sons to love life, to respect man, and to hate only one thing – war.'

(all extracts from Isabella Leitner's *Fragments of Isabella*, New English Library, 1978)

FOR YOUR FOLDERS

▶ Write a few sentences on the following:
Anti-Semitism in Hungary
The Aryans
'The Germans were always in such a hurry'

▶ Write a paragraph on:
Isabella's childhood
Auschwitz
Richard

▶ In the death camp, Treblinka, over one million Jews were gassed. A survivor, Samuel Rajzman, who lost 70 members of his family, wrote: 'The world is a prostitute – today it believes, tomorrow it forgets.' Try to explain in your own words what he means.

FOR DISCUSSION

▶ 'The victims were Jews. The murderers were Christians.'

▶ 'The Holocaust story should be untiringly told and retold, making the world aware of its lessons.'

(from *The Holocaust Library*, Schocken, 1980)

In July 1941 three prisoners escaped from the Nazi concentration camp of Auschwitz. The Nazis picked ten men in reprisal to starve to death in the underground bunker. One of the men was Franciszek Gajowniczek. When he realized his fate he cried out, 'O my poor wife, my poor children, I shall never see them again.' It was then that the unexpected happened. From the ranks of watching inmates, prisoner 16670 stepped out and offered himself in the other man's place. Then he was taken with the other nine condemned men to the dreaded Bunker, an airless underground cell, to die slowly without food or water.

Prisoner 16670 was a Polish Catholic priest called Maximilian Kolbe. He was 47 years old. Before the war he had founded one of the largest monasteries in the world which was dedicated to the Virgin Mary. It was called Niepokalanow. He had also travelled as a missionary to the Far East and Russia. In 1930 he helped to start a monastery in the Japanese town of Nagasaki. In 1939 he began helping Jewish refugees.

However, in 1941 he was arrested by the Nazis and sent to prison in Warsaw and then deported to Auschwitz.

Auschwitz was a terrible place. Human beings were treated in the most inhuman ways imaginable. Thousands died every day from beatings, floggings, torture, disease, starvation and in the gas chambers. Father Kolbe dedicated his life in Auschwitz to helping his fellow prisoners. He would console them, share his food with them, organize secret church services. He tried to show others, by his own example, that even in such a hellish place God still loved and cared for them. He once said: 'Every man has an aim in life. For most men it is to return home to their wives and families, or to their mothers. For my part, I give my life for the good of all men.'

An eye-witness of those last terrible days of Father Kolbe's life tells us what happened.

'In the cell of the poor wretches there were daily loud prayers, the rosary and singing, in which prisoners from neighbouring cells also joined. When no SS men were in the Block I went to the Bunker to talk to the men and comfort them. Fervent prayers and songs to the Holy Mother resounded in all the corridors of the Bunker. I had the impression I was in a church. Fr Kolbe was leading and the prisoners responded in unison. They were often so deep in prayer that they did not even hear that inspecting SS men

Auschwitz Concentration Camp

had descended to the Bunker; and the voices fell silent only at the loud yelling of their visitors. When the cells were opened the poor wretches cried loudly and begged for a piece of bread and for water, which they did not receive. If any of the stronger ones approached the door he was immediately kicked in the stomach by the SS men, so that falling backwards on the cement floor he was instantly killed; or he was shot to death . . . Fr Kolbe bore up bravely, he did not beg and did not complain but raised the spirits of the others . . . Since they had grown very weak, prayers were now only whispered. At every inspection, when almost all the others were now lying on the floor, Fr Kolbe was seen kneeling or standing in the centre as he looked cheerfully in the face of the SS men. Two weeks passed in this way. Meanwhile one after another they died, until only Fr Kolbe was left. This the authorities felt was too long; the cell was needed for new victims. So one day they brought in the head of the sick-quarters, a German, a common criminal named Bock who gave Fr Kolbe an injection of carbolic acid in the vein of his left arm. Fr Kolbe, with a prayer on his lips, himself gave his arm to the executioner. Unable to watch this I left under the pretext of work to be done. Immediately after, the SS men with the executioner had left I returned to the cell, where I found Fr Kolbe leaning in a sitting position against the back wall with his eyes open and his head drooping sideways. His face was calm and radiant.'

(The Catholic Truth Society)

The heroism of Father Kolbe echoed throughout Auschwitz and other death camps. Later a Polish bishop wrote: 'The life and death of this one man alone can be proof and witness of the fact that the love of God can overcome the greatest hatred, the greatest injustice, even death itself.'

In 1982 Pope John Paul II, also a Pole, declared that Maximilian was a saint. He opened his speech with the words of Jesus in *John 15: 13*: 'Greater love hath no man than this, that a man should lay down his life for his friends.'

THINGS TO DO

Franciszek Gajowniczek
Niepokalanow
Nagasaki
Auschwitz
The Bunker
John 15: 13
Martyrdom

Look at these words and phrases. How do they fit into the story of Father Maximilian Kolbe? What does each one mean?

FOR YOUR FOLDERS

▶ Write a few sentences describing the photo of Auschwitz.

▶ Write a diary of events plotting Father Kolbe's life.

▶ Imagine that you survived Auschwitz. Write a short newspaper report (about 100 words) about Father Kolbe's sacrifice.

▶ Make a list of other people you've heard of who have been martyrs.

▶ How did Father Kolbe's faith as a Christian affect his behaviour at Auschwitz?

FOR DISCUSSION

▶ 'If a man hasn't discovered something he will die for, he isn't fit to live.'

(Martin Luther King)

 ▶ 'Self-survival, not self-sacrifice.'

> **Sexism** – 'the opinion that one sex is not as good as the other, especially that women are less able in most ways than men'.
>
> *(Longman's Dictionary)*

Throughout most of human history, societies have been ruled by men. It is difficult to examine the status of women because normally they have had none. Historical and religious writings over the last 3,000 years show us how many societies have viewed women.

'100 women are not worth a single testicle.'

(Confucius)

'The female is a female by virtue of a certain lack of qualities.'

(Aristotle)

'I permit no woman to teach or to have authority over men; she is to keep silent.'

(St Paul's Epistle to Timothy, *I Tim 2: 12*)

'Women must accept the authority of their husbands.'

(St Paul's 1st Letter to Peter, *I Peter 3: 1*)

'Every woman should be overwhelmed with shame at the thought that she is a woman.'

(St Clement of Alexandria, 1st century AD)

'Women should remain at home, sit still, keep house, and bear and bring up children.'

(Martin Luther, 1483–1546)

'The souls of women are so small that some believe they've none at all.'

(Samuel Butler, 1612–80)

'What a misfortune to be a woman.'

(Søren Kierkegaard, 1813–55)

'When I turned out to be a mathematical genius my mother said, "Put on some lipstick and see if you can find a boyfriend".'

(20th century American authoress)

JESUS'S ATTITUDE TO WOMEN

The Christian church has been guilty of sexism. However, if we look at the life of Jesus, we find that he did not discriminate against people in a sexist way. He taught in the temple's court of women, showing that in his view women are just as intelligent as men. He startled a Samaritan woman by speaking to her (see *John 4: 4–9*) and included some women among his disciples (see *Luke 8: 2*). The story of Martha and her sister Mary demonstrates his belief that women were fit for other things besides domesticity (see *Luke 10: 38–42*) and it was to Martha that he revealed himself as the 'resurrection and the life' (*John II: 25–7*).

These incidents may not sound particularly remarkable to us, but in Jesus's day his attitude could only be described as 'revolutionary'. He lived in a very sexist society in which women were treated as second-class citizens.

SOME MILESTONES

1857 Marriage and Divorce Act – women were given rights in marriage
1865 First woman doctor qualified
1900 National Union of Woman's Suffrage Society formed
1918 Women over 30 allowed to vote
1919 First woman MP elected
1928 Women allowed to vote at 21
1975 Sex Discrimination Act – 'equal pay for work of equal value'
1979 First woman prime minister elected.

WOMEN IN THE THIRD WORLD

These facts are taken from a Christian Aid leaflet about the plight of women in the Third World.

- women are half of the world's population, do two-thirds of the world's work and produce half of the world's food. Yet women receive only one-tenth of the world's income, own only 1% of the world's property and make up 70% of the world's refugees (with their children)
- two-thirds of the world's illiterates are women
- where women belong to a paid workforce they are often underpaid, have no job security and possess few rights
- women in Africa do up to three-quarters of all agricultural work in addition to their domestic duties.

TODAY IN THE UK . . .

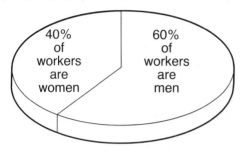

About 40% of all working people in the UK are women.

More women are doing jobs that in the past were done by men.

More men stay at home while more women are becoming the earners in the family.

FOR YOUR FOLDERS

▶ From the quotes through the ages, pick out the ones that you find most offensive.

▶ Write a short article entitled 'The plight of women in the third world'.

▶ At present there is much debate about women becoming priests in the Church of England. Write down some examples of biblical material that would support women becoming priests and of material that would *not* support women becoming priests.

◇

FOR DISCUSSION

! ▶ 'Women are capable of doing any sort of job.'
▶ 'We still live in a sexist society.'

◇

THINGS TO DO

▶ Prepare a three-minute talk to the rest of the class on any one of the following statements.
  a A woman's place is in the home.
  b A woman's work is never done.
  c If both partners work, both partners should share the housework.

Dora Black was born on 3 April 1894 in Surrey. She came from a well-off family and at 18 she won a scholarship to Girton College, Cambridge. She wanted to become an actress but instead involved herself in politics, supporting the rights of women and the Suffragettes. When she was 19 she lost her religious faith and became a Humanist.

A big influence on her life was Bertrand Russell, the famous mathematician and philosopher to whom she was married for a decade. They travelled to Russia and China, wrote books and pamphlets together and started a school called Beacon Hill, in Sussex. Beacon Hill was an extremely progressive school, especially for its time. Discipline was minimal. Boys and girls took all lessons, including PE, together. Religious instruction was excluded. The children helped to make decisions about the running of the school.

Dora Russell lived a very full life, involving herself in many issues. One of her main concerns was fighting for equality for women. She believed that women should have greater freedom to choose what they wanted as regards contraception and abortion. Many women, married and unmarried, became pregnant because they knew very little about contraceptive devices. Dora Russell campaigned for the availability of more information about contraception and for more education about different methods. She believed that it should be freely available and accessible in clinics, surgeries and hospitals. She helped to found the Workers' Birth Control Group, which aimed to help women obtain advice and information about contraception.

Linked with this desire to help give women more freedom, Dora Russell began working towards the legalization of abortion. If a woman wanted an abortion she had to have one 'illegally'. If she was rich, she could go to an expensive clinic and have it done. However, most women were poor. They could not afford to have a safe abortion, so they either had the child or risked their lives and their health in cheap 'back-street' abortion clinics. It was estimated that up to a quarter of a million illegal back-street abortions were carried out every year in Britain. In 1964 Dora helped organize the defence of a Cornish doctor who was charged with abortion.

Dora Russell

She managed to obtain 18,000 signatures on a petition, but the doctor was still sent to prison. Dora's work for the Abortion Law Reform Association played a part in the passing of the Abortion Act in 1967 which gave doctors the right to perform abortions under certain conditions.

Dora Russell also worked in other areas, including the formation of the NCCL (National Council for Civil Liberties), women's groups, Labour Party politics, the Conservation Society, CND and the Peace Movement, the Rationalist Press Association and the National Secular Society. She also wrote books, pamphlets and poems.

Dora Russell became a pacifist towards the end of her life. She believed that war was wrong and that nuclear weapons should be banned. World tension, she believed, could only be eased by negotiation and understanding. In 1958 she led the Women's Caravan of Peace across Europe to Moscow and back. Even when she was in her late eighties she would visit the women at the Greenham Common peace camp and support them in their protest at American cruise missiles being deployed in Britain. Three days before her death in 1986 she wrote: 'Had the money given to the physicists been spent on seeking to discover how the sun makes chlorophyll in green leaves, this could have been of more benefit to humanity than the research that has led to the nuclear bomb.'

(New Humanist)

At a memorial meeting for Dora Russell a quotation from her book *The Right To Be Happy* was read out. It helps us to understand not just her beliefs, but those of Humanism too.

'. . . But what of death? not of ourselves but those we love, or the agony of loss and despair which even in life may be our portion? The misery of loneliness after a vain search for companionship in love or understanding? If men and women were more free and their early life and education more secure and harmonious, there would be fewer jangled and disappointed lovers, fewer heart-broken parents, fewer desperate and rebellious sons and daughters. In a community where instinctive happiness was not rare nor suffering exalted, those whom great sorrow had visited would find some healing rather than ground for envy and malevolence in the happiness of their neighbours. Against death, disaster, and sorrow the skill and courage of all mankind would be mobilized. What we could do to avert danger and to master our environment we could do as a human society. Apart from that we must learn to meet death with quiet acceptance. Is our universe so limited, is our life so lacking in variety and mystery that we must run to take refuge in another world? Here in the universe is our home and our kingdom, not only ours, or our children's or our lover's, but belonging to all mankind. Whatever is lovely for a day, for an hour, for a moment has been worth the effort that called it into being – a flower, music, poetry, a human being.'

THINGS TO DO

Beacon Hill
Workers' Birth Control Group
Back-street abortion clinics
Abortion Law Reform Association
Women's Caravan of Peace
Greenham Common peace camp

Look at these phrases. How do they fit into the story of Dora Russell? What do they refer to?

FOR YOUR FOLDERS

▶ What do you think Dora Russell meant when she said 'women should have the right to choose'?

▶ List some of the organizations Dora Russell was involved in. Do you know what each one tries to do?

▶ In a tribute to Dora Russell, the *New Humanist* magazine said: 'she tried to make the world better every moment of her life.' What do you think this means?

! ▶ What would you say were the main beliefs that inspired Dora Russell?

IMMORTALITY

Blue, white, grey are the clouds,
And patches of grey and silver are made on the sea
And paths of blue and pearl for the ships to go.

Blue, white, grey is the house
I have made on the hilltop,
Where the clouds shall go over and winds shall blow
And we shall gaze on the sea.
Children and lawns and flowers shall blossom about us.
When we die, may we sleep in love;
Perhaps in the winds our thoughts will speak to our children.

Let people say
They were fearless in life and loved beauty
Therefore these souls are worthy
To cleanse and ride with the majestic sea
And to speak and wander the world with the murmuring winds.

Dora Russell

Ageism means discrimination against people because they are no longer young. Ageist attitudes persist in the newspapers, on radio and television, in the world of work and in advertisements.

As with all forms of discrimination, the 'stereotype' is common. 'Stereotyping' means fixing something, or an idea of something or someone, in a mould which you are not prepared to change, and then insisting that it is the only possible one. Here are some stereotypes to do with the elderly:

> 'Old people think they know best.'
> 'Old people are always talking about the good old days.'
> 'Old people are always moaning.'

If we are lucky we will grow old. However, 'old age' is often seen as being a problem. Society often tends to shunt elderly people to one side. They become 'old dears', too old to work, too old to learn anything new, too old to have a good time, too old to enjoy sex, too old to do anything except wait to die. Old age is not fashionable. We only have to look at advertisements to see that the 'good life' means being young.

Ageing is not a sudden process. It begins after 20 when we lose about 1% of the strength of our heart muscles every year. After 25 the number of our brain cells starts to decrease.

'Never too old'

- many people still enjoy sexual relations in old age
- elderly people can still play sports.
  (Recently an 82-year-old ran a marathon in just over five hours)
- many elderly people still work
- elderly people still learn. Thousands of people over 60 have studied for degrees through the Open University.

In some countries a person is 'old' earlier than in others. Average life expectancy in Ethiopia is 47, in India, 40, and in Chad, 38. In Britain, on retirement, a woman can expect to live on average to 80 and a man to 77.

'Old age is often relative'

This poem was written by Kate, who spent the last years of her life in hospital. She couldn't speak. After her death, this poem was found in her locker.

What do you see nurses, what do you see?
  Are you thinking, when you are looking at
    me:
A crabbit old woman, not very wise,
  Uncertain of habit, with far-away eyes,
Who dribbles her food and makes no reply
  When you say in a loud voice, 'I do wish
    you'd try.'
Who seems not to notice the things that you do
  And forever is losing a stocking or shoe.
Who, unresisting or not, lets you do as you
    will,
  With bathing and feeding the long day to fill.
Is that what you're thinking, is that what you
    see?
  Then open your eyes, nurse, you're not
    looking at me.
I'll tell you who I am as I sit here so still,
  As I use at your bidding, as I eat at your
    will.
I'm a small child of ten with a father and
    mother,
  Brothers and sisters who love one another.
A young girl of sixteen with wings at her feet,
  Dreaming that soon now a lover she'll meet.
A bride soon at twenty, my heart gives a leap,
  Remembering the vows that I'd promised to
    keep.
At twenty-five now, I have young of my own,
  Who need me to build a secure, happy home.
A young woman of thirty, my young now grow
    fast,
  Bound to each other with ties that should
    last.
At forty my young ones now grown, will soon
    be gone,
  But my man stays beside me to see I don't
    mourn.
At fifty once more babies play round my knee,
  Again we know children, my loved one and
    me.
Dark days are upon me, my husband is dead,
  I look at the future, I shudder with dread.
For my young are all busy rearing young of
    their own,
  I think of the years and the love I have
    known.

I'm an old woman now, but nature is cruel,
  'Tis her jest to make old age look like a fool.
The body it crumbles, grace and vigour depart,
  There now is a stone, where I once had a
  heart,
But inside this old carcase, a young girl still
  dwells,
  And now and again my battered heart
  swells.
I remember the joys, I remember the pain,
  And I'm loving and living life over again.
I think of the years, all too few – gone too fast,
  And accept the stark fact that nothing can
  last.
So open your eyes nurse, open and see,
  Not a crabbit old woman, look closer –
  see ME.

1. **One household in seven in the UK is an old person living alone.**
   Help the Aged funds day centres through out the country. For many old people, day centres are their only chance of companionship.

2. **Nearly half a million old people have no living relatives.**
   Help the Aged is aiming to place one minibus every week with voluntary groups. For no less than 20,000 old people who already use this service every week, it is a vital link with the community.

3. **One million old people have no regular visitors.**
   Help the Aged's Lifeline Appeal has already placed nearly 1,000 emergency alarm systems in the homes of old people who are vulnerable and at risk.

4. **189,000 old people cannot get in and out of bed unaided. 695,000 can't cope with stairs. 757,000 can't bath or shower without help. 1,056,000 can't walk unassisted.**
   Help the Aged is funding day hospitals where old people can recover their independence and confidence, after illness or injury.

5. **Last year, 571 old people died in their homes from hypothermia. This year, the figure will be much higher.**
   Besides campaigning for better heating subsidies and better pensions, the day centres we support provide warmth and a hot meal, for some old people their only regular hot meal.

6. **500,000 dwellings – nearly half of our most appalling housing – is inhabited by old people; who are least able to cope.**
   Help the Aged is campaigning for better housing provision for old people, both in the public and private sectors, because old people aren't "them", they're one in five of us.

7. **Winston Churchill was 65 when he became Prime Minister, Michelangelo was 71 when he started work on St Peter's, Rome.**
   A reminder that being 60+ can be the beginning, not the end of a lifetime's achievement.

8. **In 1965, 448 centenarians received a congratulatory telegram from the Queen. In 1985, the figure was 1,819.**
   Between 1981 and 2001, the number of people aged over 75 will increase from 3.1 million to 4.1 million. More and more of us are going to live to be old. Yet what is in store for us if we let things ride?

9. **Nearly two million old people depend upon supplementary benefit.**
   Put another way, that's one in five pensioners.

10. These facts paint a grim picture of what it can mean to be old in Britain today. Help the Aged is dedicated to improving this situation by campaigning for better pensions and heating allowances. Funding Day Centres, Day Hospitals and Hospices. Providing emergency alarm systems and minibuses. To find out more about our work, or if you would like to make a donation, please write to: John Mayo OBE, Director-General, Help the Aged, Freepost, St. James's Walk, London EC1B 1BD.

Help the Aged

25th ANNIVERSARY APPEAL
PATRON : HRH The Princess of Wales.

FOR YOUR FOLDERS

▶ Explain the words ageism and stereotyping.

▶ List some of the stereotypes associated with the elderly.

▶ Write a story based on Kate's life.

▶ Describe the concerns and work of Help the Aged.

▶ Prepare a three-minute talk for your class on 'The reasons for and causes of ageism', or 'The grim picture of being old in Britain'.

! ▶ Imagine that the UN are devising a Charter of Rights for the elderly. Write down some of the rights you think should be included.

◇

FOR DISCUSSION

▶ What does Kate believe the nurses think of her? Do they see her as she really is?

▶ 'Sometimes to send an old person to a hospital to be cared for is the most humane way.'

▶ 'Old age can be fun.'

Over the last 50 years the elderly population has grown faster than the population of younger ages. This is due to the rise in the birth rate in the 1920s and because of general improvements in health and social conditions.

- more than 30% of pensioners live alone
- two-thirds of the pensionable population are women
- many pensioners' homes lack basic amenities
- an estimated 200,000 elderly people are severely disabled.

Thousands of elderly people in Britain lead happy, healthy and fulfilled lives. However, many elderly people's lives are far from easy.

'I am absolutely desperate and feel like ending it all, what else can one do when one is old and hard up? Some days when it's cold I go to bed rather than put the electric fire on . . . it's so expensive.'

(George, aged 72)

'Although it's four years since dear Frank died I still miss him dreadfully, especially in the evening.'

(Sally, aged 65)

There are two major ways in which the elderly can be helped in society.

1 **Family care** – the roles are reversed. The parents look after the children in the early years and the children look after the parents in the later years. In the Muslim and Hindu world the elderly enjoy great honour and often remain as the head of the household all their lives. In the Western world many elderly people are to be found in homes or geriatric wards.
2 **Community care** – the government provides a pension and other financial assistance. It also provides homes, sheltered housing, day centres, mobile libraries, meals-on-wheels and home help services. In some areas voluntary organizations provide help.

A CHRISTIAN VIEWPOINT

'In the provision of care for elderly people, whether in their home or out of it, some principles emerge:

1 Care needs to be personal.
2 Elderly people and their families should retain as much choice as possible. (It must be recognized that the wishes of elderly people and their families may conflict.)
3 Elderly people should not be removed from their existing networks of relationships.
4 It should be made possible for elderly people to give as well as receive. This means, among other things, that they need to be guaranteed an adequate income.'

(Church of England Board for Social Responsibility)

FOR DISCUSSION

▶ 'Old age is the most unexpected of all the things that happen to a man.'

(Leon Trotsky)

▶ What problems might arise if an elderly relative came to live with your family? How might these problems be resolved?

▶ Discuss the implications of the Board for Social Responsibility's four principles.

FOR YOUR FOLDERS

▶ List some of the problems that face George and Sally.

❗▶ Write a short article entitled 'Growing old is no fun'.

THINGS TO DO

▶ Read the profile of Irene Dyer. By interviewing either an elderly relative or an elderly neighbour, design your own profile, using photos if possible.

Story of a lifetime

Irene Dyer: Important dates in her life	Important dates in the 20th century
	1901 Queen Victoria dies.
	1903 First powered flight by Wright Brothers in USA.
	1906 Free school dinners introduced.
	1908 Old Age Pension introduced.
27 January 1909 Irene Ethel Jackson born, Mitcham, Surrey.	
	1914 First World War begins.
	1918 First World War ends. Women over age of 30 first given right to vote. Education Act raises school leaving age to 14.
Irene leaves Links 1923 Road School and gets her first job in Mitcham.	
	1926 General Strike.
	1929 Stock market crash in USA. Depression spreads to Britain.
Irene marries Frank 1935 Dyer	
Irene and Frank's 1939 daughter, Delia, born.	Second World War begins.
Frank killed in 1944 action, Caen, France.	
	1945 Second World War ends. Labour Government elected.
Irene returns to 1946 work at Renshaw's Confectionery factory, Mitcham.	Socialist legislation (e.g. National Health Service Bill)
	1953 Coronation of Elizabeth II.
	1956 Suez Crisis.

Irene Dyer

Irene's daughter, 1959 Delia, marries.	
	1963 The Swinging 60s, mini-skirts, the Beatles, Carnaby Street, etc.)
Irene retires from 1969 Renshaw's.	Man lands on the moon.
	1973 Britain enters Common Market.
	1979 Margaret Thatcher elected, first woman Prime Minister of Britain.
	1982 Falklands conflict.
Irene visits Frank's 1984 grave in France.	Miner's strike in Britain.

A **disability** refers to the lack of some bodily function.

A **handicap** refers to the relationship between the disability and the environment.

Mental handicap is caused at conception, birth, or in infancy, and is a permanent disability.

Mental illness may be experienced at any stage of life and can be treated and cured.

PHYSICAL DISABILITY – A CASE STUDY

'My name is Daniel Leech and I live in Cheltenham. I was born 14 years ago, but due to a bad birth I am disabled. Cerebral palsy has left me with no speech, no use of hands, and no ability to walk.

My parents and the head teacher of my special school thought that I should try to get into a comprehensive school when I reached 11. Bournside Comprehensive School accepted me and this has meant a great deal to me. I always enjoyed the company of other children and envied their schools as they were much more interesting than small special ones.

I cope well enough thanks to my BBC computer and my left foot. I use two foot switches to write, speak and produce graphs for maths and other subjects. All the children at Bournside have made me feel very much one of them. I do not feel different at school. No one turns to look at me or my motorized wheelchair (unless I knock into them!).

I have noticed that society is becoming more aware of the needs of the disabled, providing more toilets, ramps, lifts and other facilities.

I don't know if I can believe in God. If there is a God, then why is there so much suffering in the world?'

Daniel (sitting in the middle next to the teacher) in a science lesson

FACTFILE

- among the present world population of 4.3 billion, an estimated 450 million people are disabled in some way. Some 200 million of these are children
- every year 250,000 children lose their eyesight through lack of Vitamin A alone
- 'Most disabled people agree that other people's attitudes, like embarrassment or ignorance, can be disabling in themselves.'

(*New Internationalist*, January 1981)

- one hundred million people in the world today are disabled through malnutrition.

THE MENTALLY HANDICAPPED

There are about 230,000 mentally handicapped people in Britain, of whom 60,000 are children. Taking the population as a whole, there are approximately 2.5 severely mentally handicapped people per 1,000 in the population. Sometimes the handicap is not visible, although it seriously impairs the intellectual capacity of the person. Often so-called 'normal' people have difficulty coping with mentally handicapped people and frequently confuse mental handicap with mental illness.

In the past, mentally handicapped people were shut away in homes or hospitals and this did little to break down people's prejudices and fears about them. However, today there is a steadily growing awareness that mentally handicapped people have plenty to give, and can develop within the community, and as a result more of them are taking their place in community life. The Department of Health and Social Security estimates that about 15,000 mentally handicapped people at present in hospital – about one-third of the total – could be discharged immediately if appropriate services in the community were available.

Mentally handicapped people who do live in the community live either at home, usually with their parent(s), or in hostels within the community. Many of them go out to work. In a report on the mentally handicapped, the Church of England stated:

'Mentally handicapped people have much to give, they share our common humanity and, like us all, are children of God.'

(from *The Local Church and Mentally Handicapped People,* a report by the Church of England Board for Social Responsibility, 1984)

'Mentally handicapped people can be an inspiration to others, they can help us understand ourselves and the often inhuman values of the rest of the world.'

(Jean Vanier, founder of L'Arche, a religious community concerned with helping the mentally handicapped)

FOR YOUR FOLDERS

▶ Explain the terms disability, handicap, mental handicap, mental illness.

▶ What handicaps does Daniel face? How has he learnt to overcome them?

▶ What are the advantages for Daniel and for other pupils in having Daniel attend a comprehensive school?

▶ Write an article explaining some of the problems a mentally handicapped person will have to face when living in the community.

! ▶ How might mentally handicapped people be 'an inspiration to others'? How might they 'help us understand ourselves and the often inhuman values of the rest of the world'?

FOR DISCUSSION

▶ Disabled people often encounter certain attitudes like over-protection, fear, embarrassment, stereotyping and being patronized. Discuss each of these attitudes in turn.

▶ 'It has been shown that mentally handicapped people can make their marriage promises as sincerely and with as much understanding as other people.'

(Church of England report, 1984).

THINGS TO DO

▶ Imagine that you are at Bournside School in the year before Daniel joins. In groups of four draw up a report or document entitled 'Preparing for Daniel'.

Abortion
- 'premature expulsion of the foetus from the womb'.
- 'operation to cause this'.

ABORTION ACT 1967

For many centuries it was regarded as a serious crime to destroy a baby in its mother's womb. In 1967 Parliament passed a law stating that it was no longer a criminal offence for a pregnancy to be terminated by a doctor, if two doctors agreed on either of these two conditions:

1 that to carry on with the pregnancy would involve a greater risk to the life or the physical or mental health of the mother, or of her existing children, than if she had it terminated

2 that there was a substantial risk that if the child were born it would suffer serious physical or mental handicap.

Before 1967 abortion was illegal unless there were very exceptional circumstances. So if a woman wanted an abortion she had to go to a so-called 'back-street abortionist'. Between 40,000 and 200,000 'back-street' abortions took place in Britain every year. About 30 women on average died every year.

KEY ISSUE
When does life begin? At conception? During pregnancy? At birth? Is abortion morally acceptable?

A pro-abortion march

Development of the foetus
25th day   – heart beating.
28th day   – legs and arms begin to form.
6th week   – bones appear.
7th week   – fingers, thumbs forming.
10th week – organs nearly formed.
12th week – vocal chords, sexual organs form.
16th week – half its birth length.
5th month – eyebrows, eyelashes begin.
Premature babies born as early as 25 weeks.

VIEWPOINTS

'Women must have control over their own lives. For this we must have control over our own bodies . . . Abortion must become freely available to all women who want it. We must be able to have children when we want them, and children have the right to be wanted.'

(Women's Abortion and Contraception Campaign Manifesto)

A rally of LIFE supporters

'Since human life begins at conception, i.e. fertilization, and since all human life should be equally protected by the law from conception to natural death, whether or not the human being concerned is wanted or handicapped, it follows that the destruction of unborn life is always wrong.'

(Save the Unborn Child, LIFE)

'Humanists regard abortion as better than bringing unwanted babies into the world. It is a mistake to say that Humanists are in favour of abortion; no one can be in favour of abortion, which, except in unforeseen circumstances, is the result of failed contraception. We think there will probably always be a certain number of unplanned pregnancies and that the mothers concerned should have the complete choice of either early abortion, or keeping the baby.'

(Humanist Dipper)

'We have been created by Almighty God in his own image and likeness. No pregnancy is unplanned, because no baby can be conceived unless Almighty God intends that conception and has willed that particular unique and completely individual new person into existence. What has actually happened in our society is that clever arguments have convinced those with no anchor of belief in God to cling to, that merciless slaughter of unborn babies is morally justifiable, and even essential for the happiness of the individual and the good of society.'

(Catholic Truth Society)

'The Anglican view on abortion is that although the foetus is to be specially respected and protected, nonetheless the life of the foetus is not absolutely sacrosanct if it endangers the life of its mother.'

(Church of England report, 1984)

FOR YOUR FOLDERS

▶ Explain the 1967 Abortion Act.

▶ Briefly explain why the organizations LIFE and Women's Abortion and Contraception Campaign hold the views they do on abortion.

▶ What is the Humanist view and why do Catholics believe that it is wrong?

THINGS TO DO

▶ In groups of three to four discuss reasons for and against abortion, then write your reasons down and compare them with those of the rest of the class.

CHOICES

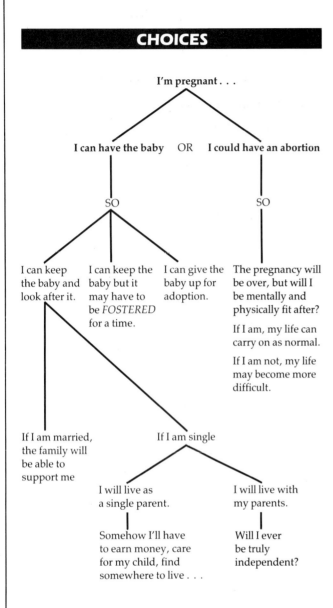

I'm pregnant . . .

I can have the baby   OR   I could have an abortion

SO   SO

I can keep the baby and look after it.

I can keep the baby but it may have to be *FOSTERED* for a time.

I can give the baby up for adoption.

The pregnancy will be over, but will I be mentally and physically fit after?

If I am, my life can carry on as normal.

If I am not, my life may become more difficult.

If I am married, the family will be able to support me

If I am single

I will live as a single parent.

I will live with my parents.

Somehow I'll have to earn money, care for my child, find somewhere to live . . .

Will I ever be truly independent?

THINGS TO DO

▶ This is only a very brief summary of the choices. Discuss them in pairs or groups of three and then write down some of the problems that these choices might create.

▶ Organize a class debate on the arguments for and against abortion, using the 'ammunition'.

NATIONAL ABORTION CAMPAIGN

A WOMANS RIGHT TO CHOOSE

! AMMUNITION FOR A CLASS DEBATE: THE CASE FOR ABORTION

- every woman has the right to choose
- abortion is often a lesser evil than overcrowding, homelessness, the problems of bringing up too many children, not having enough money for another child, the end of a career
- it is more of a trauma giving up a child for adoption than having an abortion
- the population explosion will not be solved by making abortion illegal
- if a child is going to be severely handicapped, the parents should be allowed to choose whether they want an abortion
- a foetus is not a human being in the true sense. Life begins at birth
- even if abortion were made a crime, thousands of women would still risk their lives and health in back-street abortion clinics
- if a woman is raped and becomes pregnant then abortion is the most humane way of helping her. The same goes for a woman made pregnant because of incest; or a mentally deficient girl who gets pregnant; or a schoolgirl of, say, 14
- what if the mother will die if she doesn't abort the foetus?
- the foetus feels nothing when it is aborted
- if you don't believe that life is a 'gift' from God then you shouldn't be forced into doing something that people with a faith want you to do
- abortion is an act of responsibility in that it gives people the right to choose
- every child has the right to be a wanted child. Abortion saves thousands of children from being unwanted, and saves society from many problems.

! AMMUNITION FOR A CLASS DEBATE:
THE CASE AGAINST ABORTION

- modern science proves that the unborn child is a separate human being from conception. It is never just a part of his or her mother's body

- by allowing abortion, society is taking the easy way out. It should concentrate on improving the quality of life in society

- even in the womb the unborn child has a right not to be killed

- people with the most awful handicaps can lead happy, creative and fulfilled lives

- abortion is discrimination against the weak

- abortion is not just a matter of 'religion' – it is about murder, injustice and the denial of human rights. The UN Declaration of the Rights of the Child states that children need protection before, as well as after, birth

- unborn babies are unique, different, they have potential personalities

- every aborted foetus was a potential human being, perhaps even a Beethoven or an Einstein

- abortions can go wrong. They can leave terrible mental and physical 'scars' on a woman

- if abortion is acceptable, where do we draw the line? Abortion is a form of infanticide

- if society did more in the way of contraception and education, and helped single mothers by providing counselling and places where they could seek advice, abortion would not be necessary

- killing is killing, whether done in back-streets or openly.

THREE VIEWPOINTS

Humanists say:

Abortion should be available on request.

The Catholic Church says:

Abortion is a sin in all cases.

The Protestant Church says:

Abortion in certain cases is acceptable.

TALKING POINTS

- **'If you do make a mistake, don't destroy the life . . . because also to that child God says: I have called you by your name; I have carved you in the palm of my hand; you are mine.'**

  (Mother Teresa)

- **'Circumstances which may often justify an abortion are direct threats to the life or health of the mother, or the probable birth of a severely abnormal child. The woman's environment should be considered, including children for whom she is already responsible and offensive social conditions of bad housing and family poverty.'**

  (Methodist statement, 1980)

FOR YOUR FOLDERS

! ▶ This section has been concerned with the 'rights' and 'wrongs' of the abortion issue. By now you will have formed your own opinions. Try to express them in the form of a letter to a Church, or to LIFE, or to the National Abortion Campaign.

> **Euthanasia** – 'gentle and easy death; the bringing about of this especially in cases of incurable and painful disease'.

In this section we are concerned with voluntary euthanasia, i.e. euthanasia carried out at the request of the person killed. Despite great advances in medicine, dying can be a long, painful and distressing process. In fact, advanced medical techniques can 'keep a patient alive' for much longer than in the past. Under present laws anyone (doctors included) who helps the sufferer to end their life risks the possibility of being charged with murder or manslaughter.

THE VOLUNTARY EUTHANASIA SOCIETY (EXIT)

This society aims to bring about a change in the law so that

'An adult person suffering from a severe illness, for which no relief is known, should be entitled by law to the mercy of a painless death, if and only if, that is their expressed wish.'

'Doctors should be allowed to help incurable patients to die peacefully at their own request. The patient must have signed, at least 30 days previously, a declaration making their request known.'

SOME FACTORS INFLUENCING A CHRISTIAN

- 'God made man in his own image' (*Genesis 1: 27*). Human life is a gift from God. It is sacred and has dignity
- death is an event in life, not the end of life
- Jesus in the New Testament heals the sick and the dying
- God gave man 'dominion over every living thing' (*Genesis 1: 28*). Humans have a responsibility to use God's gifts to the full
- the body *and* spirit of the patient need care and love.

THE HOSPICE MOVEMENT

In recent years the emphasis has moved from a debate about euthanasia to a concern for the care of those who are terminally ill. This has led to the growth of the Hospice movement, which tries to help the dying spend their last few days in a loving and sympathetic environment so that they can die with dignity. One of its leaders, Dame Cicely Saunders, has written: 'We have to concern ourselves with the quality of life as well as with its length.'

THE CASE FOR VOLUNTARY EUTHANASIA

- it can quickly and humanly end a patient's suffering
- it can help to shorten the grief and suffering of the patient's loved ones
- everyone has the right to decide how they should die
- if the law was changed, doctors could *legally* act on a patient's desire to die without further suffering
- it would help others to face death if they realized they could die with dignity
- it would help doctors if they knew of their patient's intentions
- the initial decision about euthanasia could be made when the individual was not under the stress of immediate suffering or anxiety.

THE CASE AGAINST VOLUNTARY EUTHANASIA

- there are many pain-killing drugs which can help the patient die with dignity
- a patient might not be able to make a rational decision or might change their mind but be incapable of telling the doctors
- many people recover after being 'written off' by doctors
- old people might feel they are a nuisance to others and opt for euthanasia when in their hearts they want to continue living
- life is a gift from God and only God can take it away
- euthanasia devalues life by making it disposable – it could be the first step on to a slippery slope
- the relationship of trust between doctors and patients could be destroyed. Under the Hippocratic Oath doctors must try to preserve life
- if there were better facilities for caring for the dying, there would be less need for euthanasia.

FOR DISCUSSION

VIEWPOINTS

'The argument for euthanasia will be answered if better methods of caring for the dying are developed. Medical skill in terminal care must be improved, pre-death loneliness must be relieved, patient and family must be supported by the statutory services and by the community. The whole of the patient's needs, including the spiritual, must be met.'

(Methodist Conference, 1974)

'Humanists believe that people have the right to end their own lives when they wish. They believe that death is final and inevitable, but nevertheless can be dignified, peaceful and painless with the aid of modern drugs. Some go to the trouble to discuss this with doctors, friends and relatives. Some sign the form available from the Voluntary Euthanasia Society which leaves no doubt whatever of the person's wishes about his last days.'

(*Humanist Dipper*)

▶ Why do many Christians, like the Methodists, argue that voluntary euthanasia is wrong?

▶ How do Methodists believe that better methods of caring for the dying can be developed?

▶ How might a Christian and a Humanist react to the following letter?
Case history (from a letter published by the Voluntary Euthanasia Society)
'I have no family commitments, I suffer from diabetes, failing eyesight, skin disorders, arthritis and chronic narrowing of the arteries which has already resulted in the amputation of a leg . . . I am not afraid of death, but I am afraid of the protracted suffering which would almost certainly precede my death in the natural course of events. Even more, I am afraid of the consequences of making an unsuccessful suicide attempt. During the six months I spent in hospital last year, numerous were the patients brought in for resuscitation after suicide attempts, and the memory of the sordid and horrifying sounds which ensued from behind the screens will never leave me. When the time comes, I shall need help, and it would be a great comfort to me to know that there is a doctor to whom I can turn.'

TO DEBATE

▶ 'This House believes that a person has a right to die.'

FOR YOUR FOLDERS

▶ Explain the following:
Exit, the hospice movement.

▶ Write a paragraph on:
a The beliefs of Exit.
b Some of the factors that influence Christians when thinking about voluntary euthanasia.

▶ From ideas collected during your debate and from the arguments for and against voluntary euthanasia, write an article of about 200 words on your own views on this matter.

What Future for Babies by Technology?

BY SPENCER REISS

*In our brave new world where already one child could have five parents,
it is time to take stock*

Since the world's first 'test-tube' baby, Louise Brown, was born in a British Hospital on 25 July 1978, well over a thousand such births have taken place. Another quarter of a million children owe their existence to artificial insemination which used sperm from men other than their legal fathers.

Today it is even possible to create a normal baby with no fewer than five parents. One would be the woman who actually bears the child. Two others, its genetic parents, would supply the sperm and the egg which are 'mixed' and then implanted as a living embryo in the surrogate mother's womb. Finally come the baby's real parents, the infertile couple who will take the baby home and call it theirs.

With doctors and researchers achieving powers over procreation that far outstrip traditional law and conventional morality, there are many questions to be answered. Should we interfere with nature? Should surrogate motherhood be allowed? What if the child is deformed? Does a sperm donor have any obligations or rights to the eventual offspring? Do all couples have a right to reproduce? Should governments regulate the new technologies – and if so, how?

It is estimated that about 2 million people are infertile in Britain. Artificial reproduction means that frustrated 'infertile' parents (by some estimates one in seven married couples) can now have children. However, many people, for moral and religious reasons, oppose artificial reproduction virtually across the board. In the Roman Catholic Church 'no procreation without sex' has been added to the older teaching 'no sex without procreation'.

One technique of artificial reproduction is 'in vitro fertilization' (IVF), involving nothing more than taking an egg from a fertile woman and sperm from a fertile man and merging them into a living embryo ready to be implanted in a waiting womb.

Artificial insemination (AI) is even simpler; live sperm are injected into a woman's uterus at the time of ovulation. Another approach, transferring embryos from a female donor, has already been used for infertile women otherwise capable of carrying a child.

IVF is most commonly employed in cases of blocked or damaged Fallopian tubes. Since it uses a married couple's own sperm and eggs, no serious legal questions arise. However, the possibilities are endless. For example, through artificial insemination by third party donors (if the husband is infertile), babies are being born to genetic parents who have never met.

'A revolution is happening', says Dr Cohen, director of the sterility clinic at Sèvres, France. 'We could see post-menopause babies, or pregnancies occurring while the husband is in prison.'

In July 1984 the government-appointed Warnock Committee recommended setting up an authority to check and control the use of IVF, sperm and egg donations, and other aspects of fertility research. The Committee also proposed a ban on surrogate motherhood agencies.

Surrogate motherhood means that an infertile couple arrange for a woman to be artificially impregnated with the man's sperm and then carry the baby until birth. The surrogate mother in many countries can charge around £3,500 to carry the baby. A surrogate mother-to-be says, 'The real parents are those who bring up a child.'

In January 1985 surrogate mother Kim Cotton was prevented by the courts from removing 'her' infant from the hospital where it was born. Eventually the High Court awarded the baby to the couple that had commissioned it, with Kim Cotton receiving a large fee. However, many aspects of commercial surrogacy have been banned.

There is much debate about embryo research, where an embryo is subjected to experiments to learn about miscarriages, genetic abnormalities, in vitro fertilization, etc. At the centre of this debate is the question, when does life begin?

Last January [1986] Dr Ian Croft of London's Cromwell Hospital held a party for some of the more than 60 IVF babies that he had personally helped bring to life. 'My concern,' he said, 'is for the people who are not at this party, who might have been if we had done more research.' Few would disagree, least of all the happy parents of children born through artificial techniques.

But the dilemma remains whether to place ultimate control over the making of life in the uncertain hands of mere mortals.

(adapted from *Newsweek International*, 18 March 1985)

A CATHOLIC VIEW OF ARTIFICIAL INSEMINATION

'Artificial insemination (AI) is different from natural intercourse. As used with animals this poses no moral problem. However, the Church teaches that among humans, AI violates the dignity of the person and the sanctity of marriage. It is therefore contrary to the Natural and Divine Law. In an address to Catholic doctors, Pope Pius XII condemned AI. It is condemned because a third party becoming involved in a marriage is like 'mechanical adultery': the donor fathers a child (with his sperm), yet he has no responsibility to the child; any process that isolates the sacred act of creating life from the marriage union is a violation of that marriage union (which alone is the way to create life). However, if the marriage act is preserved, then various clinical techniques designed to help create new life are not to be condemned.'

(adapted from *Modern Catholic Dictionary*)

The Catholic Church therefore teaches that new life should only be created by natural means within the bounds of the marriage union.

Louise Brown, the world's first test tube baby, celebrating her sixth birthday

FOR YOUR FOLDERS

Answer these questions in your folders.
1 Explain the following:
   genetic parents, procreation, IVF, AI, surrogate mothers, commercial surrogacy, embryo research.
2 Explain how it is 'even possible to create a normal baby with no fewer than five parents'.
3 What do you think are the benefits of artificial reproduction?
4 What is the Roman Catholic view of artificial reproduction?
5 What is the Warnock Committee?
6 Can you think what the problems are that face the surrogate mother and the parents who commission her?
7 What are your own views on artificial reproduction?
8 Why do some scientists wish to support and continue embryo research?
9 'God is the giver of life, not man'. In the light of this article, do you agree with this comment?

FOR DISCUSSION

▶ 'The real parents are those that bring up the baby.'
▶ 'We should not interfere with nature.'
▶ 'God has given human beings the gift of scientific knowledge. We should use it.'

INTRODUCTION

The Committee of Inquiry into Human Fertilization and Embryology was set up by the Government in 1982. The Committee was set up to:

'consider recent and potential developments in medicine and science related to human fertilization and embryology: to consider what policies and safeguards should be applied, including consideration of the social, ethical and legal implications of these developments; and to make recommendations.'

(from the Introduction by Dame Mary Warnock)

In June 1984 the Committee made the following recommendations:

- A statutory licensing authority, with substantial non-medical membership, should be set up to regulate those infertility services and research which the report regards as acceptable, including in vitro (test-tube) fertilization, semen or egg donation, embryo donation following in vitro fertilization, and the use of frozen embryos.
- There should be complete anonymity for semen, egg or embryo donors and couples requiring their services. Both partners should give written consent to treatment. The number of children born to a donor should be limited to 10. A woman giving birth as a result of egg or embryo donation should be regarded in law as the child's mother, and the donor should have no rights or duties relating to the child.
- Frozen embryos should be stored for a maximum of 10 years, after which the right to use or disposal should pass to the licensed storage authority. Up to 10 years, an embryo's parents should have the right to decide on use or disposal; if both die or fail to agree, that right should go to the storage authority.
- The establishment and operation of surrogate motherhood 'rent-a-womb' agencies should be made a criminal offence. A majority of the committee also favoured banning surrogate motherhood entirely.
- A majority of members recommended that no human embryo should be kept alive outside the womb or used for research beyond 14 days after fertilization, excluding any period when it was frozen. It should be made a criminal offence to transfer to a woman any embryo used for research, or to place a human embryo in the womb of another species.

THE CATHOLIC RESPONSE

The Catholic Truth Society called the Warnock Report 'the most important document produced in Britain in the last twenty years.'

The Catholic Church made the following comments:

1 **The human embryo has the right to proper respect. 'Test tube babies' are indeed babies, and embryos cannot be manipulated, frozen or simply left to die without bringing into question the whole area of human rights. Human beings are not to be treated as means to an end.**

2 **Marriage is the proper place for sexual activity, and our society depends on stable and loving families.**

3 **The demands of science do not take precedence over individual human persons, especially when they are defenceless.**

4 **There must be a careful weighing up of issues when deciding on the allocation of resources for the health service. It is, to say the least, doubtful that people's much-claimed 'right' to children should take precedence in the complex and difficult business of proper health provision for the nation.**

(The Catholic Truth Society, 1985)

SEVEN FRONT-LINE TECHNIQUES IN HUMAN FERTILIZATION AND EMBRYOLOGY

1 *Artificial insemination (husband) (AIH).* The putting of male seed into a female by means of an instrument.
2 *Artificial insemination (donor) (AID).* The semen (seed) is provided by an anonymous donor and not the husband.
3 *In vitro fertilization for husband and wife (IVF).* *'Test-tube babies'.* The ovum is withdrawn from the woman and fertilized with a man's semen under laboratory conditions. The embryo is then transferred to the womb.
4 *Egg donation.* A woman donates an ovum, which is then fertilized with the semen of the husband of the woman into whose uterus the resulting embryo is transferred.
5 *Embryo donation.* Similar to egg donation, except the ovum is fertilized by semen from a donor because both partners are infertile or both carry a genetic defect.

6 *Surrogacy. 'Womb-leasing'.* A woman bears a child for a wife who cannot become pregnant, and hands the child over after birth.

7 *Scientific research on human embryos.* Potential research which ranges from simple study of early embryos to increase knowledge on the beginnings of human development (for infertility, etc.) to testing new drugs on embryos.

Key questions

! Obviously these new techniques raise many religious, legal and moral questions. When does life begin? Has an embryo the same rights as you or I? Can these techniques be exploited for the wrong reasons? Have the donors or other people involved any rights? Who are the real parents? Should we interfere with God's creation? Or is nature a 'raw material' given by God to experiment with? Do these techniques help family life? What about those who suffer infertility? These are just some of the issues. There are many more.

AN ANGLICAN RESPONSE

After the Warnock Report in 1982, which dealt with these techniques, the Church of England responded in a report entitled *Human Fertilization and Embryology* (1984). Here are a few of its findings.

- It is natural for couples to want to produce and raise children. In the Bible the need and desire for an heir led to instances in which a third party was involved, e.g. Rachel's invitation to Joseph to take her slave Bilhah, so that 'I may also obtain children by her'. *(Genesis 30: 3)*.

- Human beings are made in the image of God *(Genesis 1: 26)*. This bestows on them a unique status in creation. To treat them, not as persons to be respected, but as things which may be manipulated, is to violate this God-given nature.

- On AIH, the Board took the same stance as on contraception, accepting that often intercourse and procreation are separate. AIH is therefore acceptable.

- ON AID, 'those engaging in AID are involved in a positive affirmation of the family'. AID was therefore regarded as an acceptable practice, so long as: donors do not sell their sperm; central records are kept so that no more than 10 children can be fathered by one donor; at 18 the child can have access to information about the donor.

- On IVF, the Board accepted this practice in cases of infertility and inheritable disorders.

- The report said: 'It violates the dignity of motherhood that a woman should be paid for bearing a child.' Also, 'strong bonding may take place between a woman and the child she bears in her womb and she may be unwilling to give the baby up' (at birth). The Anglican report therefore agreed with the Warnock Report that all surrogate agreements should be illegal.

- As for research on the embryo, the Anglican report said: 'We support the recommendation that research, under licence, be permitted on embryos up to 14 days old and agree that embryos should not be created purely for scientific research.'

TALKING POINTS

! • Look at the key questions. How would you answer them?

FOR YOUR FOLDERS

▶ Write an article entitled 'Babies in the Front Line of Medical Technology'.

▶ List some of the ways that the seven techniques could be misused.

▶ List some of the advantages of the techniques.

▶ Try and explain in your own words the Catholic response.

▶ List the techniques that the Anglican Church accepts and doesn't accept, and write a sentence about why each is acceptable or unacceptable to the Church.

! ▶ Write a letter to the Warnock Committee outlining your own views on these techniques.

The earliest laws known to us are those of Hammurabi, ruler of Babylon in 1790 BC. These include:

'If a man blinds a freeman in one eye, he shall lose his own eye.'

Laws are bad when they protect the privileges of the few at the expense of the many

A HUMANIST VIEW OF THE LAW

"Law and order are the framework for personal security and responsible action and it is therefore important that the law shall command general assent and respect. It should enhance the scope of responsible freedom. Personal morality is not a proper subject for legislation unless actions infringe the basic rights of others. The Law must achieve a balance between individual freedom and protection of the vulnerable."

(British Humanist Association General Statement of Policy)

THE LAW IN THE BIBLE

The first five books of the Old Testament are called the Torah (the Law). As well as including the Ten Commandments they contain many laws about ritual and about personal morality. The community was responsible for punishing law-breakers. In Jesus's day there was much discussion as to whether ritual and moral laws were of the same importance. Jesus summed up his views in *Mark 12 : 29–31.*

THINKING ABOUT LAWS

1   laws change and vary from age to age and in different cultures

2   laws change according to changes in people's attitudes

3   laws require people to do things that society considers necessary

4   laws are concerned with stability and justice and prohibit anti-social behaviour

5   policemen, magistrates and judges are servants of the law (law enforcers)

6   laws are beneficial when they protect liberty

7   laws are bad when they only protect the privileges of the few at the expense of the many

8   laws are underwritten with the threat of punishment

9   laws are not always fair

10   laws don't tell us how we ought to act in terms of personal morality.

Primitive law   In early societies the tribe would judge arguments and disputes. As society developed, this right to judge and impose punishments shifted over to officials representing society.

Common law   There are laws that have not necessarily been written down but are based on decisions given by courts through the ages. Judges will base their decisions on precedents for past cases.

Statute law   These laws are written down by the authority of Parliament and have to be followed as they are written.

??? QUIZ ???

HOW WELL DO YOU KNOW THE LAW?

1 A child is not criminally responsible for its actions under 10 years of age. *True/False?*

2 A child must not be sold fireworks under 13. *True/False?*

3 A boy under 14 cannot be convicted of rape. *True/False?*

4 Fingerprints can be taken by the police on children of 13. *True/False?*

5 A child under 14 shall not be admitted to or remain in an abattoir during slaughtering. *True/False?*

6 Children over 14 can buy tobacco. *True/False?*

7 Children over 16 can buy alcohol. *True/False?*

8 A 16-year-old can drive a 125 cc motor-bike *True/False?*

9 It is legal for two consenting male homosexuals to have sex, if they are over 18. *True/False?*

10 Religious education is the only subject that must be taught by law in schools. *True/False?*

11 At 14 you can go into a pub as long as you don't buy alcohol. *True/False?*

12 You can obtain a tattoo at 16. *True/False?*

ANSWERS TO QUIZ

1 True; 2 True; 3 True; 4 False – they must be over 14; 5 True; 6 False – 16; 7 False – 18; 8 False – 16-year-olds can only drive 50 cc; 9 False – they must be over 21; 10 True; 11 True; 12 False – at 18.

How many did you score?

FOR YOUR FOLDERS

▶ You are the Supreme Lawmaker on the island of Nirvana. The population of 1,000 people is self-sufficient and able to live off the fertile land. Draw up what you consider to be the 10 most important laws for the islanders. How would you make sure these laws were followed?

▶ Look up *Mark 12 : 29–31* and write down Jesus's words.

▶ Look at the 10 points 'Thinking about laws'. Can you think of an example for each one?

Example
1 Laws change and vary from age to age and in different cultures. → It used to be a crime, punishable by death, to steal a sheep.

▶ List some laws you know that are designed to protect:
a the individual from themself.
b the individual from others.

! ▶ Are there any of the 10 statements about laws that you disagree with? List them, giving reasons.

TALKING POINTS

- **Discuss and compare your 10 laws of Nirvana.**
- **Discuss some of your examples from 'Thinking about laws'.**

A crime is committed when a law made by the state is broken. One of the main aims of punishing an offender is that of reform. If society is to help offenders to reform, it must study the causes of the crime. However, there are immediate causes and deeper underlying causes. Immediate causes might include thrill, boredom, jealousy, lust, greed, frustration or anger. The deeper underlying causes of crime need to be studied. Often crime is not caused by just one thing but rather by a combination of factors.

Circumstances – Crime can be caused by the type of environment one lives in such as housing, unemployment or a deprived upbringing.
Conflict with others – e.g. marriage problems; difficult parents; a violent family.
Mental or emotional disturbances in the offender – such as lack of confidence; loneliness; sexual problems; psychological disorders; depression; bad experiences (e.g. accidents, being beaten as a child).
Social pressures – living in a materialistic and consumer society; keeping up with the Joneses; advertizing – the creation of false ideals and impressions; mixing with potential criminals; TV images.

In 1876 an Italian criminologist maintained that you could tell who was a criminal by studying their features. These included large jaws, the shape of the ear and large eye sockets. Other people, like the seventeenth-century British thinker John Locke, believed that a newly born baby was like a blank piece of paper and its character was formed by the experiences it went through.

NOTIFIABLE OFFENCES

Recorded by the police, by offence group, 1986			
Offence group	1986		
	number recorded	% change*	% cleared up
Violence against the person	125,500	+3	71
Sexual offences	22,700	+6	71
Burglary	936,400	+7	26
Robbery	30,000	+9	20
Theft and handling stolen goods	2,003,900	+6	31
Fraud and forgery	133,400	−1	67
Criminal damage	583,600	+8	21
Other offences	11,900	−3	92
Total	3,847,400	+7	32

*(from previous year)
(from Home Office statistics)

CHRISTIAN AND HUMANIST ATTITUDES

Many Christians and Humanists would agree that as human beings we are to a certain extent responsible for our actions and we have a duty to be responsible to others. However, many Christians and Humanists would also agree that often crime is the result of the influences that we experience. Both Christians and Humanists in all walks of life are actively involved in trying to create a better and fairer society where people don't feel the need to, or don't have to, turn to crime. They are therefore as much involved in trying to get to the causes of crime as they are in trying to find ways of reforming the criminal.

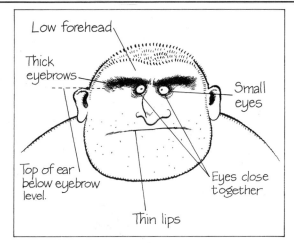

Low forehead
Thick eyebrows
Small eyes
Top of ear below eyebrow level.
Eyes close together
Thin lips

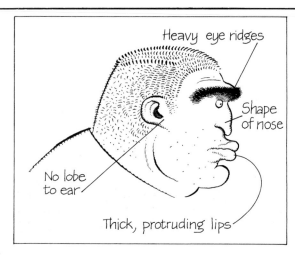

Heavy eye ridges
Shape of nose
No lobe to ear
Thick, protruding lips

'You've only got to look at him to know he's a criminal!'

Put more police on our streets, say angry MPs

By ALAN COCHRANE
Deputy Political Editor

A MAJOR crime wave is sweeping the country. And two out of three villans are getting away with it.

Official Home Office figures confirm a steep rise in virtually every category of serious crime, and a sharp fall in the rate of detection.

Crime rose 8% cent last year compared with 1983.

And over the past five years the detection rate has dropped from 40% to 35%. This means that roughly two crimes in every three go unpunished.

BURGLARIES soared 10% to just under 900,000. Over the last five years, the increase is nearly 50%.

And last year's detection rate was only 28% – just over one in four crimes solved.

THEFTS, covering all offences from pick-pocketing to armed robbery, were up by 6% to 1.8 million. They accounted for roughly half of the 3.5 million offences committed last year.

DRUG TRAFFICKING rose by a chilly 30% to more than 6,500 offences.

London's top detective, Assistant Commissioner John Dellow, said his CID force was simply too small to halt the tidal wave of heroin and cocaine flooding into Britain.

"It was a bad year," said Mr Dellow. "Some very, very evil men are making a massive amount of money."

RAPES were up 8% to 1,433. But Women Against Rape claimed the true figure was far, far higher.

They say that only one woman in 12 who has been sexually assaulted reports the crime.

WAR urges police to be more sympathetic to victims to encourage them to come forward.

ROBBERIES – which include muggings – were up 13% to 24,900.

MURDERS were up 8% to 620.

VANDALISM, which continued to soar, was up 12% last year.

And **FRAUD** and **FORGERY** rose 4%.

Daily Express, 13 March 1985

Myra Hindley and Ian Brady, two of Britain's most notorious criminals

FOR YOUR FOLDERS

! ▶ Read the newspaper cutting that appeared in the *Daily Express* on 13 March 1985 and try to answer the questions.

1   How many 'villains' are apparently 'getting away with it'?

2   What are they getting away with?

3   Do you think the answer is to 'Put more police on our streets'?

4   Do you think the article is accurate? Give reasons for you answer.

5   What do you think are the reasons for the 'crime wave'?

6   Why do you think that some types of crime are not 'cleared up' by the police?

TALKING POINTS

! • **Discuss the following statements:**
  a   **'Violence breeds violence.'**
  b   **'Society gets the criminals it deserves.'**
  c   **'Criminals are made, not born.'**

> 'My object all sublime
> I shall achieve in time
> To make the punishment fit the crime –
> The punishment fit the crime.'
>
> *(The Mikado)*

Crime – 'an offence punishable in a criminal court'.

There are two types of **offence**:

1 **Indictable** – serious crimes (e.g. forgery, theft, murder)
2 **Non-indictable** – less serious crimes (e.g. illegal parking, no TV licence)

There are two types of **court**:

1 **Civil** – dealing in cases where no crime has been committed (e.g. debts, divorce, wills)
2 **Criminal** – dealing in cases where the law has been broken.

Getting a parking ticket is a non-indictable crime

A HUMANIST VIEW

Humanists support the penal system and other forms of punishment but stress that they should aim to reform the wrong-doer and also act at a deterrent to potential criminals. Many Humanists belong to organizations like the Howard League for Penal Reform, which work to improve conditions for prisoners.

CHRISTIAN ATTITUDES

Christians believe that Jesus taught forgiveness and compassion. This is not an easy option because it means that society needs to change its attitudes towards wrong-doers. The criminal might have reasons for breaking the law and these Christians believe they need help just as the victim needs help. Some New Testament references that can be applied to punishment include:

Luke 15: 11-32	The Parable of the Prodigal Son (a parable about forgiveness)
Romans 12: 17	'Never pay back evil for evil.'
Luke 23: 34	'Father, forgive them; they do not know what they are doing.' (Jesus's words on the Cross)
Matthew 18: 21	'How often am I to forgive my brother if he goes on wronging me?' Jesus replied: 'Seventy times seventy.'
Matthew 7: 1	'Pass no judgement, and you will not be judged.'
John 8: 1-11	Jesus's attitude to sin.

FACTFILE

97% of criminal proceedings take place in the *Magistrates' Court*. More serious offences are dealt with in the *Crown Court*. Young offenders are dealt with in *Juvenile Courts*. Civil proceedings are dealt with in *County and High Courts*.

METHODS OF PUNISHMENT

In the eighteenth century, prisons did not exist. Offenders were banished from the country, fined, or executed. Prisons grew out of the nineteenth-century Christian belief in redemption for sinners. Some modern forms of punishment are:

- attendance centre
- binding over
- capital punishment
- community service order
- compensation
- corporal punishment
- day training centre
- deferment
- deprivation of property
- detoxification centre
- discharge
- disqualification
- fine
- imprisonment
- probation order.

TALKING POINTS

- **Many people think that the Old Testament 'an eye for an eye, and a tooth for a tooth' view should be adopted in our society. Do you agree?**

! - **In your opinion, are there some crimes that are not punished severely enough and some where the punishment is too severe?**

FOR YOUR FOLDERS

! ▶ Study the following five cases. In your opinion, what sort of punishment would 'fit the crime'? Give reasons for each suggestion.

1 Judy, aged 63, is suddenly widowed. She begins shoplifting.
2 A man returns from work early to find his wife in bed with another man. He stabs him through the heart with a kitchen knife, killing him.
3 Four football 'fans' who've been drinking kick a man to death outside the ground.
4 An unemployed lad of 17 mugs an old lady and takes her pension. She is not hurt physically.
5 A middle-aged man returns home after a couple of drinks. He knocks over and kills a pedestrian. He is breathalyzed and found to be just over the limit.

▶ Which of these offences are non-indictable?
- refusing to pay for a TV licence
- parking on double yellow lines
- riding a motorbike without tax
- dropping litter
- grievous bodily harm (GBH)
- burglary.

▶ Make a list of some offences that you'd expect to see tried in a criminal court.

▶ Explain, using biblical references, how a Christian might view punishment for crimes.

! ▶ In your opinion, would society be a better place if we literally applied Jesus's teachings on forgiveness to law breakers?

53 THE AIMS OF PUNISHMENT

What is society trying to do when it punishes an offender (somebody who has broken the law and therefore 'offended' society)? There are five main aims of punishment.

1   The theory of PROTECTION

Punishments are used to protect society from somebody's anti-social behaviour. This punishment takes many forms, the most obvious being imprisonment. Also this type of punishment can be designed to protect the offender against themself.

2   The theory of RETRIBUTION

If somebody does something wrong then they should receive a punishment that is fitting for the crime they have committed. 'An eye for an eye'.

3   The theory of DETERRENCE

If a person who commits a crime is punished then they will not (hopefully) commit such a crime, or any other crime, again. Also the punishment they receive will put others off (deter them from) committing crimes.

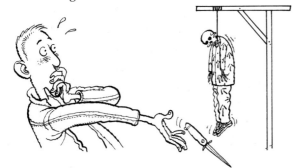

Deterrent punishment

4   The theory of REFORM

People who commit crimes often need all sorts of help. The punishments that they receive should be of a kind that will prevent them from committing further crimes, and make them responsible citizens who have something to offer society.

Reformative punishment

5   The theory of VINDICATION

In order that society is able to function securely, crime must be punished so that the law will be respected.

WHAT SORTS OF PUNISHMENT CAN YOUNG PEOPLE EXPECT IF THEY END UP IN A JUVENILE COURT?

Absolute or conditional discharge

If the magistrates find that you have committed the offence but that it is such a small matter that you should not be punished, they can give you an absolute discharge which means there is a conviction but no punishment. A conditional discharge means that there is no punishment given at the time but if you offend again you can be punished for the present office as well.

Bindover

If you are given a bindover you have to sign a bond (a written promise) saying that you will be of good behaviour for up to one year. If you break the bond you have to pay the amount of money shown in the bond.

Fine, compensation, costs

All these mean someone has to pay money to the court.

Disqualification

You can be disqualified from driving even if you do not hold a licence.

Supervision order

The magistrates can place you under supervision of someone – usually a social worker but maybe a probation officer – to 'advise, befriend and assist' you for up to three years.

Supervised activity or intermediate treatment
These are schemes run by the local authority under which you have to take part in organized activities for up to a total of 90 days.

Detention centre
Males between 14 and 20 can be sent to detention centre, normally for between 21 days and four months.

Youth custody
Only for young people aged 15 to 20. You can be locked up for between four and six months for one offence or 12 months in total.

Deferred sentences
Courts may postpone sentencing (with your consent) for up to six months and will then take into account how you have behaved during that time.

Serious offences
For very serious crimes like murder or rape, young people can be locked up for a number of years or even for an indefinite period.

Attendance centre orders
You may be given an order to go to an attendance centre for between 12 and 24 hours.

Community service
This can be ordered for a 16-year-old who has committed a serious offence. You have to do unpaid work in the community for between 40 and 120 hours.

Care orders
These can be made on 10- to 16-year-olds who have committed serious offences. The local authority (social services) can make nearly all decisions about you which your parents would usually make. You can be placed in a children's home or with a foster family.

A CHRISTIAN VIEWPOINT

Much of Jesus's teaching is about forgiveness. Peter once asked him how many times a person should suffer injustice before hitting back. He replied 'seventy times seven' *(Matthew 18: 22)*, which was his was of saying, 'keep forgiving and stop counting'. However, Jesus did believe in justice. He also often spoke about God's punishment for wrong-doers, in a next life.

Many Christians believe that punishment and forgiveness can go together. They also lay great stress on trying to look at the motives and reasons for crime. Over the last 150 years many Christians have worked towards the idea of reforming criminals, as they see the theory of reform as being perhaps the most important theory.

A HUMANIST VIEWPOINT

Humanists believe that society has a duty to try and destroy the conditions that lead to crime. Also, society must try and look at the motives for crime.

Humanists condemn any punishment that takes away human dignity and is in any way cruel.

FOR YOUR FOLDERS

▶ Read these biblical quotes. Copy them down and explain which theory of punishment they could refer to.

'A person will reap exactly what he sows.'

(Galatians 9: 6)

'Then everyone will hear of it (the death penalty) and be afraid, and no one will dare to act in such a way.'

(Deuteronomy 17: 13)

▶ In your own words explain the five aims of punishment.

▶ Look at the list of punishments and sentences for juveniles. Can you work out which theories of punishment they fit?

! ▶ What do you consider to be the most important aim of punishment? Give reasons for your answer.

FOR DISCUSSION

▶ 'The theories of punishment can't be working . . . look at the alarming crime rate.'

▶ 'Much crime is linked to social factors like the area you live in, unemployment or bad housing. The real criminals are those who keep people in poverty, yet they are the ones who walk free.'

The crucifixion of Christ by Salvador Dali

In the ancient world one of the most common methods of capital punishment was crucifixion. Death was caused by exhaustion, heart failure, or sometimes by having the legs shattered by an iron club. In 519 BC Darius, King of Persia, crucified 3,000 political opponents in Babylon. The Emperor Constantine abolished crucifixion in the Roman Empire during the fourth century but it was still practised in Japan until the nineteenth century.

Other forms of capital punishment through the ages have included being stoned to death; decapitation; being burnt alive; hanging; being fed alive to wild animals; being ripped apart by horses running in opposite directions; being hurled from rocks; drowning, drawing and quartering.

Offenders were drawn and quartered by being partly strangled and then disembowelled while still alive, having their entrails burnt in front of them, being decapitated and then having their body butchered into four pieces. Many of these punishments were carried out in public.

In the eighteenth century you could be hanged in Britain for over 200 offences. In 1957 the British government ruled that only certain types of murder were punishable by the gallows (killing police officers; using guns or explosives; killing two or more people; killing during a robbery). In 1965, after much debate, capital punishment was suspended for a five-year trial period. In 1970 it was permanently abolished.

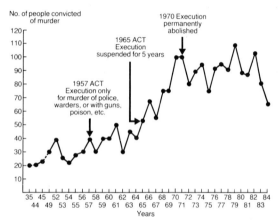

A   *Convictions for murder in the UK, 1935–84*

Relationship	1974	1984
Son or daughter	18%	12%
Parent	3%	5%
Spouse, cohabitant	21%	20%
Other family	4%	2%
Lover or former lover	5%	3%
Friend/acquaintance	22%	35%
Not acquainted	25%	23%

B   *The relationships of victims to their murderers*

CLASS DEBATE

▶ 'This House believes that capital punishment should be reintroduced.' Using some of the following arguments, organize a class debate. (You need someone to propose and second the motion of both sides plus a chairperson.)

The case for capital punishment

- terrorists who indiscriminately kill people should be hanged
- it deters (puts off) potential murderers
- it has been in existence since the beginning of time, so why abolish it now?
- it protects civilians and police
- it adequately expresses society's total abhorrence of murder
- a so-called life sentence is not punishment enough
- some 'lifers' are back on the streets in a few years
- the law should be based on 'An eye for an eye, a tooth for a tooth'
- revenge is a natural human emotion
- capital punishment helps the victim's family to get over their loss.

The case against capital punishment

- capital punishment may make convicted terrorists into martyrs
- the law condemns murder and then goes on to murder in the name of the law
- it does not necessarily deter (see graph **A**)
- the death penalty is inhumane
- society turns the executioner into a murderer
- in the past the wrong person has been hanged
- in 77% of murders in 1984 the murderer knew the victim well (e.g. family rows, loss of temper)
- it makes a mockery of the idea of reform
- rather than kill so-called murderers we should begin to study their motives and the pressures society has put them under
- all life is sacred – what right has society to judge that a person's life should end?

A HUMANIST VIEWPOINT

'The abolition of capital punishment has been the concern of humanists for years. Revenge, whether divine or human, is always destructive; never creative. It has no place in any society claiming to be civilized.'

(from Kit Mouat, *What Humanism Is About,* Barrie & Rockliff/Pemberton, 1963)

AN ANGLICAN VIEWPOINT

In 1983 some of the speakers of the Church of England's General Synod made the following points:

'God is merciful and man shares in God's merciful nature.'

'The taking of life as a penalty devalues human life.'

'There is substantial doubt that capital punishment has any significant deterrent effect.'

'The abolition of capital punishment gave prison chaplains a chance to work for the reform of all prisoners rather than just some of them.'

(Report on Proceedings)

FOR YOUR FOLDERS

▶ Write a paragraph on what you think graph **A** and table **B** show.

❗▶ A local newspaper has recently had a section on whether hanging should be brought back. Write a letter to the editor either supporting or rejecting reintroduction.

❗▶ Look at the Anglican viewpoint. Write something
  a explaining what is meant,
  b on your views of each statement.

FOR DISCUSSION

▶ Capital punishment 'has no place in any society claiming to be "civilized" '. Do you agree?

▶ To hang terrorists would only make them martyrs.

James Hemming, a Humanist writer, talks about what he sees as some of the causes of violence in *our* society.

A HUMANIST VIEW ON TEENAGE VIOLENCE

'H. G. Wells pointed out that any society will be in trouble if it fails to give its young men something significant to do. This is so because young men are physically strong and vigorous and crave to make a mark, prove themselves, gain prestige. If an outlet for this need is denied them, there is sure to be an explosive reaction of some kind.

Another factor is that young males are subject to a powerful sex drive. They are at their most virile in their late teens and early twenties. This, too, can be a source of tension, frustration and revolt.

Young women are also subject to stresses in plenty, but their stresses are different from those which affect young men. For one thing, young women have a built-in source of obvious value as the bearers of children. Because of the male's much slighter role in procreation, the drive of young men to prove their value is all the more intense. Statistically, at any rate, young males are far more often the source of physically violent behaviour than young women. I shall, then, concentrate mainly, tonight, on the male teenagers.

Social anthropologists have shown us that simpler societies were well aware of the importance of offering outlets for the physical vigour and sex drive of young males, and of meeting their hunger for significance and status. The tribal communities always provided their young men with some sort of initiation period, which was a challenge to courage and vigour, and then followed this by a ceremony of welcome and rejoicing which bestowed adult status on the initiates. The failure rate was negligible. Senseless violence among the young men was never a problem because they were assured of personal dignity and value.

I shall have more to say on adolescent cultures in tribal society but, for the moment, let us notice the difference between the road to adulthood in simple communities and what we have on offer. Our young people spend much of their adolescence boxed up in school pursuing courses of study that are often experienced as boring because they lack interest, activity, and relevance to life. The often unwilling students are then thrown, after months of tortuous preparation, into a once-for-all

A clash between police and rioter during the Brixton riots in 1985

examination which stamps many of them as inferior. These rejects can find themselves out in society without any rewarding sense of social significance. They may even be unwanted in the job market. They are, in fact, left to drift.

There is, however, one quick way into the limelight for the young men – by using their muscles. A fracas with other young men, or the police, easily gives them star status among their pals, and at least some recognition that they exist from society as a whole.

In the Xhosa society adolescents run their own culture. This includes dances, trips, discussions, club-fighting and love-making. All the boys carry clubs and may challenge one another to duels, under precribed rules and supervision. In these bouts – for settling disputes, status issues or just letting off high spirits – bruises are exchanged but real damage is rare. It is no more lethal than, say, a tough game of football. After initiation, in the late teens, the young men put away their clubs because "only boys settle things with the stick". In future, differences are to be accommodated by discussion. This system helps the young males to test one another and find out where each fits in.

Sex life among Xhosa youth is active and friendly. The young pair off, and sleep together, in an uninhibited but caring way. Penetration is not approved of because of the need to avoid pregnancy before marriage, but sexual relief is attained. The girls keeps her vagina covered throughout. Boys who become uppish, and seek complete penetration, get a bad name among the girls and are ostracized until they learn to be more thoughtful.

Sex love, in the kind of simple societies I have mentioned, is uninhibited but orderly. In our society, it is pseudo-free and disorderly; nobody knows what the rules are. This leads to stress and tension which, on top of other frustrations, may provoke either violent demonstration or retreat into fantasy and drug dependence.

'We see, then, that the prevailing school system, social indifference to youth's hunger for significance, and the experience of sexual rejection may all be components in generating a violent response among our less fortunate young males.'

(An abridged version of James Hemming's talk at the British Humanist Association in April 1986.)

23-YEAR SURVEY THAT LINKS ADULT CRIME TO VIOLENCE ON SCREEN
By LIZ LIGHTFOOT
Education Correspondent

TV VIOLENCE turns children into classroom bullies and then into violent adults, according to a major new study.

The survey, to be published in the summer, is the longest project of its kind. Carried out over 23 years in America, it documents the lives and behaviour of hundreds of people from the age of ten.

It shows that children who regularly watched violent TV programmes have turned into adults – now in their early thirties – who are:
AGGRESSIVE compared to 'non violence' viewers;
CRIMINAL, with 25% more convictions;
ANTI-SOCIAL, often with records of bad driving or assault.

(*Daily Mail*, September 1986)

Priests hit out on jobs plight that led to riot
BRIXTON

IN AN EXTRAORDINARY public statement yesterday, nine Anglican clergymen in Brixton came together to issue a joint declaration in the wake of the Brixton riots.

THE STATISTICS tell the story:
● Since the 1981 riots, unemployment has doubled in the borough of Lambeth and now stands at 22%. In Brixton it is 33%.
● The rate of house-building has fallen. In 1981, 1,022 new homes were completed. Last year, it was only 552. In 1981, the council spent £51 million on housing. This year it is spending £34 million.

Yesterday, the nine Brixton Anglican priests were forthright in their condemnation: 'We deplore the conditions of life which have persisted and worsened in Brixton since the 1981 riots. We deplore the fact that no effective steps have been taken by the Government in the past four years to alleviate unemployment.'

(*Observer*, 6 October 1985)

FOR YOUR FOLDERS

▶ Write down what the causes of violence are, according to James Hemming, the American survey, and the nine Anglican churchmen.

▶ What 'conditions of life' that led to the Brixton riots are deplored by the nine Anglican churchmen?

▶ Why does James Hemming believe that many young men in our society are not 'assured of personal dignity and value'?

! ▶ Young men are generally more violent than young women. Do you agree? Give reasons for your opinion.

! ▶ Write an article entitled 'Why we live in a violent society'.

PROFILE

19: *How do you respond when managers like Brian Clough, who say you're threatening to destroy football in this country altogether, appeal to you to stop?*

RICK: 'Don't bother. Don't take no notice.'

19: *How do you feel about the Italians who died in the Brussels stadium last year?*

RICK: 'Well, it was tragic and all that. I suppose if they'd been hard-core Juventus fans it'd have been justified.'

19: *Do you think the police will stop you?*

RICK: 'They're trying. But, if they stop us on the terraces, we'll just fight in the car park.'

19: *What's your typical week like? How do you pass your time?*

RICK: 'Well, I see me girlfriend regular, but mostly I live for the match. Sunday to Tuesday I spend thinking about the last one. Wednesday onwards, I start thinking about the next match. Otherwise, there's nothing, really. Work. Go to bed.'

19: *There has been violence at football grounds since the 'Sixties. What is different about it now?*

RICK: 'It's got more serious. Most of the kids carry knives, now, and a lot use CS gas. You can't take chances, like. If you can't take a weapon with you, you'll find something on the terraces anyway – seats, bits of concrete, bricks. The press call it "mindless", but it ain't – a lot of planning goes into it.'

19: *Who does the planning?*

RICK: 'The leaders. There always was leaders, but there's a new type of leadership on the terraces now. They're older than us. Most of them are in their late twenties, early thirties. Most of them are white, some of them are black, especially in the Midlands. The leaders all work, or have got money. To see them in the street, you wouldn't credit it. I mean, they look dead smart. They've got style.'

19: *You say some of the leaders are black. Isn't it odd, then, that you hear racist chanting at football grounds?*

RICK: 'Yeah, put like that, it is odd. But is just happens. Just happens.'

19: *What is the point of all the fighting?*

RICK: 'It's the whole point. You've got to get the respect of other Firms. That's what street credibility is. Your Firm has got to establish a reputation for being hard, then earn and keep it.'

19: *Why do you do it?*

RICK: 'I enjoy it. The experience of being in a fight – there ain't nothing like it. You never think, *I might get stabbed*. That never enters your mind. The excitement is that you never know what's going to happen. All your worries go away.'

(from *19*, March 1986)

RETURN OF THE HARD MEN

The press once described Manchester United fans as 'animals'. The following Saturday, during the match, the fans replied by chanting: "We hate humans". David Robins took the chant as the title for his own study of football hooliganism, which is published by Penguin Books.

In *We Hate Humans*, Robins offers a striking analysis. At the end of the war, communities that had been shattered by the bombing were in the process of being redeveloped. The new estates and tower blocks gave no sense of belonging. One focus of self-identity had always been the traditional support of the local football club. It had meaning, then, to say 'united'. But, increasingly, through the resettlements and redevelopments, the sense of a 'united city' disappeared. The emergence of working-class youth culture – through rock 'n' roll and the teddy boys – filled the need for an identity.

By the 'Sixties, the already difficult relations between the older and younger generations of the working class came under the further strain of automation. The skills, crafts and apprenticeships which the fathers had prided themselves on were suddenly of no use to their sons. In a real sense, the young were growing up in a different world. A section of the working-class youth who emerged in the 'Sixties had no sense of their own roots in society. It was also the time of the 'Sixties 'revolution' – flower power, Beatlemania, love and peace. A time of dreams: one dream being that Britain had at long last ceased to be a class-ridden society. The stark truth, however was already lacing its bovver boots. What Robins points out is that the 'Sixties 'revolution' was essentially a middle-class movement to which the working class lacked the cultural ticket that would have enabled them to join in. For them there was no place to drop out *to*. So the terraces became the place where they asserted their own identity. It was an ugly identity, too, because they were saying they had nothing.

Other factors have since compounded the problem. The money footballers earn, and the superstar status they enjoy, makes them remote from their traditional working-class supporters. The televizing of football has had the effect of turning what was a local event into a national institution. This has made the supporter feel that the game has been taken from him. Soccer gangs have been called 'tribes', but to be more accurate they could be termed 'lost tribes'.

Robins highlights one very important development, what he calls "the return of the hard men". What must be remembered is that hooliganism is not new. References to ruffians in Britain can be traced back as far as the 14th century. It is a phase which is usually grown out of.

The disturbing development Robins found is that the hard men who left the terraces in order to settle down went on to find life hard. Their marriages broke up; they couldn't cope with work; or they lost their jobs. As a way of trying to cope with their lives they returned to the terraces and became the new leaders. That's how – from the mid-'Seventies onwards – the Firms became organized and frightening.

That's the pattern of organization we have today and of which Rick is a member.

(from *19*, March 1986)

Death on the terraces but the riot goes on

FORTY-TWO soccer fans were killed last night at the European Cup final between Liverpool and Juventus.

Most were trampled to death after fences at the Brussels stadium collapsed under the weight of rioting fans.

Italians and Belgians were among the dead. Some were believed to be women and children.

Another 350 people were injured, 150 of them seriously. Brussels police said: "We fear the death toll could reach 60 by tomorrow."

One spectator who survived the carnage said: "I saw a little boy of six or seven whose father was lying dead next to him."

Another horrified policeman said: "It was like Hiroshima."

(*Daily Mirror*, 31 May 1985)

'Make these louts suffer'

DAVID HALL needed 170 stitches after he was attacked by a mob of Chelsea supporters.

Newcastle fan David, 22, who still suffers nightmares following his ordeal, said:

"Those found guilty of violence at soccer matches should suffer lasting punishment for their crime."

(*Daily Mirror*, 2 April 1985)

'Jail the boot boys'

BRISTOL Rovers fan David Burnham lay senseless for five days after a beating from "boot boys".

David, 20, said: "If they beat someone up, they should be locked away.

"It's not enough to ban them from grounds. They'll still turn up and cause trouble.

"I hope Mrs Thatcher really cracks down . . . but it's too late for me. I'll never go to a match again."

(*Daily Mirror*, 2 April 1985)

'Put them in the stocks'

DENNIS Midwinter, who lives near the Luton ground, received a gaping head wound and saw his car and front windows smashed when Millwall fans went on the rampage last month.

He said: "We should humiliate them in public to wipe the smiles off their faces.

"They should put up stocks around the grounds."

(*Daily Mirror*, 2 April 1985)

POPE JOHN PAUL'S VIEW OF VIOLENCE

'Peace cannot be established by violence, peace can never flourish in a climate of terror, intimidation and death. It is Jesus himself who said: "All who take the sword will perish by the sword" (*Mt. 26: 52*). This is the word of God, and it commands this generation of violent men to desist from hatred and violence and to repent.

Violence is a lie, for it goes against the truth of our faith, the truth of our humanity.

Violence destroys what it claims to defend: the dignity, the life, the freedom of human beings.

Violence is a crime against humanity, for it destroys the very fabric of society' (29.9.79).

(*The Teachings of Pope John Paul II – PEACE*, The Catholic Truth Society, 1982)

CHRISTIAN ATTITUDES

Like most people, Christians condemn the violence in society. However, as with other issues, Christians disagree about how offenders should be treated. Some base their ideas on the Old Testament teaching, believing that only severe punishments can prevent people from being violent to others. Other Christians believe that we have a duty to try and understand the root causes of violence, and the reasons why young men feel it necessary to inflict violence on others. The hooligan may be violent because he is sick in mind, or deprived, or incompetent, or bitterly resentful, but whatever his reason he needs help, just as his victims need help and society needs protection.

FOR DISCUSSION

▶ 'Soccer hooligans are able to find an identity on the terraces, that they will never find during the rest of the week.'

▶ 'One reason for the soccer hooligan's violence is that the game has been "taken from him".'

▶ Some MPs have called for corporal punishment to be used against soccer hooligans. Do you think this would solve the problem?

COMMENTS

'Prisons are the nearest things to hell on earth that have ever been created.'

(Prison Governor)

'The first time I went to prison I couldn't believe it. The sadists, the firm, the nutters, the gays – Christ, I won't last here a week, I thought! The screws [prison officers] were tough bastards too. There was one law – survive! there were three ways of doing it: being rich, having an influential "friend" or just being bloody hard. The one thing I'll always remember (I've never been back) is lying in your peter [cell] with the lights out and feeling like you'd arrived in hell.'

(John, aged 30)

'I've been in and out of nick for the last 35 years. I reckon to have spent no more than five of them free. I can never get a job, I've no family – it's the only place I really know. I feel secure inside – I'll die inside, I know that.'

(Billy, aged 55)

'When Mum told me that me Dad was inside – I felt kinda proud . . . that was until the kids at school started calling him names.'

(Joe, aged 12)

'The worst thing is waiting outside until they open the gates – people stare at you. You're so excited before you go in . . . that is until you see him and look at his eyes. He looks like a trapped animal . . . I always leave in tears which must make him feel terrible . . . perhaps I ought to stop going.'

(Joan, wife of prisoner)

TEN PRISONERS' RIGHTS

1 **Books** Library facilities are available. Reading material sent to the prisoner is allowed but may be censored.

2 **Clothing** Men must wear uniforms. (Women don't have to.)

3 **Discharge grant** A prisoner will be given a small sum of money to help him on release.

A day in a local prison

After being sentenced most offenders are taken to a local prison...

 REVEILLE

 SLOPPING OUT

 BREAKFAST

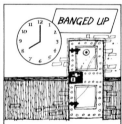 BANGED UP

 EXERCISE

 WORK

 LUNCH

TUES. 22nd JUNE	
B'FAST	PORRIDGE BEANS ON TOAST
DINNER	SOUP, BREAD, CURRY RICE JAM ROLL, CUSTARD
TEA	CORNISH PASTY
SUPPER	COCOA, BREAD

 BANGED UP

 EXERCISE

 WORK

 TEA

 RECREATION

 CLASSES

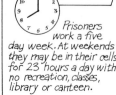 BANGED UP

Prisoners work a five day week. At weekends they may be in their cells for 23 hours a day with no recreation, classes, library or canteen.

4 **Discipline** Punishments include punishment cells, withdrawn privileges, loss of remission and earnings, confinement.

5 **Food** Three meals a day. (Bread and water punishments no longer exist.)

6 **Letters** Prisoners may send and receive one letter a week. The authorities read *all* letters except legal ones.

7 **Parole** After serving one third of a sentence a prisoner can be considered for parole.

8 **Remission** One third of a sentence can be reduced for good conduct.

9 **Visits** One visit per month of at least 30 minutes.

10 **Work** On average, 24 hours a week for small pay.

SOME STATISTICS

- 1,500 prisoners are serving life sentences
- 8 million working days a year are lost by men being in prison
- many prisoners are confined to cells for 23 hours a day because of overcrowding
- 82% of women in prison for the first time never return
- 75% of men discharged after serving 18 months or more will return
- the size of the prison population doubled between 1951 and 1981
- it is estimated that another 40 new prisons are needed to replace existing worn-out buildings
- 16,000 prisoners (in England and Wales) crowd two to three in a cell built for one in Victorian times.

CONCERNED ORGANIZATIONS

RAP (Radical Alternatives to Prison) – an organization which believes that prisons do more harm than good.

NACRO (National Association for the Care and Resettlement of Offenders) – gives prisoners advice and help on their release.

Howard League for Penal Reform – presses to make prisons more humane and fairer places.

PROP (Preservation of the Right of Prisoners) – organization of prisoners and ex-prisoners helping to acquire more rights.

'Keep in mind those who are in prison as though you were in prison with them.'
(St Paul, in *Hebrews* 13: 3)

. . . and in prison you did not visit me . . .'
(Jesus, in *Matthew* 25: 43)

TALKING POINTS

- **What are the main problems facing the present prison sysem?**
- **How can Christians help improve the system?**
- **Prisons are universities of crime.**

FOR YOUR FOLDERS

▶ Pretend you are in prison for the first time. Write a letter home describing your experiences.

▶ Write a paragraph on the sayings of Jesus and St Paul about prisons.

▶ Read through the 'Comments'. List some of the problems facing prisoners and their families.

▶ 'The use of imprisonment should be minimized to reduce isolation from society and weaken the society of crime.'
(British Humanist Association General Statement of Policy)

Explain what you think this means.

▶ Do you think prison sentences for minor crimes should be scrapped?

WHAT IS WORK?

On the one hand, work is part of living and doing the things that are essential to stay alive. It is an activity natural to people. But not all human activity is work of this sort. Some of it is play or rest and some of it is thought and using the mind. For many people, work is what they get paid for, but often people do not stop working when they are not paid for it. Work has been described as 'purposeful activity'.

WHAT PURPOSES DOES WORK SERVE?

In *Work and the Future,* a report by the Industrial Committee of the General Synod Board for Social Responsibility (Church Information Office, 1979), the Church of England outlines the five purposes of work.

1   Work is NECESSARY

'It is, first of all, necessary for human survival. It more primitive times, humans would have died out without the hunting, fishing and gathering which enabled them to feed and clothe themselves. At a later stage of development, herding flocks, farming the land and making simple tools to build useful objects like tables and chairs were also essential aspects of the struggle to survive. Without them there could have been no family or community life.'

This idea of work as being necessary is reflected in *Genesis 2: 15*:

'The Lord God took the man and put him in the garden of Eden to till it and care for it.'

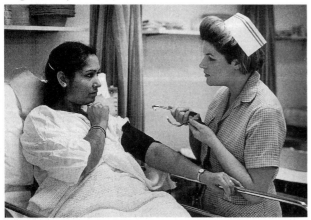

Work usually brings us into relationship with other people, as with this nurse

2   Work is CREATIVE

By mastering the elements of nature, humans are able to create things. In *Genesis 1: 28*, Adam and Eve are told:

'Be fruitful and increase, fill the earth and subdue it, rule over the fish in the sea, the birds of the air, and every living thing that moves upon the earth.'

This is a picture of humans being creative and exercizing control, sharing with God in the further development of his creation.

Pope John Paul has stressed that, in spite of the heavy toil that sometimes accompanies it, work is a good thing for people:

*'Work is a good thing for man – a good thing for his humanity – because through work man **not only transforms nature**, adapting it to his own needs, but he also **achieves fulfilment** as a human being and, indeed, in a sense, becomes "more a human being".'*

(The Teachings of Pope John Paul II – Human Work, The Catholic Truth Society, 1982)

3   Work is PAINFUL

Working on the land was very hard and back-breaking. Factory work can be repetitive, boring, meaningless, monotonous and soul-destroying. Work is tiring. Work can cause mental illness and physical illness. People can sometimes get killed doing their jobs.

Two thinkers of the past have commented:

'The division of labour in factories can erode the qualities of reason, imagination, sympathy and fellow feeling.'

(Adam Smith, 1723–90)

'The work is external to the worker . . . it is not a part of his nature . . . he does not fulfil himself in his work . . . has a feeling of misery not of well-being . . . but is physically exhausted and mentally debased.'

(Karl Marx, 1818–83)

This painful aspect of work is again reflected in *Genesis (3: 17–19)*:

'Because . . . you have eaten from the tree I forbade you, accursed shall be the ground on your account. It will grown thorns and thistles for you . . . You shall gain your bread by the sweat of your brow.'

So work is seen as being a punishment for disobeying God.

4   Work is HEALTHY

Work brings us into relationship with other people. It helps us to belong to a community, by giving us a place, status, belonging and value. So it is vital for our mental and spiritual health. We are who we are very much as a result of our relationship with others. Not working and being unemployed is:

'The worst evil, in the sense that the unemployed feel that they have fallen out of the common life . . . they are not wanted. That is the thing that has the power to corrupt the soul of any man.'

(William Temple, 1881–1944, Archbishop of Canterbury 1942–44)

5   Work is GOOD

Work is a way of obtaining the necessities of life and enriching our lives with beauty and enjoyment. It is regarded as a means of sharing with God in being creative in the world. During the centuries, work, to some Christians, especially Protestants, became a sort of religious duty. Hard work was seen as being a virtue. This became known as the 'Protestant Work Ethic'.

Martin Luther (1483-1546) was an Augustinian monk and professor of scripture in Wittenberg in Germany. He was particularly interested in the concept of **vocation**, believing that every Christian had a calling, not just those monks who devoted themselves to the life of contemplation. He found a passage in *Ecclesiasticus 11: 21* which ran, 'Do not envy a rogue his success; trust the Lord and stick to your job. It is no difficult thing for the Lord to make a poor man rich in a moment. The Lord's blessing is the reward of piety, which blossoms in one short hour.'

FOR YOUR FOLDERS

▶ 'Many people do not stop working when they are not paid for it.' List some examples of these types of 'work'.

▶ Write a sentence in your own words to explain the purposes of work as outlined by the Church of England.

▶ List some types of work that *you* would regard as being 'painful', 'creative', 'sociable'.

! ▶ Write a sentence on the sayings of Adam Smith, Karl Marx, Martin Luther, Pope John Paul II and William Temple. Do you agree with their ideas? Give reasons for your opinions.

FOR DISCUSSION

▶ Look at these two different accounts of people's experiences at work. Discuss them in relation to some of the above ideas.

'Every day is different. It's exciting. You never know what a new day will bring. The patients are all individuals with their own experiences, beliefs and characters. It is a privilege to work with and for so many interesting people.'

(Nurse in London hospital)

'You don't achieve anything here. A robot could do it. The line here is made for morons. It doesn't need any thought. They tell you that. "We don't pay you for thinking," they say. Everyone comes to realize that they're not doing a worthwhile job. They're just on the line. For the money.'

(An assembly line worker at Fords)

> **Vocation** – 'a job which one does because one thinks one has a special fitness or ability to give service to other people . . . a special call from, or choosing by, God for the religious life.'
>
> *(Longman's Dictionary of Contemporary English)*

For many people work could be described as 'the way we earn our leisure'. However, most Christians believe that work should be a vocation, a calling. Many Humanists, too, believe that working in itself should be a fulfilling and valuable thing.

Some examples of jobs that are recognizable as callings include: nursing, the priesthood, social work, teaching, working with the deprived and the disabled and working in areas of extreme poverty. For a Christian, however, every job that serves God and other human beings is a vocation. For a Humanist any honest job that helps others and contributes to the well-being of society could be said to be vocational. Humanists do not believe that they are 'called by God', but rather that their conscience and reason help them to find worthwhile and fulfilling work.

A METHODIST DEFINITION

'VOCATION   Through the right use of his time, a Christian offers his life, gifts and effort to God. A sense of vocation means that we see what we do as an expression of our faith and a response to God's love for us. Ideally it should be possible to have a sense of vocation about the whole of life, but many must work in ways that do not allow the exercize of personal qualities. In these situations a sense of vocation is difficult or impossible to achieve. Those who work like this will want to take the opportunity of leisure to find activities in which a real sense of vocation is possible.'

(What Does Methodism Think? 1980)

UNACCEPTABLE OCCUPATIONS

There are many types of occupations that both Humanists and Christians would find unacceptable. Humanists would only do work that improves the quality of life for others and does not harm anyone directly or indirectly. Christians, too, would take these factors into account, as well as thinking about the teachings in the Bible and their responsibilities as 'creatures of God'.

THINGS TO DO

▶ Consider which of the following occupations both Humanists and Christians would find morally unacceptable:

nursing, teaching, working in a weapons factory, striptease artist, making pornographic films, experimenting on animals for cosmetics, pilot of a bomber, researching into chemical weapons, police force, working in a shop that sells 'girlie' magazines, working in a tobacco factory, landlord of a pub, experimenting on animals for medical research, priesthood, working in a slaughterhouse, prostitution.

Are there some occupations that some Humanists would accept but Christians might not, or vice versa?

▶ Discuss your findings.

RESPONSIBILITY

Work involves being responsible, for both the employer and the employed. The employee (a person who is employed) has a responsibility to:

- be punctual for work
- attend work regularly
- avoid laziness and sciving
- get on with all work colleagues
- be honest if dealing with money
- use non-working time to rest.

A hundred years ago employees were in a fairly weak position at work. Poor wages, poor working conditions, long hours, few holidays, the threat of instant dismissal and no sick pay all made work a miserable reality for millions of people. This is still the case in many parts of the world today. Few employers were responsible. Their main concern was making as much profit as they could. However, this century the rise of the Trade Union movement and the passing of laws in Parliament have meant that employers must now keep to their responsibilities. An employer should see that their employees:

- receive a fair wage
- have good working conditions
- take no health or safety risks at work
- get decent holidays

- don't work too long hours
- can have some sort of pension scheme,
- are not discriminated against (sex, colour, creed)
- are not under a constant threat of redundancy
- have the right to withdraw their labour (strike) if they feel some injustice has occurred.

SOME THOUGHTS ON WORK

'So I came to hate all my labour and toil here under the sun, since I should have to leave its fruits to my successor.'

(Ecclesiastes 2: 18 – Old Testament)

'Whatever you do, work at it with all your heart, as though you were working for the Lord and not for men.'

(Colossians 3: 23 – New Testament)

TO EACH ACCORDING TO HIS NEEDS

FROM EACH ACCORDING TO HIS ABILITY

Karl Marx

'A person's work is his contribution to the community; he needs to respect his work in order to respect himself, and the quality of his work will reflect how he values his contribution.'

(James Hemming, a leading Humanist)

FOR YOUR FOLDERS

▶ Explain in your own words the meaning of 'vocation'.

▶ Write a paragraph on 'Work and responsibility'.

▶ Can you list some jobs that could be regarded as vocations?

▶ Explain what you think James Hemming says about work. Do you think there are some jobs which do not deserve respect?

TALKING POINTS

- Is it important to work?
- If you had the choice of a well-paid but boring job, or a low paid but rewarding job, which would you choose?

IN GROUPS

▶ In pairs or groups of three, decide which of the following jobs should be the highest paid. Put them in order.

Teaching, nursing, refuse collecting, judge, hospital porter, soldier, fireman, police officer, vicar, social worker, bank clerk, typist, rock musician, train driver.

Give reasons for your choices.

In *Three Men in a Boat* Jerome K. Jerome says: 'I like work; it fascinates me. I can sit and look at it for hours.'

In Britain, and throughout the world, a very large number of people have no alternative but to look at work from the outside – they are unemployed.

What causes high unemployment? The answer is very complicated, but includes:

- the decline in the demand for manufactured goods – often called the 'World Recession'
- increase in the working population (more women in the workforce and more young people eligible for work)
- low-priced goods from countries like Japan, Hong Kong, Taiwan and Singapore where often 'cheap labour' is employed
- lack of investment into new products
- technological change . . . more is produced but less people are needed to produce it. Robots, automated machines, micro processors, micro-electronic components and computers have all been introduced in the workplace.

As a result

- in 1970 there were 618,000 unemployed people in the UK. By 1986 an estimated 4 million people were out of work
- unskilled workers, black people, young people, people living in inner cities; disabled people and ex-offenders are especially hit by unemployment
- unemployment costs the government an estimated £15 billion a year
- more people are becoming unemployed for longer periods (in 1986 over 1 million people had been without work for more than a year) . . . often people become so-called 'unemployable'
- *'There are social and personal costs. Local communities and amenities decline; social order is threatened; crime increases; the integrating effect of having a job and belonging in society is lost; individuals suffer psychological shock; they feel humiliated, angry and depressed; health problems increase; families suffer extra strain [there are] increases in heart disease, suicide and other deaths, mental illness, loss of self-esteem, violence, the use of alcohol and tobacco . . .'*

(Church of England report, 1982)

> 'Everyone has the right to work, to free choice of employment, to just and favourable conditions of work and to protection from unemployment.'
>
> *(Universal Declaration of Human Rights)*

PROFILE

'Besides looking for jobs, you read comics, watch television, play records, go looking in shop windows. You can't afford the bus fares to visit your mates if they live out of walking distance. You make yourself useful doing the housework. At first, I used to keep the house absolutely clean and tidy, for something to do.

You do anything to occupy your mind. Sometimes my mum gives me money for doing the housework. I have to cook my brother's meals, and if I've been out on a course or something, he has a go at me when it's not ready.

For money, I've got a boyfriend who will pay when we go out. But that means I've got to be nice to him.

I just go to my mum, and now I owe her a lot of money. But I wouldn't go on at her for it when I know she doesn't have it. It's not easy to borrow money from people.

We can't get money for clothes. Sometimes we get money for cigarettes, but it all adds up. If I've fags

Robots are taking over many people's jobs

and my sister hasn't I give her some, and the same for me. But if my mum was unemployed I'd be completely stuck.'

Your family and friends
'People ask what you do and you say nothing and they say never mind and that's the end of the subject – nothing more to talk about. You might lie because you're embarrassed about it to try to cover up, and make excuses if they ask more.

They look down on you as if you're a layabout, especially if they're working. You feel you're the only one because all your friends seem to have jobs. You get very lonely, and you have no topic of conversation. My boyfriend says, "Why don't you get a job, at least you'd have something to talk about".

At home it's really depressing. You tend to get moody and unsociable. You lose confidence in yourself so that when you do get an interview you don't expect to get the job. At first you feel angry but after a while you lose interest. People keep telling me to get married and have children but there's no point in that. You're really tied down then and you still have to go out to work.

Often your parents think it's easy to get a job, but it's not. You can go out virtually all day, tramping around, killing yourself, going for interviews and getting turned down. And all your parents say is, "Oh, never mind, at least you've had an interview." They're pushing you out all the time. My brother says to me, "Why haven't you got a job? I've got one." But there's many more jobs open to boys than to girls. You mother says, "Never mind, there'll be another," but you feel like giving up because you're so rejected.'

(Susan Hemmings, ed., *Girls Are Powerful*, Sheba, 1982)

Why the dole leads to depression

'Why do many people feel depressed and "down" when they are unemployed?

When you are in a job, or in regular training or education, your job gives you important personal support in five basic ways.

If you lose that job, or just don't have one, you may also lose these important supports. The result: Depression.

These are the five basic supports:

1 A job brings you a sense of *purpose and direction*.
2 A job brings *regular daily activity*.
3 A job brings a personal sense of *identity and self-respect*.
4 A job provides us with *companions and friendship*.
5 A job provides *money*.

(*The Unemployment Handbook*, National Extension College, 1981)

TALKING POINTS

- **Read this advice in *Proverbs 6: 6–11*.**

  'Go to the ant, you sluggard,
  watch her ways and get wisdom.
  She has no overseer,
  no governor or ruler;
  but in summer she prepares her store of food
  and lays in her supplies at harvest.
  How long, you sluggard, will you lie abed?
  When will you rouse yourself from sleep?
  A little sleep, a little slumber,
  a little folding of the hands in rest,
  and poverty will come upon you like a robber,
  want like a ruffian.'

  Does unemployment necessarily mean idleness?

- **How can somebody who is unemployed spend their time in a creative and fulfilling way?**

- **What does it mean to be unemployed? Is a laid-off factory worker who rebuilds his house unemployed in the same way as a laid-off factory worker who sits idly at home watching television all day?**

FOR YOUR FOLDERS

▶ Look at the Church of England report. Write an article about 'The hidden cost of unemployment'.

▶ Explain in your own words what unemployment means for the writer in *Girls Are Powerful*.

▶ What do you think are the main problems that unemployment causes?

BIBLICAL ATTITUDES TO LEISURE

'You have six days in which to do your work, but the seventh day is a day of rest dedicated to me. On that day no one is to work.'

(4th Commandment, Exodus 20: 9–10)

'There were so many people coming and going that Jesus and his disciples didn't even have time to eat. So he said to them, "Let us go off by ourselves to some place where we will be alone and you can rest for a while".'

(Mark 6: 31–32)

SOME GENERAL IDEAS ABOUT LEISURE

- leisure can relax our minds, bodies and spirits
- leisure time is generally on the increase
- leisure gives us time to get to know ourselves
- leisure gives us time to meet people outside work
- leisure helps us to face our work, refreshed
- catering for people's leisure time has become an industry.

As well as these ideas, a Christian and a Humanist might add:

- leisure time can be spent in helping others in the community
- leisure time can give us the time to think about and meditate upon some of the more important things of life
- leisure should really be spent in doing worthwhile, creative and fulfilling things in order that we can grow as human beings.

SUNDAY

Sunday is traditionally a day of rest in our society. During the Reformation in Britain, Sunday, as a 'divinely ordained day of rest' was strictly followed. In 1781, a Lord's Day Observance Act was passed, making it illegal for places of entertainment to be opened on a Sunday. Slowly the rules have become more relaxed until in 1985 the Auld Committee proposals, which could lead to the removal of most of the present restrictions about shops opening on Sundays, were debated in Parliament. The Church of England, along with other Churches, strongly opposes these proposals.

'Every society needs a publicly expressed day of rest and "re-creation", such as the Christian Sunday has provided, and that society needs symbols which point beyond market forces as the determining aspects of our lives in community.'

(Church of England response to the Auld Committee, 1985)

TELEVISION

Without a doubt the biggest single leisure activity in Britain among all age groups is watching television. A BBC survey found that at 9 pm 70% of the population were at home, and that 40% of the population were watching 'the box'.

This means that on average a person in Britain from the age of five to 70 will watch, in total, a staggering 3,927,540 minutes of TV. (This works out at about **seven and a half years**.)

Hours and minutes of TV watched daily

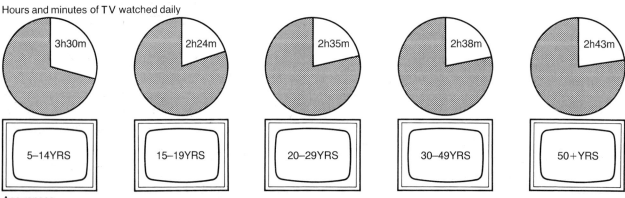

3h30m — 5–14YRS
2h24m — 15–19YRS
2h35m — 20–29YRS
2h38m — 30–49YRS
2h43m — 50+YRS

Age ranges

THE SPORTS COUNCIL

The aims of this Council, set up in 1972, are to involve more people in sport, to increase sports facilities and to show people how important sport is.

PREDICTION

'In the very near future we are all going to spend more and more time in leisure. Unless young people are taught how to spend their leisure time constructively then the result might well be boredom, frustration and despair.'

(from an essay by a 16-year-old)

THINGS TO DO

▶ Organize a survey in your class to find out
  a   how many hours of leisure people have in an average week,
  b   what sort of things they do during their leisure time.
  Make a class display of your results.

▶ From the survey, work out individually how many hours a week people spend watching the video or TV.

▶ Now try and work out how many days, months and years each individual will spend between the ages of five and 70 watching TV.

A CHRISTIAN STATEMENT

'As far as possible opportunities of work and leisure should be evenly shared in the community. There is particular value in a leisure day which is common to as many members of the community as possible.

Unemployment, redundancy and retirement are forms of involuntary leisure. In these cases it is especially important that the Church should combat any sense of guilt or uselessness by emphasizing the positive opportunities which even enforced leisure provides.

The traditional concept that work is good while leisure is a necessary breathing-space must be replaced by the understanding that both work and leisure are good if used for the glory of God.'

(Methodist Conference, 1974)

FOR YOUR FOLDERS

▶ The Church of England talks about 're-creation'. Write down what you think this might mean.

▶ Make a list of some of the 'educational' type TV programmes (when you learn something) that you watch in an average week.

▶ About one third of our time and money is spent on leisure. Say how you think schools could help 'educate us for leisure'.

▶ What do you understand by the Methodist statement on leisure?

▶ Write a piece about leisure like the one in 'Prediction'.

▶ Why do you think leisure time is so important?

TALKING POINTS

● 'Leisure can sometimes be "work".'
● 'It is more important for our society to spend money on 'Leisure Centres' than on schemes that try to get the unemployment figures down.'
● 'If everyone shared a job then we'd all have more time and more money to enjoy our hobbies.'
● 'Really, only the well-off can enjoy leisure activities.'
● 'We live in a so-called Christian society, so Sunday should remain a holy day of rest and "re-creation" '.

We have virtually conquered the planet, explored the moon, overcome the natural limits of travel and communication; we stand at the dawn of a new age, ready to move farther into space and perhaps inhabit other planets. Using technology wisely, we can control our environment, conquer poverty, markedly reduce disease, extend our life span, significantly modify our behaviour, alter the course of human evolution, unlock vast new powers, and provide humankind with an unparalleled opportunity for achieving an abundant and meaningful life. The future is, however, filled with dangers.

In learning to apply science to life, we have opened the doors to ecological damage, over-population, political repression and nuclear and biochemical disaster. Humanity, to survive, requires bold and daring measures. The ultimate goal should be the fulfilment of the potential for growth in each human personality – not for the favoured few, but for all of humankind.

For these reasons Humanists have submitted this new 'Humanist Manifesto', for the future of humankind: for them it is a vision of hope, a direction for satisfying survival.

1st   While there is much that we do not know, humans are responsible for what we are or will become. No deity will save us. We must save ourselves.

2nd   There is no evidence that life survives the death of the body.

3rd   Human life has meaning because we create and develop our futures. We strive for the good life here and now.

4th   Reason and intelligence are the best instruments humankind possesses. We also believe in the cultivation of feeling and love.

5th   All human life is precious and dignified. Also, whenever possible, freedom of choice should be increased.

6th   The right to birth control, abortion and divorce should be recognized. We wish to cultivate the development of a responsible attitude towards sexuality, in which humans are not exploited as sexual

'The developed world has a moral obligation to assist the developing world.'

objects, and in which intimacy, sensitivity, respect and honesty in interpersonal relations are encouraged.

7th The individual must experience a full range of civil liberties in all societies (e.g. freedom of speech and the press, democracy, religious liberty). It also includes a recognition of an individual's right to die with dignity, euthanasia and the right to suicide.

8th We are committed to an open and democratic society. People are more important than rules and regulations.

9th The church and the state, and the state and any other ideologies, should be separate.

10th A humane society should only have economic systems that improve the quality of life.

11th All discrimination should cease. Everyone should have equal opportunity and recognition of their talents. We are concerned for the aged, the infirm, the disadvantaged, the outcasts (addicts, prisoners, abused children, mentally retarded, the abandoned) — for all who are neglected or ignored by society. We believe in the right to universal education. We are critical of sexism, or sexual chauvinism — male or female.

12th We deplore the division of humankind on nationalistic grounds.

13th The world community must condemn the resort to violence and force as a way of solving international disputes. With the possession of biological, nuclear and chemical weapons, war is obsolete. Military spending must be reduced and these savings put to peaceful and people-orientated uses.

14th We must free our world from needless pollution and waste . . . exploitation of natural resources uncurbed by social conscience must end.

15th The developed world has a moral obligation to assist the developing world.

16th Technology must be used humanely and carefully.

17th Travel restrictions across frontiers must cease. We must learn to live openly together or we shall perish together.

(adapted from an article first published in *The Humanist*, September/October 1973)

FOR YOUR FOLDERS

▶ Make a list of the things Humanists would like to see in the future.

▶ Think of some things that are happening in the world today that Humanists believe are wrong.

 ▶ What do you consider the five most important points in the Humanist Manifesto?

THINGS TO DO

▶ Design a poster with the theme 'A Humanist view of the future of humankind'.

TALKING POINT

- 'Using technology wisely we can control our environment.'
- 'We must learn to live openly together or we shall perish together.'

1 ORIGINS

The name 'United Nations' was devised by President Franklin D. Roosevelt of the United States and was first used in 1942. The UN Charter was drawn up by representatives of 51 countries in 1945, on 24 October. That date is now celebrated all over the world and is called United Nations Day.

2 PURPOSES AND PRINCIPLES

The *purposes* of the UN are:

- to maintain international peace and security
- to develop friendly relations among nations
- to cooperate internationally in solving economic, social, cultural and humanitarian problems and in promoting respect for human rights and fundamental freedoms
- to be a centre for helping nations achieve their ends.

The UN acts on the following *principles*:

- all member countries are equal
- all member countries must fulfil their obligations
- countries must try and settle their differences by peaceful means
- they must avoid using force or threatening to use force

The *United Nations Headquarters in New York*

- the UN will not interfere with the domestic affairs and problems of any country
- countries should try to assist the UN.

So the UN's main concern is with world peace. Also, it aims to secure a world of justice, peace and progress for all people. It seeks to make nations think 'globally', not nationally, when facing the problems of the twentieth century (e.g. arms race, poverty, pollution, human rights, wars, nuclear weapons and conservation).

3 THE CHARTER

The Charter of the UN helps us to understand its hopes and aims.

PREAMBLE TO THE CHARTER OF THE
UNITED NATIONS

We the peoples of the United Nations determined

- to save succeeding generations from the scourge of war, which twice in our lifetime has brought untold sorrow to mankind and
- to reaffirm faith in fundamental human rights, in the dignity and worth of the human person, in the equal rights of men and women and of nations large and small, and
- to establish conditions under which justice and respect for the obligations arising from treaties and other sources of international law can be maintained, and
- to promote social progress and better standards of life in larger freedom.

And for these ends

- to practise tolerance and live together in peace with one another as good neighbours, and
- to unite our strength to maintain international peace and security, and
- to ensure, by the acceptance of principles and the institution of methods, that armed force shall not be used, save in the common interest, and
- to employ international machinery for the promotion of the economic and social advancement of all peoples.

4 ORGANIZATION

The General Assembly

The General Assembly is composed of all **member states**. It makes recommendations to governments on a variety of issues.

The assembly's work includes:

- dealing with things such as peace-keeping, disarmament, apartheid and colonialism
- helping bodies within the UN (e.g. the UN Children's Fund).

The Security Council

This organization has the main responsibility for maintaining peace and security. There are 15 members. Five of these (USA, USSR, China, France, Great Britain) are permanent members. The other 10 are elected by the General Assembly for two-year terms. Each member of the Council has one vote. Any major decision requires all the five permanent members to vote the same way together. If they do not this is called the **veto**.

The Secretariat

This is the 'civil service' of the UN. It helps to administer the programmes and policies laid down by the UN. At its head is the Secretary-General.

5   SOME OTHER UN ORGANIZATIONS

- **UNCTAD – United Nations Conference on Trade and Development**

- **UNDP – United Nations Development Programme**
  This deals with the economic and social problems of low-income countries.

- **UNICEF – United Nations Children's Fund**
  The Fund's purpose is to help developing countries improve the condition of their children and youth.

- **FAO – Food and Agriculture Organization of the UN.**

International Court of Justice

- **UNESCO – United Nations Educational, Scientific and Cultural Organization**

- **WHO – World Health Organization**
  This works to promote the highest possible level of health throughout the world.

6   ACHIEVEMENTS

The UN's achievements since 1945 include:

1   helping 1 billion people gain national independence,
2   helping poorer countries,
3   providing a meeting ground and a talking place during the worst periods of the 'cold war',
4   providing a code of international morality,
5   containing would-be conflicts,
6   producing more understanding around the world, proving that talking and listening are the beginning of wisdom and peace in human relations,
7   providing a platform for the hopes of humanity including liberty, equality and fraternity (brotherhood),
8   helping racial equality throughout the world,
9   warning people that they are capable of destroying the world if they are not careful,
10   generally helping the world to be a more ordered and safe place.

THINGS TO DO

▶ Think of some modern-day examples where work still needs to be done to fulfil the 10 achievements of the UN.

▶ **Role play**. Each one of you represents a country of the security council. A small country in Asia has been invaded by one of the permanent members. Organize a discussion on what should be done. What problem might the **veto** cause?

FOR YOUR FOLDERS

! ▶ What do you think the purposes of the UN are? What is their order of importance in your opinion? Give reasons for your choices.

▶ After reading this section write an essay describing the work and importance of the UN.

TALKING POINTS

- **What are the most important problems facing humankind?**
- **What can be done to solve them?**

In December 1948 the United Nations produced its Universal Declaration of Human Rights.

- All human beings are born free and equal.
- Everyone has the right to life, liberty and freedom from fear and violence.
- Everyone has the right to protection of the law without discrimination.
- No one shall be subjected to arbitrary arrest, detention or exile.
- Everyone has the right to a fair and public trial.
- Everyone charged with a penal offence has the right to be assumed innocent until proved guilty.
- No one shall be subjected to arbitary interference with his privacy, family, home or correspondence, nor to attacks on his reputation.
- Everyone has the right to freedom of movement within his own country and abroad.
- Everyone has the right to a nationality.
- Adult men and women have the right to marry and found a family regardless of their race or religion.
- Both men and women are entitled to equal rights within marriage and in divorce.
- Everyone has the right to own property. No one should be arbitrarily deprived of his property.
- Everyone has the right to freedom of thought, conscience and religion and the right to express their opinion both privately and publicly.
- Everyone has the right to attend meetings and join associations.
- No one should be forced to join an association.
- Everyone has the right to take part in the government of his country.
- Everyone has the right to work and to just and favourable conditions of employment.
- Everyone has the right to equal pay for equal work.
- Everyone has the right to fair pay to enable him and his family to live with self respect.
- Everyone has the right to form and join a trades union.
- Everyone has the right to rest and leisure, including reasonable working hours and holidays with pay.
- Everyone has the right to a standard of living adequate for their health and well-being, including housing, medical care and social security in the event of unemployment, sickness, widowhood and old age.
- Everyone has the right to an education.
- Everyone has the right to enjoy the cultural life of the community and to share in its scientific advancements and benefits.
- Everyone has duties to the community to ensure the full recognition and respect for the rights and freedoms of others.

CHRISTIAN VIEWPOINTS

'Rights can be established on the basis of the doctrine of the image of God when we consider those human characteristics which are both distinctively human and shared with God.'

(Church of England report, 1977)

'Each individual man is truly a person. He has a nature that is endowed with intelligence and free will. As such he has rights and duties . . . these rights and duties are universal and inviolable.'

(Encyclical letter of Pope John XXIII, 1963)

FOR YOUR FOLDERS

▶ Describe in your own words what each picture opposite shows.

▶ Look at the Universal Declaration of Human Rights. Write down which part of the Declaration is being violated in each case.

▶ Design a poster illustrating a violation of human rights. On your poster write down the relevant words of the Declaration.

! ▶ Why do you think the UN Declaration of Human Rights is so important?

FOR DISCUSSION

▶ 'Human rights are fundamental to our nature. Without them we cannot live as human beings.'

(UN Office of Information)

▶ 'No rights are possible without the basic guarantees for life, including the right . . . to adequate food, to guaranteed health care, to decent housing . . .'

(Declaration of the 5th Assembly of the World Council of Churches, Nairobi, 1975)

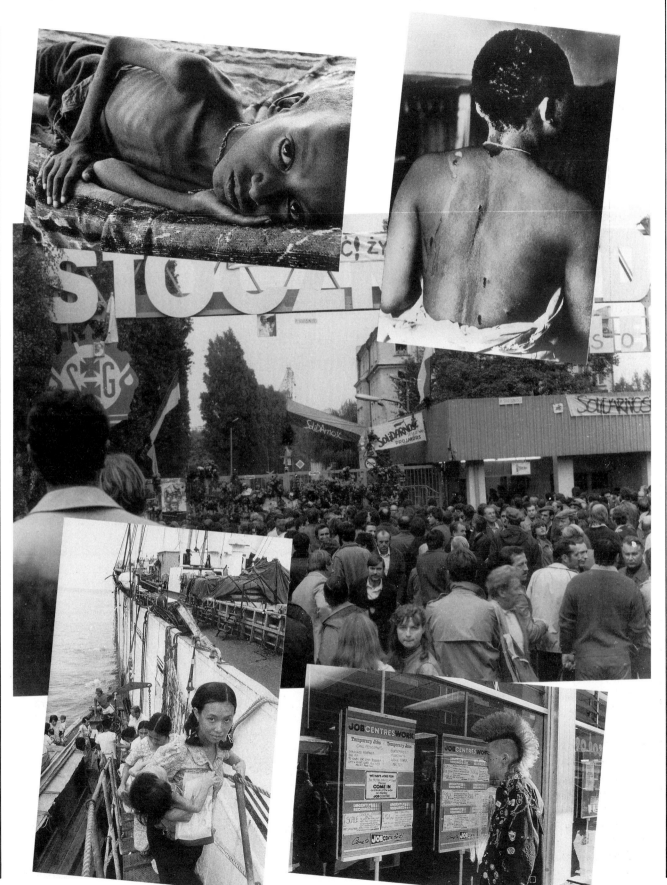

In some countries the rule of law exists and human rights are respected. However, this is not the case in others. In many countries civil and political rights are consistently denied or violated. Some of the reasons why this happens include:

- some governments refuse to admit the value of human rights
- in a time of 'emergency', rights are denied (e.g. in 1986 in South Africa's state of emergency)
- ruling groups who want to keep their power and wealth pretend there is an 'emergency' which justifies their violating human rights
- ruling groups fear democracy because it will reduce their power.

What happens when these rights are violated?

- critics of the government are threatened, tortured, punished
- People are imprisoned, often without trial
- People are killed for their beliefs
- Sometimes people are kidnapped and 'disappear'.

ILLUSTRATIONS OF SUCH SUFFERING ARE NOT HARD TO FIND

El Salvador
During 1981 and 1982 human rights violations in El Salvador became a source of world outrage. Reports of illegal detention, torture, 'disappearance', and cold-blooded murder came out of El Salvador almost every day. The victims included children, priests, nuns, medical workers and other non-violent and non-military individuals.

South Africa
In South Africa many people of all races have been restricted or imprisoned because of their conscientious opposition to 'apartheid'. By its very nature, the apartheid system restricts the human rights of the majority of South Africans. Opposition to apartheid is increasing all over the world. Police action in places like Soweto have resulted in many deaths and injuries.

Philippines
Disappearance and the torture and killing of political prisoners known as 'salvaging' became acute during the Marcos regime. The victims are the poor, students and young professional people. The military avoid as much as possible the international condemnation which would follow if the deeds or the extent of their brutality were accurately known.

Northern Ireland
Fourteen men were interrogated by British Security Forces in Northern Ireland in 1971. They were suspected of supporting the IRA. Black hoods, like pillowcases, were kept over their heads, except during actual questioning. They were forced to stand at a wall in a search position, supported only by their fingertips for up to 16 hours continuously and returned to position forcibly when they fell; they were subjected to continous loud 'white noise'; they had no sleep during the first few days of interrogation; and they had no food except a slice of bread and a pint of water at six hourly intervals.

FOR DISCUSSION

▶ 'If you want to establish what any society is like, visit its prisons.'

(Dewey)

TO DEBATE

▶ 'This House believes that sometimes torture is justified.'

FOR YOUR FOLDERS

▶ Read and study the four illustrations of suffering. Devise a telegram (maximum 25 words) that might be sent to the appropriate government expressing your concern.

! ▶ 'Torture is sometimes necessary.' Write an essay either agreeing or disagreeing with this statement.

ARGUMENTS FOR AND AGAINST TORTURE

Very few people openly support the use of torture, yet many governments allow it to be used.

We must use torture to keep people afraid. If they don't fear us they won't obey us.

Torture is prohibited by all international human rights treaties.

Torture is a regrettable act, but it is necessary for the good of everyone. If we are threatened by evil people, we have to use ruthless methods, too.

Torture degrades the torturer as well as the victim.

It's not really torture – just intensive interrogation. We need to find out about enemy agents and their friends.

Torture is never limited to "just once." Once we start to use it it spreads to more and more cases.

You can make anyone confess if you hurt them enough. As a result you are bound to hurt innocent people.

Torture may be useful in the short term. But some short-term methods must be forbidden in order to save the more important values of civilization.

A terrorist is not an ordinary soldier or criminal. If he gives information quickly, OK — if not his secret must be forced from him. He must face suffering as part of his job.

Torture is inhumane and is always wrong. It can never be justified.

WHEN DID AMNESTY INTERNATIONAL START?

In 1961, British lawyer Peter Benenson started Amnesty International from a tiny office in London. It started with seven people from Europe working to find ways of discovering the facts about people being illegally imprisoned, ill-treated and often killed outright by the authorities in different parts of the world. When the facts became clear, the Amnesty team sent written appeals to those governments asking for the release of those prisoners of conscience and for torture and killing to stop.

HOW BIG IS AMNESTY TODAY?

Today there are over 500,000 people (almost all volunteers) working for Amnesty in 160 different countries.

WHAT ARE THE AIMS OF AMNESTY?

1   It seeks the release of all prisoners of conscience.
2   It asks for a fair and prompt trial for all political prisoners detained without charge or trial.
3   It opposes torture and the death penalty in all cases.

HOW DOES AMNESTY CAMPAIGN?

An amnesty group usually 'adopts' two prisoners from two countries with very different governments. It either writes letters to the government of the particular country or raises funds to publicize the plight of its prisoners. The letters aim to put pressure on the governments to improve their treatment of prisoners. In 1977 Amnesty International was awarded the Nobel Peace Prize. Since 1961 over half of the prisoners of conscience adopted have been released. More than 1,400 of Amnesty's adopted prisoners are released every year.

Ten hints for writing letters

1   Be brief.
2   Be simple.
3   Write politely.
4   Be accurate.
5   Write in your own words.
6   Keep writing.
7   Get others to write too.
8   Say who you are.
9   Write in English.
10   Write also when there is good news.

Letter from a prisoner:

Dear Friend
    My first words are to thank you and all your friends for the moral support and material help you have given me and my family during the time I was in prison. Only someone who has spent nearly five years behind bars under a severe prison regime parted from those they love, can know how important it is to feel that far away in another country there are friends who do not forget and do all they can to soften the hard and unfair sentence.

Prisoners are often imprisoned because of their religion. The story started 2,000 years ago. Even in 1980 the Guatemalan newspaper *La Nacion* wrote: 'Today, as was the case a thousand years ago, it seems that to be a Christian is dangerous . . . very dangerous.'

'First they came for the Jews
and I did not speak out –
because I was not a Jew.
Then they came for the communists
and I did not speak out –
because I was not a communist.
Then they came for the trade
unionists and I did not speak out –
because I was not a trade unionist.

Then they came for me –
and there was no one left
to speak out for me.'

*These words were written by a
victim of the Nazis.*

Throughout the world people's freedom is still under threat

FOR YOUR FOLDERS

▸ Read and study the case study files of Nelson and Winnie Mandela in South Africa and Father Alfonsas Svarinskas in the USSR in the next chapter.

▸ Using the 'Ten hints for writing letters' and looking at the sample letter, construct a letter of about 200 words to

1 His Excellency the Chairman of the Presidium of the Supreme Soviet of the USSR, Kremlin, MOSCOW, USSR
2 The Minister of Justice, Government Buildings, Pretoria, South Africa

   a explaining who you are,
   b explaining the facts about the prisoners of conscience,
   c explaining your views,
   d quoting part of the UN Declaration that is relevant,
   e asking for justice and for freedom,
   f requesting a reply,
   g finishing your letter with 'Yours respectfully and sincerely'.

TALKING POINTS

- 'When evil men plot, good men must plan.'
- 'Freedom is never voluntarily given by the oppressor; it must be demanded by the oppressed.'

  (both quotes by Martin Luther King)

Nelson Mandela's wife, Winnie, has campaigned since 1962 for the release of her husband and for apartheid to end

NELSON AND WINNIE MANDELA

'South Africa is the richest country in Africa, and could be one of the richest in the world. But it is a land of extremes and remarkable contrasts. The whites enjoy what may be the highest standard of living in the world, whilst Africans live in poverty and misery. 40% of the Africans live in hopelessly overcrowded and, in some cases, drought-ridden reserves . . . 30% are labourers, labour tenants and squatters on white farms and live under conditions similar to those of the serfs in the middle ages. In the towns 50% do not earn enough to keep them going. Mortality rate is five times greater for black children than for white.'

These words were spoken by Nelson Mandela just before he was sentenced to life imprisonment in 1962. He was accused of 'high treason' because he was one of the leaders of the banned organization the ANC (African National Congress). The ANC was formed in 1912 and has worked for justice, and an end to apartheid, in South Africa. Nelson's wife, Winnie, has campaigned since 1962 for the release of her husband and for apartheid to end. She has been banned, put under house arrest, imprisoned and banished from her home town Soweto. The Mandelas have two daughters. The family has only been together once since 1962. Today, Nelson Mandela is still in Robben Island top security prison. Millions of black South Africans see him as their leader in their struggle against apartheid. However, the authorities refuse to release him.

FATHER ALFONSAS SVARINSKAS

In the Soviet Union there are many restrictions on religious believers. This means that religious believers have to register their congregations with the State and in doing so they lose, among other things, the right to teach religion to children, to appoint their own clergy, to publish 'unofficial' material and to choose the contents of their sermons. Hundreds of Christians from all denominations have been sent to prisons, labour camps and psychiatric hospitals for protesting peacefully against this lack of religious freedom.

In 1983 a Catholic priest called Father Alfonsas Svarinskas was sentenced to spend 10 years in a labour camp. Father Svarinskas had previously spent a total of 16 years in labour camps and prisons for standing up for the religious rights of believers in the Soviet Union. He had produced journals about religious persecution, continued to give religious instruction to children, led 'illegal' religious processions and pilgrimages, and spoken out in his sermons about the lack of freedom and the need for reform. For years he was a target for criticism by the State-controlled press and he was often arrested and interrogated by the KGB, the secret police. Despite having massive support in the community, he was arrested on 25 January 1983 and charged with 'anti-Soviet agitation and propaganda'. Within five days of his arrest, 50,000 people had signed a petition calling for his release.

Although international standards proclaim the right of every convicted person to lodge an appeal against their sentence, Father Svarinskas was sent to a labour camp. He is due for release in 1993, when he will be 68 years old. Amnesty International have adopted him as prisoner of conscience.

◇

THINGS TO DO

▶ Design a poster to support the release of either Nelson Mandela or Father Svarinskas.

FOR YOUR FOLDERS

▶ Write an article entitled 'Poverty and black South Africans'.

▶ Write to one of the organizations concerned with apartheid (see the important addresses section on page 190) and find out more about South Africa.

▶ Find out the meaning of the following: ANC, apartheid, banning, house arrest.

▶ How many years will Father Svarinskas have spent in prison by the time he is released in 1993?

▶ Find out the meaning of the following: psychiatric hospitals, propaganda, KGB, petitions.

TALKING POINTS

• 'Mandela will only be released if he condemns revolutionary violence.'
(P. W. Botha, President of South Africa)

Should Mandela do this considering the desperate plight of millions of black South Africans?

• Christians at all times should obey the authorities.

• 'The leader of the Soviet Union, Mr Gorbachov, is concerned with giving people more freedom. This has been the result of years of pressure by people like Father Svarinskas.'

In 1959 the United Nations presented the 'Declaration of the Rights of the Child', so that governments could make new laws or enforce existing laws enabling each child to have the following rights: the right to an identity; the right not be to discriminated against by reason of birth; the right to equal treatment at home and in the community; the right to family life; education, including sex education; the right to grow up in a family atmosphere; and the right not to be abused or exploited in any way.

The rights, in full, are:

'1   *The enjoyment of the rights mentioned, without any exception whatsoever, regardless of race, colour, sex, religion or nationality.*

2   *Special protection, opportunities and facilities to enable them to develop in a healthy and normal manner, in freedom and dignity.*

3   *A name and nationality.*

4   *Social security, including adequate nutrition, housing, recreation and medical services.*

5   *Special treatment, education and care if handicapped.*

6   *Love and understanding and an atmosphere of affection and security, in the care and under the responsibility of their parents whenever possible.*

7   *Free education and recreation and equal opportunity to develop their individual abilities.*

8   *Prompt protection and relief in times of disaster.*

9   *Protection against all forms of neglect, cruelty and exploitation.*

10   *Protection from any form of racial, religious or other discrimination, and an upbringing in a spirit of peace and universal brotherhood.'*

CHILDREN'S RIGHTS IN THE BIBLE

'And they were bringing children to him, that he might touch them; and the disciples rebuked them. But when Jesus saw it he became indignant, and said to them, "Let the children come to me, do not hinder them; for to such belongs the Kingdom of God".'

(Mark 10: 13–15)

'Fathers, do not exasperate your children, for fear they grow disheartened.'

(Colossians 3: 21)

Children have the right to protection and relief in times of disaster

HUMANIST POLICY ON CHILDREN

'Children are individual people, not private possessions of their parents. The community must ensure that children receive certain basic opportunities.'

(British Humanist Association General Statement of Policy)

VIOLENCE AGAINST CHILDREN

Much violence against children takes place in the home. Often we read of terrible beatings that children have suffered at the hands of their parents. Sadly, many of these crimes are 'hidden' crimes and go unpunished. In November 1986 the BBC launched a programme called *Child Watch*. It dealt with one particular form of violence, 'child sex abuse'. It invited people, especially children, to 'phone in' about experiences of sexual assault. Over 60,000 calls were made over a few days.

CHILD SEX ABUSE

8 years for sex abuse of daughter

Sex beast gets 12 years

...an who committed sex-offences against young ...en was jailed for 12 ...at Leeds Crown Court

...ear old Horsforth.

Two cases from the *Yorkshire Evening Post* in Leeds last week where the doctors below gave evidence.

THERE are many myths about child sexual abuse: perpetrators are all men – usually stepfathers – the victim is only one child in a family, a girl, usually a teenager. They live in overcrowded, poor conditions.

Child sexual abuse is much commoner than that. There are abused children in every neighbourhood, nursery, playgroup and school. They visit GPs' surgeries, paediatric outpatients' clinics and child guidance clinics. Where there are many children there are perpetrators.

This year in Leeds we (the two consultant community paediatricians) have seen over 800 children referred because of possible abuse. In over half, the main concern of the referring agency has been sexual abuse.

The emerging pattern shows that stepfathers, natural fathers and cohabitees are an equal risk to the child. Not only fathers abuse but mothers do too. Fathers abuse boys and girls, mothers do too. Not only grandfathers but grandmothers, uncles and aunts, older boy and girl cousins, boy babysitters and girl babysitters all may abuse.

In our most recent analysis at Leeds, the ratio of boys to girls as victims was two to three. The abuse of boys is even more likely to be hidden.

Children of all ages are equally at risk. The youngest child we have seen was four months, and one third of all sexually abused children were pre-school children.

(*The Observer*, 9 November 1986)

TALKING POINTS

'The child is father of the man.'

(Wordsworth)

'Children begin by loving their parents; after a time they judge them; rarely, if ever, do they forgive them.'

(Oscar Wilde)

Using the article on 'Child Sex Abuse', try to answer the following:
- What are the myths about child sexual abuse?
- Why is child sex abuse so often a 'hidden crime'?
- What can be done to protect children in their own homes?

FOR YOUR FOLDERS

▶ Copy out the words of Jesus and St Paul.

▶ Write a paragraph on some of the ideas that came up from your Talking Points.

▶ Try to think of some examples where children's rights are violated in the world today.

! ▶ What do you consider to be the most important parts of the 'Declaration of the Rights of the Child'?

Key questions

- should we use animals for scientific experiments?
- should we kill animals for things like fur coats?
- should we inflict pain on animals?
- should animals be subjected to undignified slaughterhouses and battery farms?
- should animals be locked up in zoos and circuses?
- have we the right to destroy whole species of animals?

DEAD AS A DODO

Since 1900 alone, 100 species of wild animal have followed the dodo (a bird which died out in 1681) into extinction. One example is the buffalo. In 1840 there were about 60 million buffalo in North America, but in 1898 only 26 survivors were left. Many species in the tropical rain forests have not yet even been 'discovered' but are threatened with extinction because of the massive destruction of their habitats.

The World Wildlife Fund raises money and campaigns to save animals in danger of extinction.

CHRISTIAN VIEWPOINTS

'God blessed them and said to them, Be fruitful and increase, fill the earth and subdue it, rule over the fish in the sea, the birds of heaven and every living thing that moves upon the earth.'

(Genesis 1: 28)

Christians believe that:

- God created all things. All life has a purpose.
- God cares for all of his creation.
- Human beings are responsible to God for the way they treat creation. In the Bible it says: 'A righteous man is merciful to the life of his beast'.

(Proverbs 12: 10)

- There is a unity between all living things.

The Royal Society for the Prevention of Cruelty to Animals (RSPCA) was founded in 1824 by a group of Christians.

Battery hens

TEN LAWS FOR ANIMALS

An organization called Compassion in World Farming lists 'Ten Laws' for animals.

1   movement – not tied up all day
2   exercise – daily exercise
3   rest – access to clean bedded area
4   water – access to clean water
5   food – no drugs or chemicals
6   environment – as comfortable as possible
7   light – adequate lighting
8   mutilations – only carried out by a vet (if necessary)
9   transport – no more than 60 miles
10 slaughter – must be painless.

OUR ROAST DINNER IS SOMEBODY ELSE'S HUNGER!

Some people do not eat meat. They are called vegetarians. Some refuse to eat meat because they think it is wrong to kill animals. Others think meat is not good for you (it is estimated that 90% of food poisoning is caused by meat). Others do not eat meat because they argue that our massive meat consumption is one of the causes of world hunger. They argue that 10 times more people can be sustained on vegetarian food than on meat. At present 90% of our agricultural land is used to grow food for farm animals, instead of food for humans.

BATTERY HENS

'Battery hens are packed so tightly that they lose their feathers, attack each other, lose the use of their legs and even go blind. Often to stop cannibalism their beaks are cut off. They are transported to the slaughterhouse stuffed into crates like rags. Sometimes lids or flaps are shut with wings or legs trapped.

Birds are wrenched from their crates and hung upside down on a moving conveyor belt. Their feet are thrust through a metal shackle and they are taken by a conveyor belt towards their death, hung upside down. Their heads are brought into contact with an electrically charged water bath. This is supposed to stun them before their throats are cut. However this stunning is not reliable and every day thousands die still conscious.'

(adapted from an Animal Aid report)

THINGS TO DO

▶ Find out more about the World Wildlife Fund, the RSPCA, Compassion in World Farming and the Animal Aid society (see the Important Addresses section on page 190).

TALKING POINTS

'Zoos are concentration camps for animals. The lords of creation are imprisoned in them by men who perhaps mean well, but who are really no better than grinning tormentors.'

(James Kirkup)

FOR YOUR FOLDERS

▶ Give examples of the way human beings use animals.

▶ Design a poster on the theme 'Compassion in farming'.

! ▶ How would *you* answer the 'Key Questions'? Write a paragraph on each.

! ▶ 'If more people saw what happens in slaughterhouses, more people would stop eating meat tomorrow.' Do you agree? What are your views on vegetarianism?

Key question
Are we entitled to make experiments on living animals, causing them pain, to benefit humankind?

Today 3½ million animal experiments take place every year, about 80% of them without anaesthetic. In May 1985 the Government published a report outlining proposed legislation for the control of scientific experiments on living animals. Most of the regulations in force on animal experiments dated back to the Cruelty to Animals Act 1876. Since then scientific experiments have become more sophisticated. Also various pressure groups (e.g. the Anti-Vivisection Society, Beauty without Cruelty, Animal Aid) have alerted the public about what may be happening behind the padlocked doors of research laboratories.

The Animal Rights Movement says	The Government says	The Scientists say
'All experiments should be banned.'	'Animal experiments must be watched carefully and suffering kept to a minimum.'	'Animal experiments are necessary for advancing medical knowledge.'

'Animals feel pain
animals feel fear
animals can feel bored
and lonely –
just like us.
Animals want to live . . .
not to be killed and dissected
animals want to be free . . .
not imprisoned in small cages.'

('*Just Like Us*' from the Animal Aid Youth Group)

'Nearly half a million experiments a year are for cancer research. Every year thousands of human beings in Britain die of cancer. It is only by experimenting with animals that we can begin to understand and hopefully one day make cancer a thing of the past. We have no alternative.'

(scientist)

More and more people are objecting to experiments on animals

LOOKING AND SMELLING GOOD

Firms that put new products like shampoos and perfumes on the market every year have to make sure they're safe. Most test them on animals first. These tests include dropping neat shampoos into rabbits' eyes held open with clamps (the Draize Test). However, some firms refuse to have their cosmetics tested on animals. These include The Body Shop and Cruelty Free Cosmetics.

SPORT OR SADISM

'If you ever saw the damage a fox can do to chickens or how it can rip a lamb to bits you'd call them pests too.'

(Wiltshire farmer)

'Foxes are an integral part of the ecology and food-chain of the countryside. The damage they do is less than that caused by the horses and hounds that chase them.'

(fox hunt saboteur)

FASHION

'Four hundred million animals a year, unfortunate enough to have been born with beautiful fur coats, are ruthlessly trapped and killed or imprisoned in factory farms. Their skins are ripped from their bodies to satisfy ignorant vanity and to make fat profits for people. The traps can kill "non-target animals", like pets.'

(Lynx)

CHRISTIAN CONCERN

'In the end, lack of respect for the life and wellbeing of an animal must bring with it a lowering of man's own self-respect. "In as much as ye do it to these the least of my little ones ye do it unto me." '

(Robert Runcie, Archbishop of Canterbury)

'God has the right to have all his creatures treated with proper respect.'

(Cardinal Heenan, Catholic Archbishop)

'Scientists must abandon laboratories and factories of death.'

(Pope John Paul II)

'Animals, as part of God's creation, have rights which must be respected.'

(Dr Donald Coggan, Archbishop of Canterbury in 1977 and President of the RSPCA)

ANIMAL ABUSE CASES HIGHEST FOR 150 YEARS
By GERALD BARTLETT

CRUELTY investigations by the Royal Society for the Prevention of Cruelty to Animals have reached their highest level for more than 150 years. They cover everything from neglect to malnutrition and sadistic treatment.

Announcing the latest figures from inspectorate records in London yesterday, the Society said it had investigated 64,678 complaints last year compared with 47,362 in 1984.

Animal cruelty convictions reached a post-war record, 2,112 against 1,889 in 1984.

For the second year running the number of calls dealt with topped the million mark. The majority of cases involved dogs and cats and the most common offence was neglect.

(The Daily Telegraph, 18 February 1986)

TALKING POINTS

• 'People have a right to go fox-hunting.'

• 'If one human being can be saved from a disease it is worth all the animal experiments put together.'

FOR YOUR FOLDERS

! ▶ There are many controversial issues here. Try to write something about *your* views on animal experiments for medical knowledge; fox-hunting; wearing fur coats.

▶ In light of the statements from the Christian leaders, what do you think a Christian view should be on these issues?

▶ Write an article (about 100 words) called 'Human rights before animal rights'.

! ▶ After reading these two units on Animal Rights, write an article (using pictures if possible) explaining why animal rights are thought to be so important.

'The Church's primary role must be a spiritual one. I say this as a member of the Anglican Church.'

(Patrick Jenkin, MP)

'I believe that the revolutionary struggle is appropriate for the Christian. Only by changing the concrete conditions of our country can we enable men to practise love for each other.'

(Father Camilo Torres)

Key question

Should a Christian become involved in politics?

THINGS TO DO

▶ Look at these eight biblical quotes. Decide whether they answer 'yes' or 'no' to the Key Question.

1 'You shall love your neighbour as yourself' *(Leviticus 19: 18)*.
2 'You who oppress the poor and crush the destitute . . . the Lord has sworn by his holiness that your time is coming' *(Amos 4: 1–2)*.
3 'The Lord will answer . . . "Here I am" if you cease to pervert justice, to point the accusing finger and lay false charges. If you feed the hungry from your plenty and satisfy the needs of the wretched, then your light will rise like dawn out of darkness' *(Isaiah 58: 9–10)*.
4 'Pay the Emperor what belongs to the Emperor, and pay God what belongs to God' *(Mark 12: 13–17)*.
5 'He has sent me to proclaim liberty to the captives . . . set free the oppressed' *(Luke 4: 18)*.
6 'Every person must submit to the supreme authorities. There is no authority but by act of God . . .' *(Romans 13: 1)*.
7 'I have come not to bring peace but a sword . . .' *(Matthew 10: 34)*.
8 'My kingdom does not belong to this world.' *(John 18: 36)*.

JESUS AND POLITICS

The political climate of Judea during Jesus's life was dangerous and often violent. The Romans ruled with strength and most Jews deeply resented their presence. A group of Jews formed a terrorist and revolutionary type organization called the **Zealots**, who were determined to rid themselves of Roman rule. Many Jews thought that Jesus would be a political Messiah who would lead them against the Romans. However, Jesus opted for a peaceful role as can be seen in the temptation *(Matthew 4)* and his entry into Jerusalem on a donkey (an animal of peace, *Mark 11: 1–10*). He went to his death asking that his persecutors be forgiven *(Luke 23: 34)*. Many people argue that Jesus was therefore not concerned with politics but with spiritual matters.

However, many events and sayings of Jesus point to the fact that he was concerned with improving people's lives and bringing God's kingdom to earth. He was not afraid to challenge those in authority; he was on the side of the disadvantaged members of society; he tried to make people aware and concerned about each other's needs.

THE WORLD COUNCIL OF CHURCHES (WCC)

The Geneva-based WCC includes Christians of Orthodox, Protestant, Lutheran, Reformed, Anglican, Pentecostal and independent traditions. Its membership brings together 400 million of the world's 985 million Christians. The WCC is concerned with Christianity in the modern world. Practical action includes funding emergency aid and long-term development programmes, research and study; conferences; and dialogues with other faiths.

The WCC provides an essential platform for the Churches of the world to talk and work together for a better future.

WANTED: JESUS CHRIST

ALIAS: THE MESSIAH, SON OF GOD, SON OF MAN, LORD OF LORDS, PRINCE OF PEACE.

★ Notorious leader of an underground liberation movement.

★ Wanted for the following charges:

– Practising medicine, wine-making and food distribution without a licence.

– Interfering with businessmen in the Temple.

– Associating with known criminals, radicals, subversives, prostitutes and street people.

– Claiming to have the authority to make people into God's children.

★ **APPEARANCE:** long hair, beard, robe, sandals, etc.

★ Hangs around slum areas, few rich friends, often sneaks out into the desert.

★ Has a group of disreputable followers, formerly known as 'apostles'.

BEWARE – This man is extremely dangerous. His message is particularly dangerous to young people who haven't been taught to ignore him yet. He changes men and claims to set them free.

WARNING: HE IS STILL AT LARGE!

There was political opposition to Jesus

LIBERATION THEOLOGY

In South Africa, Latin America and Poland the Church is active in giving a voice to those who would otherwise be unheard. In South America a movement called Liberation Theology has emerged. These Christians believe that the gospels demand them to stand up and fight against poverty, exploitation, and lack of human rights. Liberation Theologians are inspired by the words of Jesus:

> 'He has sent me to bring good news to the poor, to proclaim liberty to the captives and to set free the oppressed.'

(Luke 4: 18–19)

In the past the Catholic Church in South America did little to alleviate injustice. Many priests today, however, have identified themselves with the poor, as Jesus did. One leading theologian, Gustavo Gutiérrez, said:

> 'The poverty of the poor is not a summons to alleviate their plight with acts of generosity but rather a compelling obligation to fashion an entirely different social order.'

FOR YOUR FOLDERS

▶ Why might some Christians regard political involvement as being

(a) right

(b) wrong?

Use some of the Biblical quotes to back up your arguments.

▶ What is the WCC?

▶ What is Liberation Theology?

▶ Write a sentence explaining your reasons for answering 'yes' or 'no' to each of the eight quotes.

Desmond Tutu blesses Cape Town after the ceremony when he became Archbishop

In 1984 a black man, Desmond Mpilo Tutu, was awarded the Nobel Peace Prize. In September 1986 the same man became South Africa's first black archbishop. People from all over the world attended the ceremony and guests included Stevie Wonder, the Archbishop of Canterbury and Coretta King, wife of the late Dr Martin Luther King.

Born on 7 October 1931, Desmond Tutu became a priest at the age of 25. After working in Britain and in South Africa he became Bishop of Lesotho in 1976 and secretary of the South Africa Council of Churches (SACC) in 1978. The SACC represents some 13 million Christians in South Africa, mostly black. In the same year, the Dutch Reform Church which generally supports the government's 'apartheid' system, withdrew from the Council.

During his ministry Archbishop Tutu has consistently spoken out against apartheid, believing it to be evil and totally unchristian. Even before he became Bishop of Johannesburg, he found himself increasingly in conflict with the authorities as he organized non-violent protests against apartheid. In 1976, for instance, he led a march through the slums of Soweto during the riots when more than 600 blacks were shot dead. In 1982 he saved the life of a black policeman by flinging himself across the man's body when an angry crowd tried to stone the man to death.

Archbishop Tutu believes that being a Christian means working for justice and equality in South Africa. For him the Bible is the 'most revolutionary book' ever written, demanding that people fight against injustice. Many people believe that it is only because he is so well known that the government has not tried to ban him, or even have him killed.

Some people argue that Christians should not become involved in politics.

Archbishop Tutu, in a sermon called 'Divine Intervention' (1979), has argued otherwise:

> *'Christian worship can never let us be indifferent to the needs of others, to the cries of the hungry, of the naked and the homeless, of the sick and the prisoner, of the oppressed and the disadvantaged. Our Lord said, "As much as you have done this [i.e. fed the hungry, clothed the naked, visited the sick and the prisoners] to the least of my brethren, you have done it to me, and in as much as you have not done it to the least of these my brethren you have not done it to me." [Matthew 25: 31–46]*

> *True Christian worship includes the love of God and the love of neighbour. The two must go together or your Christianity is false. St John asks, in his First Epistle, how you can say you love God who you have not seen if you hate your brother whom you have. Our love for God is tested and proved by our love for our neighbour. This is what the churches, and perhaps especially the South African Council of Churches, attempt to do in our beautiful but sadly unhappy land which is South Africa. It has a vicious political system of segregation called apartheid. There are many victims of this system: the family who are bereft of their father who must be a migrant labourer in the White man's cities, living in single-sex hostels, the*

persons who provide cheap unskilled labour to swell investment income; the marginalized, the disadvantaged who are treated often as objects and not subjects. Many have protested against this system and for their pains they are often detained for long periods without trial, or banned for five years at a time to a twilight existence when they can't attend any gathering. A gathering, I would have you know, is more than one person, so they can't speak to more than one person at a time, and they can't be quoted; others are brought to trial under a system where you are presumed guilty until you can prove you are innocent. These detained persons, these banned people, these political prisoners, are the least of Christ's brothers and sisters He referred to, and we try, with the very generous help of people overseas, to minister to them – this we contend is deeply religious work, others call it political.

*We are Christian not only in church on Sunday. Our Christianity is not something we put on, like our Sunday best, only for Sundays. It is for every day. We are Christians from Monday to Monday. We have no off day. We are Christians at play, at work and at prayer. They are all rolled into one. It is not **either** worship **or** trying to do all the good works in our community. It is both. The wise men came to the Child and worshipped. Then they gave him their gifts. We too must worship our God for ever and ever, and serve him by serving our neighbour today and always.'*

(Desmond Tutu's *Hope and Suffering*, Collins, 1983)

Tutu becomes an archbishop

CAPETOWN: Nobel Peace Prize winner Desmond Tutu was enthroned yesterday as South Africa's first black archbishop.

Surrounded by celebrities and world church leaders he called President P. W. Botha 'my brother' for whom he said he had to pray whether either of them liked it or not.

His charge, delivered in a shrill cant at Capetown's St George's Cathedral, was as controversial as most of his sayings. And he roundly condemned apartheid – 'this vicious evil' – which he said was the cause of all South Africa's problems.

(*Daily Mail*, 23 September 1986)

THINGS TO DO

Nobel Peace Prize
SACC
Dutch Reform Church
Soweto
Victims of apartheid
Matthew 25: 31–46

Look at these phrases. How do they fit into the story of Archbishop Tutu? What does each one mean?

FOR YOUR FOLDERS

▶ Write a paragraph explaining why Archbishop Tutu believes Christians have a duty to become involved in politics.

▶ What have you learnt about apartheid after reading Archbishop Tutu's sermon?

FOR DISCUSSION

▶ Tutu often quotes Martin Luther King's words: 'Together we must learn to live as brothers or together we will be forced to perish as fools.' Discuss them in the context of South Africa.

▶ Do you agree with what Archbishop Tutu said in his sermon in 1979?

73 FATHER CAMILO TORRES

Father Camilo Torres lived in Colombia in South America. He was a Roman Catholic priest who worked in Bogota, the capital city of Colombia. The vast majority of the people in Colombia are very poor – living off the land at barely a subsistence level. Sixty-five per cent of the land is owned by just a handful of powerful families. Torres believed that the vast division of wealth in his country was very unjust and he became involved in politics to try and bring about a fairer society.

Torres believed that the New Testament teachings of Jesus were directed towards the poor and the oppressed and that a Christian revolution was acceptable to bring about change. He said:

'Revolution is necessary to free the hungry, give drink to the thirsty, clothe the naked and procure a life of well-being for the needy majority of our people. I believe that the revolutionary struggle is appropriate for the Christian and the priest. Only by revolution, by changing the concrete conditions of our country, can we enable men to practise love for each other.'

(from Camilo Torres, *Revolutionary Priest*, edited by John Geriffi, Penguin, 1973)

The Catholic Church did not support Torres's revolutionary fervour and told him to choose either his cause or the priesthood. He left the ministry and founded the United Front of the Colombian people. He became known as 'Padre Camilo' wherever he travelled around the countryside, talking to and teaching the people. He tried to make the peasants aware of their rights and as a result his life was under constant threat from the government. Torres came to believe that the government would crush any non-violent and peaceful protest. It would put up violent resistance to prevent the people from gaining a share of power.

Torres believed that there was, therefore, no other choice for him but to join a guerrilla movement and to fight against the government. The guerrillas hid in the vast mountains and waged a campaign against the government. They had the support of many peasants but the government used harsh and cruel measures to try and defeat the guerrilla movement. The fighting was often bloody and in 1966, when he was 36 years old, Torres was killed in a small skirmish.

The Cathedral at Bolivar Square in Bogota, Columbia, the city where Father Camilo Torres worked

The authorities buried him in a secret grave. They feared that his grave would become a shrine because the people saw Torres as a beloved martyr. However, his influence continued after his death. In 1968 many priests followed his example and pledged their support for revolutionary struggle against the evils of the State. They, like Torres, believed that when confronted by an evil, the only response was to fight against that evil. Also, in other Latin American countries other priests and bishops, some inspired by Torres, joined movements that were committed to overthrowing dictatorships and unjust governments that exploited millions of poor people. To them, Christians have a moral duty to become involved in worldly affairs especially when innocent people are oppressed and exploited.

Many believed that the *only* response was violence. Nothing would be changed, they believed, until the corrupt and evil governments were overthrown. Non-violent direct action would not work. It would be crushed by the State.

In Nicaragua in 1979 a movement involving priests and bishops fought a war against the corrupt Somoza regime and overthrew it. Many of the priests were inspired in Nicaragua and Colombia by Jesus's words in *Luke 4: 18–19:* 'He has sent me to bring good news to the poor, to proclaim liberty to the captives and to set free the oppressed.'

QUOTES FROM CAMILO TORRES

'I chose Christianity because I felt that in it I had found the best way of serving my neighbour. I was elected by Christ to be a priest for ever, motivated by the desire to devote myself full time to loving my fellow men.'

'The Catholic who is not a revolutionary is living in mortal sin.'

'The basic thing in Catholicism is loving one's neighbour. For this love to be true it has to be effective . . . we must take power from the privileged minorities in order to give it to the poor majority. The revolution can be peaceful if the minorities do not offer violent resistance.'

FOR YOUR FOLDERS

▶ Copy down the two of the following statements that you think say the most about the piece you have read:
1 Torres was right to become involved in politics.
2 The Church should keep out of politics.
3 Torres was a martyr.
4 Torres was a troublemaker.

▶ Why did Torres join the guerrillas?

▶ Write down the words of Jesus that inspired Torres and others.

In many countries in Latin America ordinary people and Catholic priests have decided to stand up and fight against injustice and poverty. They refuse to accept the power and oppression of rich landowners and corrupt military dictatorships. In this extract a Salvadorean peasant explains why he has decided to fight against the rulers of his country.

'People are always worried about the violence done with machine guns and machetes. But there is another kind of violence that you must be aware of too. To watch your children die of sickness and hunger while you can do nothing is a violence of the spirit. We have suffered silently for too many years.'

(*New Internationalist*, September 1986)

THINGS TO DO

Christian revolution
United Front
guerrilla movement
martyr
revolutionary struggle
(Luke 4: 18–19)

Look at these words and phrases. How do they fit into the story of Camilo Torres? What does each one mean?

FOR DISCUSSION

▶ 'When you are up against a violent state, the only way to change things is by using violence.'

▶ 'Every person shall submit to the supreme authorities' (St Paul, in *Romans 13: 1*). How might Torres have replied to St Paul?

! ▶ Discuss the comments of the El Salvadorean peasant. Do you agree that he is right to take up the gun and the machete?

The twentieth century has seen the largest and bloodiest wars in history. The main reason is that weapons have evolved over the centuries from clubs: swords – bows – gunpowder – guns – cannons – tanks – bombs – missiles. Weapons today are from the military point of view very efficient – they can kill more people.

The First World War (1914–18), for instance, saw the death of 8,538,315 men and the serious wounding of 21,219,452 men. Of 7,750,919 taken prisoner or missing, well over 1 million were presumed dead; so the total deaths of combatants (soldiers), not including civilians, approached 10 million.

The Second World War (1939–45) saw the death of 15,600,000 soldiers and 39,200,000 civilians. The total death count of people from all countries was 54,800,000.

These figures are hard to imagine. Even more difficult to imagine are some of the other facts about twentieth-century warfare.

In the first battle of the Somme (1 July to 19 November 1916) over 1,030,000 men died in the trenches.

It is estimated that 6,000 Jews died in one day in the death camp known as Auschwitz.

On Monday 6 August at 8.15, a B29 bomber called 'Enola Gay' dropped a uranium bomb called 'Little Boy' over the Japanese city of Hiroshima. It is estimated that 140,000 people died as a result. In 1978, 2,000 people died from its long-delayed effects.

In one night in Tokyo in 1945, 279 B29 superfortresses, each carrying about 7 tons of incendiary bombs, burnt 15 square miles to the ground, killing over 100,000 people.

Again, during the Second World War on 13 February 1945, Allied planes bombed the beautiful city of Dresden in Germany, killing 135,000 people, mostly civilians, in 14 hours.

However, since 1945 there have been other wars. The Second World War did not end wars (nor did the First World War, which claimed to be the 'war to end all wars') and since 1945 it is estimated that 21 million people have been killed using 'conventional' (non-nuclear) arms. The average death toll from armed conflict is put at between 33,000 and 41,000 *a month* since 1945. It has been estimated that the

A child caught up in the war in Beirut

world has only seen 36 *minutes* of peace since 1945. The Korean War (1950–53) claimed nearly 4 million lives, most of them civilian. The Vietnam War (1965–73) saw an average 164 massive bombing missions by the Americans *every day*. During the war some 2½ million tons of bombs of all kinds were dropped on the country of Laos. In China from 1949 onwards it is estimated that between a staggering 33 million and 61 million people died at the hands of the regime of Mao Tse-Tung.

The list of the waste that war causes could go on and on. The grief and suffering that millions upon millions of people have endured during times of war is impossible to calculate and impossible to begin to imagine. Whole generations of people have been wiped out. Billions and billions of pounds have been poured into wars all over the world. Millions of people have been maimed and tortured. Even today babies are being born terribly deformed, years after their parents or grandparents suffered the effects of chemical and nuclear weapons. As well as shattered bodies there are shattered minds. Even after a relatively small conflict like the Falklands War doctors and psychiatrists estimated that 1,000 British troops needed treatment due to the psychological effects of the war.

The cost of modern arms in economic terms is enormous. **Total global military expenditure during 1986 was £634 billion or just over £1.2 million a minute.** This took place in a world full of people crying out for improved health care, food, shelter, housing, sanitation, hospitals, irrigation and social services.

FOR YOUR FOLDERS

▶ Make a history chart of war in the twentieth century (include in it some statistics).

▶ Design a poster on the theme 'War in the twentieth century'.

FOR DISCUSSION

▶ 'And you will hear of wars and rumours of wars . . . this must take place . . . For nation will rise against nation' (Jesus, in *Matthew 22: 6–7*).
Are wars ever going to end?
Will war destroy the human race one day?

THINGS TO DO

▶ Make a list of all the wars going on in the world today.
Can you find out the causes of these wars?

A victim of civil war in Sri Lanka

> **War** – 'armed fighting between nations'.
>
> (*Longman's Dictionary of Contemporary English*)

DEFINITION

'What is war, my lord?
War is empire.

What is war, general?
War is manhood.

What is war, teacher?
War is inevitable.

What is war, preacher?
War is unfortunate.

What is war, fellow?
War is escape.

What is war, kind employer?
War is profit.

Sister, what is war?
War is a telegram.

Brother, what is war?
War is my powerlessness.

Father, what is war?
War is my trembling hand.

Mother, what is war?
War is undiscovered graves.'

L. Collinson

'War has been constant in human affairs since the earliest societies of which there is record. In 7000 BC Jericho was strongly fortified by a wall 21 feet high; out of 2,500 citizens 600 would have been fighting men armed with the bow and arrow. But the art of warfare had clearly been evolving for long before these days. How then did war first arise?

War is a basic part of history because it is concerned with the essentials of life. Food, and a secure place in which to live, were the two basic necessities for primeval man – just as they are for us. But these things which man needs, as well as many other things which he desires, such as mates, wealth, power and prestige, are often available only in short supply. The basic reason why individual men and societies have almost incessantly fought each other lies in this economic fact – they have always had to compete for the minimum conditions of existence. Animals fight each other for the same reason. Human beings, of course, have been much less successful than animals in avoiding the resort to violence.'

(Field Marshall Viscount Montgomery of Alamein, *A Concise History of Warfare*, Collins, 1968)

'The destruction of Guernica went on altogether for two hours and 45 minutes. When the bombing was over the people left their shelters. Eyes fixed on Guernica, we were completely incapable of believing what we saw. We could see no more than 500 metres. Everywhere there were flames and thick black smoke. Around me people were praying and some stretched out their arms in the form of a cross, imploring mercy from heaven . . . when it grew dark the flames of Guernica were reaching to the sky, and the clouds took on the colour of blood, and our faces too shone with the colour of blood.'

(Father Alberto de Onaindia, 1937; quoted in *The Civil War in Spain* by Robert Payne, Secker & Warburg, 1962)

Picasso's 'Guernica'

'Within My Lai Four the killings had become more sadistic. Several old men were stabbed with bayonets and one was thrown down a well to be followed by a hand-grenade. Some women and children praying outside of the local were killed by shooting them in the back of the head with rifles. Occasionally a solder would drag a girl, often a mere child, to a ditch where he would rape her . . . the young were slaughtered with the same impartiality as the old.'

(*The Tarnished Shield: A Report on Today's Army* by George Walton, New York, Dodd, 1973)

CHRISTMAS 1914

'I climbed over the parapet and saw the strangest sight which can ever be seen by any soldier in any war.

All along the line groups of British and German soldiers were laughing and singing together.

Just imagine it: English, Scots, Irish, Prussians, Wurtemburgers in a chorus.

I wrote a report on the whole fantastic episode and ended by saying that if I had seen it on film I would have sworn it was a fake.'

(Captain Sir John Hulse, 2nd Battalion Scots Guards, in a letter to his mother)

'Go now and fall upon the Amalekites and destroy them, and put their property under ban. Spare no one; put them all to death, men and women, children and babes in arms, herds and flocks, camels and asses.'

(I Samuel 15: 2–4)

'While he was still speaking, Judas, one of the twelve, appeared: with him was a great army with swords and cudgels, sent by the chief priests and elders of the nation . . . they came forward, seized Jesus, and held him fast. At that moment one of those with Jesus reached for his sword and drew it, and he struck at the High Priest's servant, and cut off his ear. But Jesus said to him, "Put up your sword. All who take the sword die by the sword." '

(Matthew 26: 47–52)

FOR YOUR FOLDERS

▸ Write a paragraph explaining:
  1 L. Collinson's attitude to war.
  2 Montgomery's reasons for war.
  3 Samuel's attitude to victory.
  4 Jesus's attitude to violence.
  5 The difference between 3 and 4.

▸ The bombing of Guernica by the German air force during the Spanish Civil War was the first time people had witnessed massive aerial bombing.
  1 Write a short newspaper article entitled 'Guernica . . . the still after the storm'.
  2 Write an art review of Picasso's *Guernica*.

THINGS TO DO

▸ *The Tarnished Shield* is a factual account of the My Lai massacres by American troops during the Vietnam War. Compare its very real description with the images of war you have seen in films.

FOR DISCUSSION

▸ 'Human beings, of course, have been much less successful than animals in avoiding the resort to violence.'

(Montgomery)

IN PAIRS

▸ *Brainstorming.* Work with a partner and write down as many words as you can thing of in three minutes, to do with, or suggested by, (a) the word 'peace', (b) the word 'war'. What are your findings? e.g. peace, co-operation, love; war, hate, killing.

'Peace' does not just mean absence of war. Peace also means a world in which justice, freedom, basic needs and harmony are the order of the day. There is therefore no real global peace in the world today.

Many individuals are not at peace with themselves, their families and their neighbours. Many groups of people and nations are not at peace with other groups of people and other nations.

Human beings have created weapons of war that threaten not only this generation but the very existence of life on earth.

Here are some quotes about peace. Read through them and try and understand what they mean for us today, and then discuss them.

'But once more God will send us His Spirit. The waste land will become fertile, and fields will produce rich crops. Everywhere in the land, righteousness and justice will be done. Because everyone will do what is right, there will be peace and security forever. God's people will be free from worries, and their homes peaceful and safe.'

(Isaiah 32: 15–18)

'He will be judge between many peoples and arbiter among mighty nations afar. They shall beat their swords into mattocks and their spears into pruning-knives; nation shall not lift sword against nation nor ever again be trained for war.'

(Micah 4: 3)

'How blest are the peacemakers;
God shall call them his sons.'

(Matthew 5: 9)

'You have learned that they were told "Eye for eye, tooth for tooth". But what I tell you is this: Do not set yourself against the man who wrongs you. If someone slaps you on the right cheek, turn and offer him your left.'

(Matthew 5: 38–39)

'Let him who desires peace, prepare for war.'

(Vegetius, Roman, 4 AD)

'Violence is the way of barbarians, non-violence is the way of men.'

(Mahatma Gandhi)

'It is one of the strangest things that all the great military geniuses of the world have talked about peace.'

(Martin Luther King)

'Since wars begin in the minds of men, it is in the minds of men that peace must be constructed.'

(UNESCO)

'Peace can't be kept by force, it can only be achieved by understanding.'

(Albert Einstein)

FOR DISCUSSION

▶ Everyone, not just Christians, has a responsibility to work for peace.'

The dove is a traditional symbol of peace

SOME ORGANIZATIONS CONCERNED WITH PEACE

United Nations
The UN's main concern is world peace. It works to 'unite our strength to maintain international peace'.

World Council of Churches (WCC)
This brings together Christians of all denominations except Catholics and works for peace.

Anglican Pacifist Fellowship
Anglican peace movement.

World Disarmament Campaign
Set up in 1980, this comprises distinguished people trying to pressurize governments to disarm.

END
European Nuclear Disarmament.

(CND)
Campaign for Nuclear Disarmament in Britain.

Pax Christi
An international Roman Catholic organization with a section in Britain.

Pax Christi

United Nations

Logos of some organizations concerned with peace

TREATIES

Tlatelolco Treaty (1968) – prohibits nuclear weapons in Latin America.

Convention on Biological and Toxin Weapons (1972)

The Geneva Convention (1864)

Non-Proliferation Treaty (1970) – forbids transfer of nuclear weapons

'SALT' – Strategic Arms Limitation Treaty calling for a balance of nuclear weapons between the superpowers.

FOR YOUR FOLDERS

▶ 'Peace is not just the absence of war.' Explain what you think this means.

▶ Design a poster about peace on earth.

! ▶ *'Above all else* Christians have a duty to bring about peace on earth.' Do you agree with this statement? How can peace on earth be achieved? (A clue might be the statement from UNESCO.)

THINGS TO DO

▶ Try and find out more about some of the above organizations concerned with peace (see the Important Addresses section on page 190).

THE 'JUST WAR'

Many Christians believe that there is such a thing as a 'Just War'. This is a war which it is morally right to fight.

For a war to be just, three conditions were laid down in the thirteenth century by St Thomas Aquinas. There were:

1   The war must only be started and controlled by the authority of the state or the ruler.

2   There must be a just cause; those attacked are attacked because they deserve it.

3   The war must be fought to promote good or avoid evil. Peace and justice must be restored afterwards.

Later, two other conditions were added:

4   The war must be the last resort; all other possible ways of solving the problem must have been tried out.

5   There must be 'proportionality' in the way the war is fought, e.g. innocent civilians should not be killed. You must use only enough force to achieve your goals, not more. (It would not be 'proportionate', for example, to bomb a whole village because the enemy was hiding in one house.)

THE 'HOLY WAR'

'Declare a Holy War, call the troops to arms.'

(Joel 3: 9)

Holy Wars are wars fought by people who believe either that God is on their side or that they have righteousness on their side. The Crusades were Holy Wars. They were campaigns against the Turks, in the eleventh and twelfth centuries, to liberate the Holy Places of Palestine from the Muslims. The Christian Church identified the Muslims with Satan and the Crusades with God. However, from a Muslim point of view their wars were holy too. Often Holy Wars are very viciously fought wars and the people who fight them are stirred up by their church or religion.

Holy Wars have been fought through the centuries but morally they pose many questions:

- who really knows what is right?
- is it right to kill for a religion of a set of beliefs?
- how can anyone know that 'God is on their side'?

'The Lord said to Joshua, "Look, I have delivered Jericho and her King into your hands. You shall march round the city with all your fighting, making the circuit of it once for six days running . . . thus the Lord was with Joshua.'

(Joshua 6: 2–4)

A victim of a modern Holy War, between Iran and Iraq

With God on Our Side

by Bob Dylan

Oh my name it is nothin'
My age it means less
The country I come from
Is called the Midwest
I's taught and brought up there
The laws to abide
And that land that I live in
Has God on its side.

Oh the history books tell it
They tell it so well
The cavalries charged
The Indians fell
The cavalries charged
The Indians died
Oh the country was young
With God on its side.

Oh the Spanish-American
War had its day
And the Civil War too
Was soon laid away
And the names of the heroes
I's made to memorize
With guns in their hands
And God on their side

Oh the First World War, boys
It closed out its fate
The reason for fighting
I never got straight
But I learned to accept it
Accept it with pride
For you don't count the dead
When God's on your side.

When the Second World War
Came to an end
We forgave the Germans
And we were friends
Though they murdered six million
In the ovens they fried
The Germans now too
Have God on their side.

I've learned to hate Russians
All through my whole life
If another war starts
It's them we must fight
To hate them and fear them
To run and to hide
And accept it all bravely
With God on my side.

But now we've got weapons
Of the chemical dust
If fire them we're forced to
Then fire them we must
One push of the button
And a shot the world wide
And you never ask questions
When God's on your side.

In a many dark hour
I've been thinkin' about this
That Jesus Christ
Was betrayed by a kiss
But I can't think for you
You'll have to decide
Whether Judas Iscariot
Had God on his side.

So now as I'm leavin'
I'm weary as Hell
The confusion I'm feelin'
Ain't no tongue can tell
The words fill my head
And fall to the floor
If God's on our side
He'll stop the next war.

FOR YOUR FOLDERS

▶ Explain in your own words the difference between a Just War and a Holy War.

!▶ Do you think there are circumstances when it is morally justifiable for Christians to take part in a war?

FOR DISCUSSION

▶ What do you think Bob Dylan is trying to say in his song above?

▶ Could a nuclear war ever be called a Just War?

THE OLD TESTAMENT

War and other forms of organized mass violence
receive a great deal of attention in the Old
Testament. Indeed, the history of Israel is one of
military victories and defeats. Moses was one of the
the world's first leaders of a national liberation
movement. He opposed one of the world's first
superpowers, Egypt, which had advanced military
technology, especially the chariot. The Jews escaped
by the use of guerrilla warfare. They had to use
force both to obtain and to maintain Israel.

By the time of David and Solomon, about
1,000 BC, priests often accompanied Israel's armies
into battle. The Old Testament provides detailed
accounts of how wars were fought in terms of both
weapons used and number of soldiers.

THE NEW TESTAMENT

Many Jews expected Jesus to be a great military
leader who would free them from the occupying
armies of the Romans. At the time a group of
revolutionaries called the Zealots were using
guerrilla tactics to try to overthrow the Romans.
However, throughout the gospels Jesus is portrayed
as a man of peace. During his temptation (*Matthew
4: 8–10*) the devil offers him political and military
power but Jesus refuses to accept. He travels in a
country where armed bandits are active but he
never has an armed guard. Even during the most
dangerous trip into Jerusalem, his disciples were
only lightly armed (*Luke 22: 49*) and when one of
them wounds an official's ear, Jesus stops the
violence and heals the man (*Luke 22: 51*). Indeed, it
may be Jesus's pacifism which turns the citizens
against him and results in their call for his
crucifixion (*Luke 23: 13–25*).

A soldier prepared for modern warfare

A HUMANIST VIEW ON MODERN WAR

'The world community must renounce the resort to violence and force as a method of solving international disputes. We believe in the peaceful adjudication of differences by international Courts and by the development of the arts of negotiation and compromise. War is obsolete. So is the use of nuclear, biological, and chemical weapons. It is a planetary duty to reduce the level of military expenditure and turn these savings into peaceful and people-orientated uses.'

(A Humanist manifesto for the future of humankind, 1973)

torn by civil war, the Society of
ere formed by George Fox in
ace Testimony which still
d other Christians today:

MONY
TY OF FRIENDS

all outward wars and
ings with outward
y end, or under any
ver; this is our testimony to
the whole world. The Spirit of Christ by which we are guided is not changeable, so as once to command us from a thing as evil, and again to move unto it; and we certainly know, and testify to the world, that the Spirit of Christ, which leads us into all truth, will never move us to fight and war against any man with outward weapons, neither for the kingdom of Christ, nor for the kingdoms of the world.

(from *A Declaration from the Harmless and Innocent People of God, called Quakers*, presented to Charles II, 1660)

FOR YOUR FOLDERS

▶ Look up and read the story of the capture of Jericho in *Joshua 6*.

▶ Imagine that you are a newspaper reporter with Joshua's troops. Write an article of about 200 words describing what happens. (Date it 1500 BC.)

▶ Look up and read the four quotes from the New Testament section.

TALKING POINTS

- Quakers 'will never more fight and war against any man with outward weapons'. What do you think they mean?
- 'There will always be wars and rumours of wars.' Do you think this will always be the case? Are Christians and Humanists who reject war being unrealistic?

TALKING POINTS

- 'To love one's country does not really imply that one must hate other countries or adopt a slogan – "My country right or wrong".'
(Dr Samuel Johnson)

- 'All mankind are my brethren; to do good is my religion.'
(Thomas Paine)

- 'War is obsolete because of chemical and nuclear weapons.' Do you agree? Look at the picture.

159

The atomic bomb explodes on Hiroshima

On the morning of 6 August 1945, a B29 bomber called the 'Enola Gay' dropped an atomic bomb on the Japanese city of Hiroshima. This is an account of what happened. It was written by Lord Philip Noel-Baker, Nobel Peace Prize Winner in 1959, and was read to the House of Lords in 1980.

'Hiroshima, 6th August 1945, 8.15 a.m., a perfect summer morning: gentle breezes, sunshine, a blue sky. A blue sky is for happiness in Japan. The streets are full of people: people going to work, people going to shop, children going to school. The air raid siren sounds but no one runs, no one goes to shelter. There is only a single aircraft in this enemy raid. The aircraft steers a course across the city. Above the centre, something falls – 20 seconds, 30 seconds, 40 . . . and then there is a sudden searing flash of blinding light, hotter and brighter than a thousand suns. Those who are looking at it have their eyes burned in their sockets. They will never look on men or things again.

In the streets below, other people are walking – a lady as beautiful as she is elegant, a businessman in charge of great affairs, a clever student, the leader of his class, a little girl, laughing as she runs. They are in the street walking. Then suddenly they are not there. The beautiful lady, the businessman, the brilliant student, the scampering little girl have vanished, utterly consumed in the furnace of the flash. There are no ashes, even on the pavement – nothing but their black shadows on the stones.

Then comes the blast. For two kilometres in all directions, every building, every structure is levelled to the ground. The people inside are buried in the ruins of their homes. Lorries, vans, men and women, babies, prams, are picked up and hurled like bullets, hundreds of feet through the air. The blast piles its victims in huge heaps on the corners of the street – heaps seven, eight layers of corpses deep. I know a man and woman who looked for seven days for their little grandson. When they found him, one layer below the top, he was still breathing, but all the doctors in Hiroshima could not save his life.

*Then the fireball touches the earth.
Conflagrations spring up in every quarter.
Swept by tornado winds they rush together in a
single firestorm. Tens of thousands more,
trapped by walls of flame that leap higher than
the highest tower in the city, swiftly, or in
longer agony, are burned to death. And
everything goes black. The mushroom cloud
rises to the very vault of heaven. It carries with
it many thousand tons.*

*The first atom bomb weighed two
kilogrammes – less than five pounds. It was a
little larger than a cricket ball. It killed 140,000
people on that August day. In 1978, more than
2,000 died in Hiroshima from its long-delayed
effects. Today there are very many young
adults who were only embryos in their mothers'
wombs when the bomb exploded. They have
leukaemia and shortly they will die. Babies are
being born with tiny, deformed heads – and
that first atom bomb was what the science editor
of **The Times** called a "nuclear midget".'*

('Protest and Survive', Green Party pamphlet)

There are many different theories as to why the
Allies dropped the bomb on Hiroshima and then
three days later dropped one on Nagasaki. One
thing is sure – the world has never been the same
since.

THOUGHTS FOR THE FUTURE

*'Those that survive a nuclear war would envy
the dead.'*

(Nikita Khrushchev)

*'On the assumption that a Third World War
must escalate to nuclear destruction, I can tell
you that the Fourth World War will be fought
with bows and arrows.'*

(Albert Einstein)

*'Before the bomb, man had to live with the idea
of his death as an individual; from now
onwards, mankind has to live with his idea of
death as a species.'*

(Arthur Koestler)

*'We are now faced with the fact that tomorrow
is today. There is such a thing as being too late.
Over the bleached bones of numerous
civilizations are written the pathetic words "too
late". It we do not act, we shall surely be
dragged down the dark corridors of time
reserved for those who possess power without
compassion, might without morality and
strength without sight.'*

(Martin Luther King)

*'Our future on this planet, exposed as it is to
nuclear annihilation, depends on one single
factor; humanity must make a moral about-
face.'*

(Pope John Paul II)

FOR YOUR FOLDERS

▶ Write a telegram (maximum 30 words) dated 6 August reminding a friend about 'Hiroshima Day'.

▶ Using the listed quotes write a letter to a magazine about the dangers of nuclear war.

▶ Write a paragraph answering the question 'Can a nuclear war ever be called a Just War?' (See unit 77.)

▶ It has been argued that the atomic bombings of Hiroshima and Nagasaki brought the war to a quick end and therefore saved the lives of countless people. In the light of this, do you think that the devastation of Hiroshima and Nagasaki was morally justifiable?

FOR DISCUSSION

▶ 'The use of nuclear weapons can *never* be justified.'
▶ 'The world now stands on the brink of the final abyss.'

(Lord Louis Mountbatten)

'BRITAIN MUST GET RID OF HER NUCLEAR WEAPONS'

1. The use or threatened use of nuclear weapons which can destroy everyone ('genocide') and everything ('omnicide') is simply wrong. Morally we must give them up.

2. One fleet of British submarines can deliver 192 warheads, each 15 times the size of the Hiroshima bomb, and a drop in the ocean compared with the superpowers' fire power. It is 'overkill'.

3. Because we have got nuclear weapons (including American ones) we are a 'number one target'.

4. The Americans have never had a major war on their own ground – they are using Britain and Western Europe as their aircraft carrier.

5. The Americans have the ability to have a 'first strike'. This makes things more unstable.

6. In the nuclear exchange Britain would be totally obliterated. The government has not even given us 'civil defence'. *But* there is no defence against nuclear weapons.

7. The siting of American missiles in Britain increases the danger. Some other NATO countries have restricted such siting.

8. The Russians do not want war – 36% of all casualties in the Second World War were Russians, and they were on our side.

9. Multilateral disarmament – everyone disarming step-by-step – must start somewhere.

10. The huge cost of our weapons ought be be spent on the real needs of people in this country and in the Third World.

11. There are safer alternative defence policies. Will nuclear weapons keep the peace for the future?

12. A nuclear weapon could be launched by mistake through a computer error.

(Adapted from the Campaign for Nuclear Disarmament's arguments)

'BRITAIN MUST KEEP HER NUCLEAR WEAPONS'

1. We must think clearly about nuclear weapons and not just abhor (hate) them.

2. Nuclear weapons cannot be 'dis-invented' – they are a fact of life and we need to find a way of making sure of that they are not used to destroy or blackmail.

3. Conventional and chemical weapons must also be covered by action to make the world a safer place.

4. Non-nuclear war between East and West is the most likely road to nuclear war.

5. The USSR is so much stronger than Western Europe that our nuclear weapons are necessary.

6. Preventing a nuclear war through deterrence (putting the other side off) is the only safe course.

7. We must show our strength to the Soviet Union.

8. The USSR must realize that it could never win a war – if we keep nuclear weapons then it knows it can never win.

9. We must be committed to NATO (North Atlantic Treaty Organization countries in Western Europe). A weaker NATO would make the world more unstable and war more likely.

10. Nuclear weapons have kept the peace in Europe since 1945 – deterrence has seen to that.

11. We must try and get arms agreements and work slowly for disarmament. It might take a long time.

12. The Peace Movement in the USSR has been suppressed which shows us the sort of potential enemy we have.

(Adapted from the British government's official statement in 1981)

THE ROMAN CATHOLIC CHURCH – THE SECOND VATICAN COUNCIL (1962–5)

A considerable amount of the Council's time was
spend discussing peace in a document called *Pacem
in Terris*, 1965:

> 'Though the monstrous power of modern
> weapons acts as a deterrent, it is to be feared
> that the mere continuance of nuclear tests,
> undertaken with war in mind, will have fatal
> consequences for life on earth. Justice, right
> reason and humanity therefore, urgently
> demand that the arms race should cease; that
> the stockpiles that exist in various countries
> should be reduced equally and simultaneously
> by the parties concerned . . . nuclear weapons
> should be banned.'

The Council also said: 'The world is a volcano which
can erupt at any time.' Some bishops called for a ban
on all war (conventional weapons also), saying 'Any
act of war is a crime against God'.

THE CHURCH AND THE BOMB

In 1982 members of the Anglican Church published
a report *The Church and the Bomb*. It stated that
Britain should get rid of the nuclear weapons it
had. Nuclear weapons could not be looked at in
isolation from the whole problem of war, nuclear
disarmament was the most urgent task in the
process of ridding the world of any kind of a war.
In 1983 the General Synod of the Church of
England rejected the idea of unilateral
disarmament but agreed that the Church must
make every effort to help world peace and that
Britain's weapons should be purely defensive and
never be used first.

'All war and violence is morally wrong. Violence only breeds violence and it may solve a problem in the short run but not in the long run. Nothing good can come out of something evil. We have been fighting wars for thousands of years – millions of people have died. The world today is not better off, in fact we live in the most dangerous period of history ever. Pacifism has never been tried – to be unarmed means taking risks but to be armed is no less risky.

In some parts of the world people use violence to defeat injustice and evil. But if oppressors are overthrown by violence, then they themselves must be oppressed to maintain that victory. To fight is not the way to win true freedom. There are other non-violent ways.

Sometimes pacifism is hard – people are often placed in terrifying situations when violence seems the only answer. However, a commitment to pacifism means a commitment to overcome these violent impulses and look for a better way.'

(a pacifist)

Dietrich Bonhoeffer

THE CASE OF DIETRICH BONHOEFFER

Dietrich Bonhoeffer was a German theologian who lived during the rise to power of Hitler's Nazi Party in Germany. The Nazis abandoned all human rights and began persecuting the Jews and other groups of people. Thousands of people 'disappeared' and 1941 saw the first mass deportation of Jews to concentration camps like Auschwitz and Belsen.

Bonhoeffer believed that Christians had a moral duty to speak out against evil and tyranny and he helped form the 'Confessing Church' which opposed the Nazis. He also became involved in helping groups of Jews escape the death camps. In 1940 he joined the Abwehr, an organization that secretly worked to overthrow the Nazi state and assassinate Hitler. Bonhoeffer believed that the true test of faith was helping the oppressed. To him the state did not represent justice so he decided to become a conspirator. Although he was a pacifist he was prepared to sacrifice not only himself, but also his principles to rid the world of the evils of Nazism. He was prepared to take part in an assassination of Hitler, and perhaps his henchmen as well, because he saw it as being the only course of action open to him. As a Christian, he would let God pass judgement. He himself did not see the murder of Hitler as being 'good', but rather as a practical necessity.

However, in 1942 Bonhoeffer was arrested and spent the rest of his life in prison. In 1945 he was executed for treason. Today in Canterbury Cathedral there is a chapel dedicated to martyrs of the twentieth century – 'Dietrich Bonhoeffer' is the one German name there. At his service the Bishop of Chichester said Bonhoeffer's death 'represents the resistance of the believing soul against injustice and cruelty'.

FOR YOUR FOLDERS

▶ 'You shall treat him as he intended to
treat his fellow . . . life for life, eye for
eye, tooth for tooth . . .

(Deuteronomy 19: 19–21)

'You have learned that they were told:
eye for eye, tooth for tooth. But what I
tell you is this. Do not set yourself
against the man who wrongs you. If
someone slaps you on the right cheek
turn and offer him your left.'

(Jesus, in *Matthew 5: 38–40*)

Copy down the quote that applies to
pacifism.

▶ Make a list of some of the main beliefs
of a pacifist.

▶ Although Dietrich Bonhoeffer was a
pacifist, he was willing to take part in a
conspiracy to assassinate Hitler. How
did he try to justify this? Try to explain
his decision in not more than 50 words.

▶ Can you think of circumstances when a
pacifist might find it impossible *not* to
resort to violence?

◇

FOR DISCUSSION

▶ 'If the world could live for a few generations
without war, war would come to seem as
absurd as duelling has come to seem to us.'

(Bertrand Russell)

PERSONAL RESEARCH

▶ Go to the library, or hire the film *Gandhi,* and
find out as much as you can about Gandhi's
life.

'An eye for an eye and we shall soon all be blind.'

(Mahatma Gandhi)

82 NON-VIOLENT DIRECT ACTION

'To resist without bitterness
To be cursed and not reply
To be beaten and not hit back.'

(Martin Luther King, explaining the
Non-Violent Creed)

Violence is:

- wasteful – it uproots and destroys precious human lives; it consumes huge quantitites of wealth and intelligence
- indiscriminate – it is hard to limit its deadly effects to those who are 'guilty'
- sexist – historically it has been done by men
- unjust – often the innocent suffer
- destructive – it encourages brutality and treats people like objects
- a vicious circle – it sets off a spiral of violence.

Non-violence is:

- humane – it avoids killing other human beings
- creative – it cuts across barriers of sex, race, and class
- a civilian method – everyone can become involved
- voluntary – people are not forced into a miliary type machine
- radical – it can change society for the better
- dignifying – it depends on people standing up for themselves and refusing to let go of their argument however much they are provoked.

'In non-violence the masses have a weapon which enables a child, a woman, or even a decrepit old man to resist the mightiest government successfully.'

(Gandhi)

Non-violent direct action is designed to:

1 raise people's knowledge about an issue,
2 put pressure on people in authority to change things,
3 object to some injustice in society,
4 ultimately change the situation.

GROUP WORK

▶ 'Council to close youth club!'
In groups of four to five plan a campaign to prevent this (e.g. letter writing, demonstrations, petitions, publicity, meetings and posters).

FOR YOUR FOLDERS

▶ Look at the five pictures.
1 Match them up after reading the following explanations:
'Gandhi begins salt match to protest against salt tax.'
'Cruise missile convoy meets direct action.'
'Greenpeace spray a seal pup with harmless dye to spoil the value of the pelt.'
'Protest against nuclear tests in Moscow.'
'Dr Martin Luther King jailed after entering a "whites only" restaurant.'
2 Write a few sentences about each picture explaining exactly what the protestors want to change.
3 Can you think of other forms of non-violent protest?
4 List some of the things that you would like to see changed in the world today, giving your reasons.
5 Write an article on 'Violence and non-violence'.

FOR DISCUSSION

▶ 'Let every person be subject to the governing authorities. For there is no authority except from God . . . therefore he who resists the authorities resists what God has appointed.' (St Paul, in *Romans 13: 1–2*)

'Do not think that I have come to bring peace on earth; I have not come to bring peace, but a sword.' (Jesus, in *Matthew 10: 34*)

What do you think St Paul and Jesus mean?

▶ 'In a democracy it is wrong to try and change things by non-violent direct action.'

▶ 'In an undemocratic state it would be a waste of time trying to change things non-violently.'

FOOD

Food helps us grow and develop. Without the right amount of food or the right kinds of food, people suffer from malnutrition which can result in death. At least one in eight of the world's population does not have enough to eat.

> 'When you have gathered your grapes once, do not go back over the vines a second time . . . they are for the foreigners, orphans, and widows.'
>
> *(Deuteronomy 24: 19)*

WATER

Clean, safe drinking water is essential for life. It is vital for the control of diseases such as diarrhoea, typhoid and cholera. Eighty per cent of all sickness in the Third World is caused by unsafe drinking water.

> 'I am the alpha and the omega, the beginning and the end. A draught from the water-springs of life will be my free gift to the thirsty.'
>
> *(John 21: 6)*

HOUSING

Housing provides us with protection and security. Today, as more and more people in Third World countries are drawn to cities in search of work and a better life, overcrowding becomes a major problem.

> 'Everyone has the right to a standard of living adequate for their health and well being, including housing.'
>
> (UN Declaration of Human Rights)

HEALTH

Health care is important to 'ensure a state of complete physical, mental and social well-being and not merely the absence of disease or illness' (World Health Organization). This requires adequate food, access to safe drinking water, sewage disposal, health education and health care. Yet 70% of the population in Third World countries do not have access to any organized health care and 90% of child deaths are linked with malnutrition, contagious diseases and unhygienic living conditions.

> 'Heal the sick, raise the dead, cleanse those who have leprosy, drive out demons. Freely you have received, freely give.'
>
> *(Matthew 10: 10–8)*

Scavenging for grain in Ethiopia

EDUCATION

We take education for granted but in the poorest countries of the world only four adults in 10 can read and write and less than one in four children go to secondary school.

> *'Every child shall be given an education which will promote his general culture and enable him on a basis of equal opportunity to develop his abilities, his individual judgement and his sense of moral and social responsibility and to become a useful member of society.'*
>
> (UN Declaration of the Rights of the Child)

WORK

Work can give us identity, security and the means to meet many of our other basic needs. Today world unemployment stands at around 500 million – 300 million of these are in the Third World.

> *'All of us should eat and drink and enjoy what we have worked for. It is God's gift.'*
>
> (*Ecclesiastes 3: 13*)

FOR YOUR FOLDERS

▶ Write an account of some of the basic needs of the Third World.

▶ After reading the biblical passages and the UN Declarations, write a letter, using some quotes, to a friend explaining what responsibilities Christians and non-Christians have towards countries in the Third World.

▶ Write a sentence about the two photos. Why might the children in the photo on the left have a different view of basic needs from the people in the photo below?

FOR DISCUSSION

▶ 'More people have died as a consequence of hunger in the past six years than have been killed in all the wars, revolutions and murders in the past 150 years.'

(The Hunger Project, 1987)

Inside a western supermarket

We live in a world of mass communication. This means that we in the so-called 'developed world' are very much aware of the horrifying existence of world hunger – the near-starvation conditions in which a large area of the world exists at the present. However, we often make assumptions about the causes of, and real facts about, world hunger, which are not founded in reality. This section is designed not only to prompt you to think more deeply about the problems of world hunger, but also to dispel some of the myths that have been created around the subject.

THERE ARE TOO MANY PEOPLE.

Overpopulation – *the* bogey word. But which countries are overpopulated? Those which consume the most, like the USA with 6% of the world's population consuming over 25% of the world's resources? Or one of the poor countries?

THERE'S NOT ENOUGH FOOD.

There is. The world is producing enough food to feed every man, woman and child. Enough grain is produced to provide every person with more than 3,000 calories a day.

And that's without counting beans, fruit and vegetables. But that's not all! Enough food is available in those very countries where so many people are forced to go hungry.

WHERE COULD THEY GROW ALL THE FOOD?

Only 44% of the world's arable land is cultivated. The remainder is used in a variety of ways. Amongst them:

Grazing In Brazil huge cattle ranches take up some of the most fertile soil in the whole country, yet 60% of Brazilians are malnourished.

Fallow Much land in Latin America is not used at all. Over 80% of large estates is left uncultivated.

Export crops Increasingly land is being turned over to grow crops for export.

NOTHING GROWS WITH ALL THOSE DROUGHTS.

In the Third World, droughts and floods are not the unexpected disasters we always imagine. In the Sahel region of Africa drought is practically part of the environmental cycle, and in Asia everyone knows that floods will occur regularly.

The problem is that the poor have very little resistance to these shocks. And they are getting poorer and poorer.

Yes, we buy food and other crops from Third World countries. And increasingly this trade between rich and poor has encouraged more of these crops to be grown. As a result land use is changing. Land on which families lived and grew food is now growing these crops – for export. And production of them is rising. Now poor countries compete with each other in selling the same crops to the highest bidder. Prices are forced down. And it's the poorest who lose out. In the late 1960s, Tanzania had to sell 66 bags of coffee to buy a 16 tonne truck. Over 10 years later 123 bags had to be sold to buy that same truck.

Food aid is a lifesaver in many situations, but in other cases it does more harm than good. Only 10% of all food aid sent is used for vital emergency relief. The remainder is distributed in a variety of ways, but rarely gets out to the poor.

And the biggest myth of all –

It's got everything to do with us. The problem starts here, not 'out there'. The connections between us and world hunger are numerous. Take the debt crisis for one – relegated to those pages of newspapers we barely read. It is, we are told, a problem for our high street banks. The poor of the Third World don't read about it either, they live it.

Third World countries struggling under huge foreign debt are forced to take drastic measures to make regular payments. Less money is spent where it's needed most – on the poor. Health services are cut to the bone, and infant mortality and disease are rising. And they must earn more foreign exchange by boosting their exports. More and more land is used to grow export crops. This can be at the expense of the food needs of the poor.

(Adapted from Oxfam's *Seven Myths about World Hunger* leaflet)

FOR YOUR FOLDERS

▶ Write out the seven myths about world poverty. Now try to write down what Oxfam says about each of these myths.

▶ Design a poster 'Myths about world poverty'.

▶ Imagine you work for Oxfam. Try to work out a programme for educating people about world poverty. Describe how you would go about it, e.g. advertizing, TV, local radio, teenage magazines, schools and cinemas.

▶ Do you think that 'it's got nothing to do with us'?

TALKING POINTS

• 35,000 people die every day as a result of hunger.

It is widely accepted that the buying and selling of armaments – the 'Arms Trade' – is one of the major causes of world poverty. In this section you will find some facts about the arms trade. Many of these facts raise questions about the kind of world in which we want to live. It is up to you to look at the facts, to try and understand the reasons behind them and to decide for yourselves whether the arms trade is a good or bad thing.

'Two-thirds by value of all international arms transfers now go to the countries of the Third World.'

(Stockholm International Peace Research Institute)

Why do so many Third World countries acquire modern weapons?

- fear of attack
- to bolster national image
- they are involved in conflict with their neighbours
- they have territorial ambitions
- they want to crush internal unrest (often caused by poverty)
- governments are under pressure by their military to get up-to-date weapons.

underdevelopment

possibility of internal unrest

arms purchased

The poverty and arms vicious circle

SOME FIGURES

'One and a half per cent of one year's world military expenditure would pay for all the farm equipment needed to increase food production and approach self-sufficiency in food-deficit low-income countries by 1990.'

(The Brandt Report)

'Military spending, on average, has consumed $US 25 million (in current prices) every hour for the last 30 years.'

(Clyde Sanger: Safe and Sound)

The money required to provide adequate food, water, education, health and housing for everyone in the world has been estimated at $17 billion a year. It is a huge sum of money . . . about as much as the world spends on arms every two weeks.

(*New Internationalist*, January 1980)

BREAD NOT BOMBS

'World spending on military equipment alone in 1986 was a staggering £634 billion. This global arms trade fuels wars, distorts economic and social priorities, and wastes urgently needed resources.

- *A modern tank costs around £1 million. This is enough to provide storage for 100,000 tonnes of rice, or classrooms for 30,000 children.*
- *A British Aerospace Hawk fighter aircraft costs around £6 million. For the cost of one of these, one and a half million people could be provided with clean safe water.*
- *More is spent on arms in one day than the world's 2,000 million poorest people have to live on in a year.*

Britain, as the world's fourth largest arms exporter, is heavily involved in this scandalous waste. Over three-quarters of all British military exports go to Third World countries.'

(CAAT)

THINGS TO DO

BLESSED ARE THE VICTORS, FOR THEY SHALL BE CALLED PEACEMAKERS...

But Jesus Said...

▶ To find out . . . Look up the following: *Matthew 5: 9; Matthew 5: 44; Matthew 26: 52.*

▶ Find out what 'CAAT' stands for and the type of work it does (see the Important Addresses section on page 190).

FOR YOUR FOLDERS

▶ Design a poster about the link between the arms trade and world poverty.

▶ Why do you think it is important that people become aware of the link between the arms trade and world poverty?

! How do you think Christians and Humanists should respond to the arms trade?

FOR DISCUSSION

▶ Read the following comments and discuss them.

'The British Government funds over 1,000,000 people through its military spending. Yet there are only 85,000 doctors and 600,000 teachers in Britain in spite of pressing social needs. In the Third World there is now one doctor for every 1,290 people, but one soldier for every 250 people.'

(Campaign against the Arms Trade)

'I have no moral scruples about selling arms to any country with which the Government says I can deal. The Government decides the markets, I help satisfy them. I lose no sleep whatever on the moral issue. The morality lies with the user.'

(Ronald Ellis, Head of US Defence Sales Organization 1976–81)

Between 1978 and 1980 leading political figures from all over the world worked together to see if the enormous problems of world poverty could be solved.

In his introduction to the report the group's chairman, Willy Brandt, wrote:

'Our report is based on what appears to be the simplest common interest. Mankind wants to survive and, one might even add, has the moral obligation to survive. This not only raises the traditional questions of peace and war, but also how to overcome world hunger, mass misery and alarming differences between the living conditions of rich and poor . . . we want to emphasize our belief that the two decades ahead of us may be fateful for mankind.'

(*North – South: A Programme for Survival, Pan, 1980*)

Here is a brief summary of ten of the main suggestions made in the report.

- There must be an emergency programme to help the world's poorest countries in the poverty belts of Africa and Asia.
- There must be an end to mass hunger and malnutrition. This means more funds for developing agriculture, irrigation, agricultural research, crop storage, fertilizers and other aids.
- There should be more international support for family planning programmes.
- Funds and skills being put into arms production must be channelled into peaceful needs.
- World trade should be encouraging the developing countries to have more part in the processing, marketing and distribution of their own commodities, to increase their earnings.
- Flows of overseas aid should be enlarged.
- There should be an international 'income tax' to spread wealth from the rich to the poor.
- The international monetary system must be reformed, giving greater participation and advantage to poorer countries.
- A new World Development Fund could act to distribute resources raised on a universal and automatic basis.
- More attention must be paid to educating public opinion, and the young especially, about the importance of international cooperation.

KEY IDEA

North–South is a very simple way of showing how the world divides into rich and poor countries. The rich **North** includes North America, Europe, USSR, Japan, Australia, and New Zealand. The poor **South** includes most of Asia, Africa, and Latin America.

Countries of the **South** are sometimes called the **Third World** or **developing** countries because they are generally poorer.

'Even in the United States this division (between rich and poor) can be seen. In countries like India, Portugal and Brazil, the contrast between the wealth of the few privileged individuals and the dire poverty of the masses is a crying scandal. And looking at the world as a collection of nation states, we see the same problem repeated; there are a few wealthy nations which dominate the world economically and therefore politically, and a mass of smaller and poor nations.'

(Julius Nyerere, president of Tanzania)

NORTH–SOUTH

North:
- ¼ of the world's people
- ⅘ of the world's income
- a person can expect to live on average more than 70 years
- most people are educated at least through secondary school
- over 90% of the world's manufacturing industry
- about 96% of world's spending on research and development, nearly all the world's registered patents
- dominates most of the international economic system and institutions of trade, money and finance.

South:
- ¾ of the world's people
- ⅕ of the world's income
- a person can expect to live, on average, to about 50 years
- ⅕ or more of the people suffer from hunger and malnutrition
- ½ of the people still have little chance of formal education

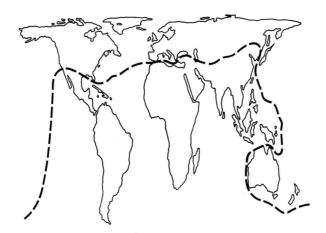

The North-South divide

FOR YOUR FOLDERS

▶ *The Rich Man and Lazarus*

'There was a rich man who was dressed in purple and fine linen and lived in luxury every day. At his gate was laid a beggar named Lazarus, covered with sores and longing to eat what fell from the rich man's table. Even the dogs came and licked his sores.

   The time came when the beggar died and the angels carried him to Abraham's side. The rich man also died and was buried. In hell, where he was in torment, he looked up and saw Abraham far away, with Lazarus by his side. So he called to him, "Father Abraham, have pity on me and send Lazarus to dip the tip of his finger in water and cool my tongue, because I am in agony in this fire."

   But Abraham replied, "Son, remember that in your lifetime you received your good things, while Lazarus received bad things, but now he is comforted here and you are in agony. And besides all this, between us and you a great chasm has been fixed, so that those who want to go from here to you cannot, nor can anyone cross over from there to us."

   He answered, "Then I beg you, father, send Lazarus to my father's house, for I have five brothers. Let him warn them, so that they will not also come to this place of torment."

   Abraham replied, "They have Moses and the Prophets; let them listen to them."

   "No, father Abraham," he said, "but if someone from the dead goes to them, they will repent."

He said to him, "If they do not listen to Moses and the Prophets, they will not be convinced even if someone rises from the dead." '

(Luke 16: 19–31)

1 Try to describe in your own words how these this parable of Jesus can be applied to the North–South divide.
2 Does it help us to understand anything about the North's responsibility to the South?
3 Now read it again and try to explain how it could apply to the following quote from the Brandt report.

   'The world is a unity and we must begin to act as members of it who depend on each other.'

▶ Read Julius Nyerere's speech. Try to list:
   (a) Some groups of rich and poor people in Britain;
   (b) Some rich countries (North) and some poor countries (South).

! ▶ Write an article of about 100 words outlining what you consider to be the most important parts of the Brandt report.

▶ 'We must learn to live together as brothers or perish together as fools.' How can this quote by Martin Luther King be applied to the findings of the Brandt report?

Some people believe that the greatest threat to the survival of the human race is overpopulation. It is predicted that by the year 2000 there will be about 6 billion people on earth. The so-called 'population explosion' creates some huge problems for humankind. Millions of people in the poor world suffer from malnutrition. Many cities are desperately overcrowded with millions of people living in terrible conditions. Millions of people throughout the world, including Britain, are homeless. Our skies, seas, wildlife and rivers have become poisoned by masses of human waste. The world's energy resources are dwindling. Our societies seem to be getting more violent and people more despairing and frightened of the future.

The population explosion also raises many moral problems. Should governments impose compulsory birth control? Why do we in the rich world consume so many of the earth's resources, yet by comparison have less of a population problem? How are poverty and population related? Should we only be allowed to have a certain number of children? Should people be sterilized? Or should we follow the teaching in *Genesis (1: 28)* which states 'Be fruitful and increase'?

It is very important to think about the relationship between overpopulation and world poverty and this section shows different aspects of this relationship. Very simply, the relationship between poverty and overpopulation can be shown like this:

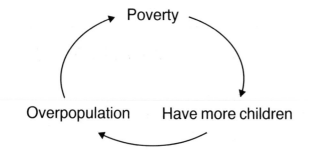

The vicious population circle

Also linked to the problem of overpopulation is the issue of birth control. The Roman Catholic Church, however, teaches that most types of birth control are unnatural (see section on contraception) and that sexual intercourse is primarily for the purpose of reproduction. Many Catholic priests working in the developing world believe that the levels of poverty cannot be reduced by birth control programmes but only by a massive redistribution of wealth.

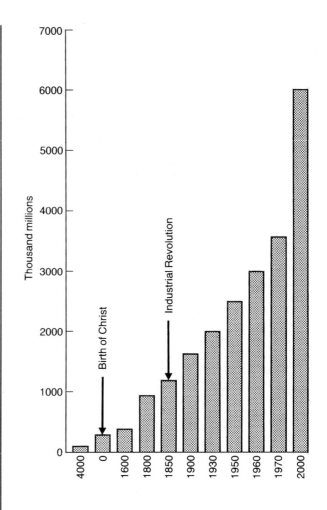

1 *The growth of the world's population: 4000 BC to 2000 AD*

Other teachings

> 'Human beings must enter into absolute control of their birth-rate. Without this they will lose their birthright.'
>
> (Church of England report)

> 'It is the moral obligation of the developed nations to provide birth control techniques to the developing portions of the globe.'
>
> (Humanist Manifesto)

Many experts believe that there is easily enough food in the world to feed everyone adequately. They also believe that people could use new techniques to feed an even more densely populated world (e.g. better farming methods, use of foods in the sea). However, at the moment the richest 10% of the world consume 90% of the world's resources.

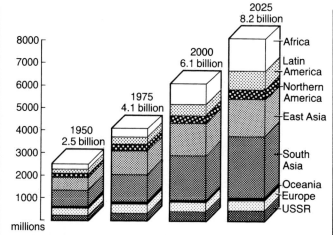

2 *The growth and distribution of the world's population: 1950 to 2025*

FACTS

- There are 3 births every 2 seconds,
  90 births every minute,
  200,000 birth each day.
  World population doubles every 35 years.

- In 1935, there were 56 cities with more than a million inhabitants.
  In 1960, there were 100.
  In 2000, there will probably be about 500.

'Why do people in poor countries go on having more children than they can afford? The answer is: they don't, usually. Where you are living without any of the aids to living which we have, where each day is a long grind of many hard jobs, just to survive, children are needed as helpers. When there is only a 50-50 chance of your children living past five years, you've got to plan to have many children. And when there is no social security, old age pension or health insurance, who else is going to look after you if not your children? If we looked at life from the point of view of those who say 'my children are my only wealth' would we still be so keen on birth control?

'We in the West are afraid that more people in the poor world will mean lower standards for us, or will cause trouble for us through revolution. We do not necessarily know best. The poor of the world will start using contraceptive devices very quickly indeed, just as soon as real development and a fairer deal in life lets them do so.'

(*How the Other Half Dies* by Susan George)

TALKING POINTS

- All Christians and Humanists would agree that the present distribution of the world's resources leads to poverty. However, they might disagree on the use or non-use of birth control. What do you think?

- 'The only way to deal with the population explosion is by compulsory birth control.'

- 'We can't expect the poor to limit their family sizes when they need children to help support their family. The real problem is not overpopulation but poverty and the unequal redistribution of wealth. This must be tackled first.'

FOR YOUR FOLDERS

▸ Equation:
  poverty ⟷ overpopulation.
  How does Susan George explain this equation?

▸ Write a paragraph about figure 1.

▸ Figure 2 shows a breakdown of world population. List the areas where the 'population explosion' is occurring.

❗▸ List some of the problems you think this will cause, especially in the developing South.

Mother Teresa believes that 'what people need even more than food and shelter is to be wanted'.

In 1973 a British TV producer reluctantly allowed a programme about the work of a 63-year-old Yugoslavian missionary working in the slums of Calcutta to be shown. To his amazement the programme caused so much interest that it had to be repeated and £20,000 was received by viewers to be sent to Calcutta. The missionary was Mother Teresa.

Twenty-seven years previously, a young nun felt that God was calling her to go among the very poor in the slums of Calcutta. She decided to spend her entire life in total service to the poor, living with them and sharing their lives. In 1948 she opened a school for the children of the slums and began teaching them. When she found dying children in filthy alleys and even in dustbins she began feeding and looking after them.

In 1952 when she found a desperately sick woman half eaten by rats she demanded that the authorities give her a building. She was given a disused temple and she began taking dying people off the streets. The temple became known as the 'Home for the Dying'. Soon she got help from other nuns and she formed the Congregation of Sisters.

She once said:

'What these people need even more than food and shelter is to be wanted. They understand that even if they only have a few hours left to live they are loved. However dirty and sick they are, someone cares for them.'

In 1957 Mother Teresa extended her work to many lepers in the city. The congregation grew in strength and spread to other towns in India and throughout the world. Mother Teresa has been an inspiration to millions and she is a remarkable woman. She gets up every day at 4 am and works tirelessly among the dying and destitute of Calcutta. She says:

'In Christ we can do all things. That's why our work is possible. Without him we can do nothing. We feel that what we are doing is just a drop in the ocean. I think that the ocean would be less because of that missing drop.'

Mother Teresa has been awarded many prizes in recognition for her work and in 1979 she was awarded the Nobel Peace Prize. She often travels all over the world with her sisters, helping victims of disasters, working around the clock, feeding and clothing an endless stream of people who have lost everything. She has brought love, peace, comfort, hope and purpose to tens of thousands of people. This is her prayer:

'Make us worthy, Lord, to serve our fellow men throughout the world who live and die poor and hungry. Give them, through our hands, this day their daily bread. By our understanding love, give them peace and joy.'

THINGS TO DO

calling
Home for the Dying
Congregation of Sisters
leprosy
Nobel Peace Prize
Mother Teresa's prayer

Look at these words and phrases. How do they fit into the story of Mother Teresa? What does each one mean?

100,000 people sleep on the streets of Calcutta every night

FOR YOUR FOLDERS

▶ Write down examples of how Mother Teresa's Christian faith has influenced her life.

! ▶ Why do think that the life of Mother Teresa has inspired many Christians in the world today?

THINGS TO DO

▶ Tape the interview. It will need an introduction. Assume that your listeners know nothing about world poverty.

GROUP WORK

▶ In pairs discuss what questions you would ask Mother Teresa if you were given the privilege of meeting her. Conduct an interview with one of you playing Mother Teresa.

FOR DISCUSSION

▶ 'When the rich young ruler asked Jesus what must he do to have eternal life, Jesus replied: "Sell what you possess and give it to the poor" *(Matthew 19)*. Christianity demands that people should follow Mother Teresa's example.'

> **Charity** – definitions include: 'kindness; the feeling of generosity; Christian love for God and humankind; help to the poor; a society or organization that gives help to the poor.'

There are some 136,000 registered charities in Britain. Generally charities try to:

- relieve hardship and suffering
- relieve poverty
- educate the public about the disadvantaged
- benefit the community
- advance religious and moral ideas.

CHARITIES – FILLING A GAP OR BAND AID?

Many people argue that charities are a good thing.
- they can 'fill a gap' by providing a service which otherwise might not exist
- they give the public a choice as to how to spend money
- they can provide new ideas for care and treatment
- they can complement, supplement and extend the influence of the welfare state
- they can help people develop talents which they might not otherwise use
- they enable people to help each other
- they help make society more caring.

However, some people believe that charities are not such a good thing. They argue that:

- in a welfare state there should be no need of charities
- charities make people less responsible. They may decide not to help others because they think it is the job of a charity to help them
- charities make governments 'pass the buck'. They might not give money or resources to an area because they know a charity will cover it
- people might tend to over rely on charity help and perhaps become less independent
- the existence of charities makes it difficult to see the real problems of society – charities act as a 'band aid on a gaping wound'.

TALKING POINTS

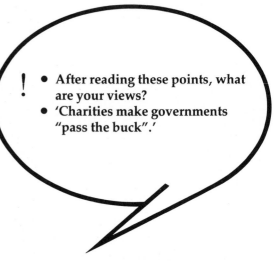

!
- After reading these points, what are your views?
- 'Charities make governments "pass the buck".'

THE HISTORY OF CHARITIES

In the middle ages the Church became involved with helping the needy, seeing this as a moral duty. Despite this, by 1600 Britain was full of desperately poor people. In 1601, the Elizabethan Poor Law was introduced, making each parish responsible for its poor. Around that time the first 'Workhouses' appeared. There were centres where the poor could go and, in return for working, receive basic shelter and food. However, with the Industrial Revolution in the nineteenth century a new wave of poverty occurred.

Many people blamed the poor themselves for their condition. (Some even thought it was 'God's will', and did little to help them.) Then in the second half of the 19th century many social reformers, often Christians, began setting up homes and orphanages for the poor. The work of charities had begun. In 1905 the Liberal Party introduced a wide range of social services which later developed into the Welfare State. The state became responsible for helping the poor and providing resources to improve the condition of the poor.

Royal National **Lifeboat** Institution

Compassion's hidden costs: How much went on overheads at leading charities

CHARITY ALL FIGURES 1984/5	VOLUNTARY DONATIONS	TOTAL INCOME 1984/5 (INC GRANTS, RENTS SALES ETC)	ADMIN	FUND-RAISING	p in £ SPENT ON ADMIN & FUND-RAISING	CHARITABLE SPENDING 1984/5	p in £ OF 84/5 INCOME SPENT ON CHARITY
	£000	£000	£000	£000	%	£000	%
BAND AID	56,500	69,000	39	—	0.056	23,000	33.33
OXFAM	49,533	57,430	1,060	3,936	8.70	42,177	73.44
SAVE THE CHILDREN	35,469	42,673	719	2,448	7.42	22,974	53.84
NATIONAL TRUST	27,701	70,219	4,783	2,932	10.99	48,649	69.28
RNLI	23,548	25,823	1,105	1,175	8.83	17,283	66.93
CANCER RESEARCH CAMPAIGN	20,051	22,321	318	1,436	7.86	21,359	95.69
SALVATION ARMY	19,743	43,264	2,589	581	7.33	26,725	61.77
DR BARNADO'S	19,473	42,753	992	4,328	12.44	26,143	61.15
IMPERIAL CANCER RESEARCH FUND	18,169	32,433	341	1,371	5.28	21,837	67.33
NSPCC	17,564	21,182	584	1,301	8.90	10,135	47.85
CHRISTIAN AID	17,374	20,357	567	1,505	10.18	17,394	85.44
SPASTICS SOCIETY	12,463	32,645	744	3,380	12.63	24,738	75.78
RNIB	11,304	23,125	278	1,799	8.98	15,947	68.96
TEAR FUND	11,019	11,790	977	—	8.29	8,175	69.34
ACTION AID	10,500	11,317	1,012	1,248	19.99	7,665	67.73
CATHOLIC FUND FOR OVERSEAS DEVELOPMENT	10,115	11,882	132	307	3.69	11,298	95.08
BRITISH HEART FOUNDATION	9,595	12,316	351	1,253	12.73	6,997	56.81
GUIDE DOGS FOR THE BLIND	9,533	14,943	439	1,579	13.50	5,796	38.79
RSPCA	9,301	12,347	1,070	454	12.34	8,157	66.06
MARIE CURIE (CANCER RESEARCH)	9,164	9,656	176	674	8.80	8,337	86.34
WAR ON WANT	9,133	9,231	70	89	1.72	6,620	71.71

Charity begins with good housekeeping

'The latest figures for Britain's top 21 charities show that, for every £1 donated to them, less than 9½p went on overheads.

Out in front is Bob Geldof's Band Aid, which kept its expenses down to a remarkable 0.056 per cent, or just under 7p for every £100 donated. Because of its unique achievement, Band Aid was not included in the calculation to avoid distortion.

During the year 1984/85, the public gave £360 million to the 21 main charities, boosting their total income to nearly £600 million.

Although the figures were helped by the massive public reponse to famine relief, they help rebuff critics who claim that many charities are over-manned and the staff over-paid.

The most popular charities were Band Aid, Oxfam and Save the Children, closely followed by the National Trust, the Royal National Lifeboat Institution and the Cancer Research Campaign.

According to our survey, based on figures supplied by the Charities Aid Foundation, only eight of the charities spent more than 10p of every pound of income on administration and fund-raising.

The income of overseas aid agencies was boosted dramatically by African famine relief appeals, which prompted more people than ever before to reach into their pockets. As the amount of money given to the charities increases, the proportion spent on staff and administration will fall.'

(*Observer*, 9 November 1986)

FOR YOUR FOLDERS

▶ How much did the public give the main charities in 1984/5?

! ▶ By studying the arguments for and against charities, write an essay expressing your own views. Give reasons.

▶ Which four organizations spent less on overheads?

▶ List the charities which are:
(a) concerned with overseas aid,
(b) concerned with causes in Britain.

! ▶ 'Charity begins at home' . . . write a paragraph on your thoughts.

▶ 'Very little actually gets to the disadvantaged.' How do the figures in the *Observer* disprove this?

Bob Geldof, one-time drifter, labourer, teacher, journalist, actor, abattoir assistant and lead singer with the 'Boomtown Rats', switched on his television to watch the 6 O'Clock News one evening in November 1984. What he saw was Michael Buerk's news report from Ethiopia. The report was to change Bob's life and literally 'rock the world'. He describes what he saw:

Bob Geldof in Africa

> *'The news report was of famine in Ethiopia. From the first seconds it was clear that this was a horror on a monumental scale. The pictures were of people who were so shrunken by starvation that they looked like beings from another planet.*
>
> *The images played and replayed in my mind. What could I do? I could send some money. Of course I could send some money. But that didn't seem enough. Did not the sheer scale of the whole thing call for something more? Buerk had used the word 'biblical'. A famine of biblical proportions. There was something terrible about the idea that 2,000 years after Christ, in a world of modern technology something like this could be allowed to happen as if the ability of mankind to influence and control the environment had not altered one jot?'*

Within weeks Geldof somehow managed to get all the biggest names in the British pop music industry together. They released 'Do They Know it's Christmas?', written by Geldof and Midge Ure of Ultravox. The musicians and artists went under the name 'Band Aid'.

Everyone worked on the record for no charge and all the proceeds went to the 'Ethiopian Appeal'. The record raised £8 million, shot to the top of the charts and became the biggest selling records ever in Britain.

Although 'Band Aid' raised £8 million, there were 22 million people starving to death in the Horn of Africa because of a massive drought. The world had been warned years ago that this could happen but very little had been done to prevent this tragedy. The point of the record had not just been to raise money but to make the world aware of what was happening. Geldof found that he had touched the consciences of millions of young people. He knew that 'Band Aid' was not the end of his work but rather the beginning. He went to America and helped to organize a similar project there. Michael Jackson and Lionel Ritchie wrote 'We Are the World' which had enormous success in the States. On Christmas Eve 1984, Geldof went to Ethiopia himself to see the tragedy and to decide how to spend the 'Band Aid' money.

GELDOF IN ETHIOPIA

'I must try and show you this.

There is a child I think maybe its's four months old. The doctor says 'No it's two years old.' It squats on baked mud a tattered dusty piece of cotton hangs from one shoulder onto its distended stomach. Its face is huge. A two year old face on a four month body.

The eyes are moons of dust and flies caked by tears so big they don't dry until they reach the navel.

The child stares. Between its legs flows a constant stream of diarrhoea. The immediate earth around its legs is damp with it.

I am watching a child die. In total silence and surrounded by its family it eventually begins to shit out its own stomach.

I am tired with grief and despair and a consuming rage for humanity.

He dies soon. He just dies. Big deal. A jumble of bones and dry skin, wet eyes, flies and shit.

In that place where humans have abandoned, humanity thrives. A handful of grain each. There is no water to boil and make a sort of porridge . . . or there is water but there is no fuel with which to boil it, . . . or there is no fuel or water, just the grain.

You eat it. It is like consuming razor blades. It tears the walls of the stomach away, then passes through you, taking your innards with it, unconsumed and useless.

Eight weeks ago the EEC spent 265 million pounds in destroying 2 million tons of vegetables and fruit.

The shame, the shame, the shame.'

(Geldof's introduction to the Live Aid programme)

On his return Geldof began to organize 'Live Aid', a sort of global juke-box – live music beamed to nearly all the countries of the world. It was a brilliant success. An estimated 500 million people watched it on television and it raised millions of pounds worldwide for the famine victims in Africa.

FOR YOUR FOLDERS

▶ Write an article on 'Geldof and Africa'. In it include:
(a) Michael Buerk's news report,
(b) what Geldof saw in Africa,
(c) his reponse.

▶ Write down what you think these two quotes mean:

'If we don't do something, then we are participants in a vast human crime.'
(Geldof)

'Nobody made a greater mistake than he who did nothing because he could only do a little.' (Edmund Burke)

▶ Band Aid was concerned with long-term aid as well as short-term aid. After studying the last few units, what do you think are the main causes of world poverty? What do you think can be done to help the problem?

Christian Aid
THE CHURCHES IN ACTION WITH THE WORLD'S POOR
PO Box No 1 London SW9 8BH

One of the largest Christian organizations concerned with trying to help improve people's lives in the 'South' is Christian Aid. In this section we will be looking at some of the ways in which it tries to create a fairer world.

'Christian Aid is seen by many as a way of showing concern for those in need by putting love into action – it enables you to love your neighbour – even when he or she is in another part of the world!

It is our task to confront men with their neighbours everywhere – and especially with those who suffer. In every human being in need we are confronted by Jesus Christ himself . . . if we deny him in this encounter we cannot belong to him.'

(Christian Aid's Policy Statement)

What does Christian Aid do?
Christian Aid raises over £10 million a year to help the neediest people in poor countries to help themselves. In times of war and disaster it also pays for relief and rehabilitation. Here at home it helps make people aware of world poverty and its causes.

Is it part of the churches?
Yes. Christian Aid is a Division of the British Council of Churches. There are other Christian and denominational agencies but Christian Aid is the only inter-denominational one appointed and controlled by the churches.

Is it only for Christians?
No. It serves people of all religions and of none, combating distress without seeking anything in return. Therefore the general public as well as church people support its work. Nearly half its income comes from the annual Christian Aid Week each May; the rest from special church collections, individual donations, covenants and legacies.

How is the money spent?
In areas of poverty Christian Aid finances agricultural training, equipment, livestock, seeds and irrigation, trade training, child welfare, instruction in nutrition and hygiene, community health schemes, education in community development and citizenship and – in a few countries – legal aid to the very poor when their human rights are threatened.

In areas of emergency it finances medical supplies, food and blankets, transport and building materials, all for use by local relief organizations and their workers. Refugees and displaced people are sheltered, fed and helped to resettle.

How much is spent on aid?
Out of every £1 donated 85p is spent on aid projects. Only 15p is needed for fund raising, advertizing, staff, offices, and other essential overheads.

(Christian Aid leaflet)

Christian Aid Week is for the World's Poor

The poor in Africa, Asia and Latin America have inherited poverty, just as Britain's present generation has inherited an industrialized economy which finances our social security, education and health benefits.

Poor nations cannot earn enough capital to finance their own development because countries like ours control most of the world's trade and consume 80% of the world's resources.

But local communities and families can escape from the poverty trap when given modest financial help. That's what Christian Aid does. Please will you make a contribution?

(Christian Aid leaflet)

This is a rubbish tip in Tondo, a slum area of Manila, capital of the Philippines. Tondo is a shanty town, the largest squatter settlement in Asia. 100,000 people live in shacks built on stilts on land reclaimed from the sea. The government had promised that the people could buy the land and keep their homes, but now the authorities want to 'beautify' the area and to move the residents to the outskirts where there are few amenities or jobs.

With unemployment in the area at 40% to 50%, the tip provides a means of survival through scavenging. It not only contains household refuse from the affluent suburbs, but also industrial waste, particularly glass, from nearby factories.

KEY IDEA

1 Christians believe in a God of love and justice revealed by Jesus Christ and who calls them to make a response of love: Christian Aid sets out to put such love into action.

2 Christians believe that Jesus Christ is to be found in our neighbours in need: Christian Aid is one way of responding to Christ's presence in our neighbours.

3 Christians believe that the coming of God's Kingdom is hindered by evil which must be fought in whatever form it appears: Christian Aid is involved in this task of building God's Kingdom.

FOR YOUR FOLDERS

▶ Christian Aid has helped the people of Tondo since 1978.
  ● What problems face the people?
  ● What do you think Christian Aid has done to help solve these problems?
  ● What do you think their main priorities were?

▶ What are the main teachings and beliefs of Christianity that inspire people who work for Christian Aid?

▶ Design a leaflet explaining the work of Christian Aid?

THINGS TO DO

Look at the five photos on the opposite page. Now match the pictures up with these five statements.

1 At the present rate of destruction, the oldest and richest expression of life on this planet – the rainforests – will be gone within 40 years. The effects of the death of the rainforests could be as severe as those of nuclear war.
2 Smoke belches out from industrial factory pollution.
3 Because of bad farming practices the amount of desert land in the world is increasing.
4 Oil leaks destroy the sea's wild life.
5 Every day millions of litres of industrial and domestic wastes and sludges are dumped into the seas.

FOR YOUR FOLDERS

▶ Write your own short descriptions of the photos shown.

▶ Design a poster on 'Polluting planet earth'.

▶ Using some of the Talking Points, write an article entitled 'Humankind's responsibility to planet earth'.

! ▶ Look at the five photos. How would you suggest humans clean up planet earth?

TALKING POINTS

● 'You appointed him ruler over everything you made; you placed him over all creation.'

(Psalms 8: 3–6)

● 'We must free ourselves from needless pollution and waste.'

(Humanist Manifesto 14)

● ' "Because of what you have done", the Lord said, "the ground will be under a curse." '

(Genesis 3: 17)

● 'The dignity of nature as creation needs to be bound up with our responsibility for the preservation of life.'

(World Council of Churches)

● 'It is tragic that our technological mastery is greater than our wisdom about ourselves.'

(Pope John Paul II)

● 'Nature is the art of God.'

(Teilhard de Chardin)

The earth's natural resources are here for us to use. We need food, water, energy, air, medicine, warmth, shelter and minerals. If we use these resources carefully and sensibly they will last, indefinitely. If we misuse them we will not last, definitely.

SOME DAMAGING FACTS

In the time it will take you to read these facts, 100 acres of tropical rainforest will be destroyed.

- 10% of flowering plants in the world are threatened with extinction
- it is estimated that by the year 2050 all supplies of oil and natural gas will be used up
- 'acid rain' from Britain and France is damaging forests and poisoning lakes in Scandinavia
- 15 million acres of land turns to desert every year
- one affluent European consumes the same amount of the world's resources as 40 poor North Africans.

TO DEBATE

▶ Use the arguments below to organize a class debate on nuclear power.

A CONTROVERSIAL ENERGY ISSUE

In the 1950s many scientists believed that nuclear energy would solve all the world's energy problems. Phrases like 'Atoms for Peace' were coined. However, public fears about nuclear energy have led to anti-nuclear groups campaigning for the abandoning of nuclear power programmes. The issue is a very complicated one but basically the arguments run like this:

Stone age? No thanks — Atoms for energy!

NUCLEAR POWER? No thanks

	FOR	AGAINST
Is nuclear energy necessary?	*Yes:* We need a replacement for fuels like coal and oil.	*No:* There are replacements – solar, wind, wave and tidal energy. Also, we can all conserve more energy.
Is nuclear energy safe?	*Yes:* No fatal accident has yet occurred in a nuclear power station. More coal miners are killed every year than nuclear power workers.	*No:* Accidents have occurred. What about Three Mile Island, Windscale and, worst of all, Chernobyl? Their effects are hard to measure.
Is nuclear energy clean?	*Yes:* Nuclear waste can be safely and securely disposed of.	*No:* Radioactive waste is being dumped in the sea. It remains active for hundreds of years.
Is nuclear energy cheap?	*Yes:* Nuclear power is cheaper than other forms of power from oil or coal.	*No:* A nuclear power station costs £1,000 million to build. This money could be put to alternative energy sources.

WHAT CHRISTIANS BELIEVE:

- God created the earth.
- God made humans his stewards and managers.
- God's world has been spoiled and exploited by greed, ignorance and selfishness.
- Humans should wisely protect what has been given to them.
- Humans should work with nature, not against it.
- Nature should never be exploited.

WHAT HUMANISTS BELIEVE:

- Humans are totally responsible for what we are or will become.
- The planet Earth is one single ecosystem.
- We have a moral duty to cultivate and conserve nature.
- We are part of nature. In conserving nature, we conserve humankind.

- Exploitation of natural resources for purely economic gain must end.
- The world must be 'freed from needless pollution and waste'.

FOR DISCUSSION

▶ 'The earth has enough for every man's need, but not for every man's greed.'

(Mahatma Gandhi)

PARADISE LOST

PLANET EARTH is 4,600,000,000 years old. If we condense this inconceivable time-span into an understandable concept, we can liken Earth to a person of 46 years of age. Nothing is known about the first 7 years of this person's life, and whilst only scattered information exists about the middle span, we know that only at the age of 42 did the Earth begin to flower. Dinosaurs and the great reptiles did not appear until one year ago, when the planet was 45. Mammals arrived only eight months ago and in the middle of last week, man-like apes evolved into ape-like men and at the weekend, the last ice age enveloped the Earth.

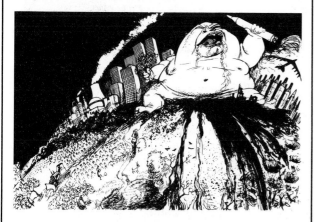

Modern Man has been around for 4 hours. During the last hour, Man discovered agriculture. The industrial revolution began a minute ago. During those sixty seconds of biological time, modern Man has made a rubbish tip of a paradise. He has multiplied his numbers to plague proportions, caused the extinction of 500 species of animals, ransacked the planet for fuels and now stands, like a brutish infant, gloating over his meteoric rise to ascendency, on the brink of a war to end all wars and of effectively destroying this oasis of life in the solar system.

(Greenpeace)

FOR YOUR FOLDERS

▶ Find out what the following words mean: ecology, ecosystem, food chain.

▶ Write a paragraph on each of the following:
   (a) a Christian view of nature,
   (b) a Humanist view of nature.

▶ Design a poster based on some of the ideas in the Greenpeace poster 'Paradise lost'.

▶ Write an article entitled 'Progress with conservation'.

! ▶ What do you think are the most important ecological problems that humankind must try and solve in the very near future?

SOME IMPORTANT ADDRESSES

Age Concern
Bernard Sunley House
60 Pitcairn Road
Mitcham
Surrey CR4 3LL

Amnesty International
5 Roberts Place
(off Bowling Green Lane)
London EC1R 0EJ

Animal Aid
7 Castle Street
Tonbridge
Kent TN9 1BH

Anti-Apartheid Movement
13 Mandela Street
London NW1 0DW

Band Aid
PO Box 4TX
London W1A 4TX

British Humanist Association
13 Prince of Wales Terrace
London W8 5PG

**EXIT (Voluntary Euthanasia
  Society)**
13 Prince of Wales Terrace
London W8 3PG

Family Planning Clinics
27/35 Mortimer Street
London W1N 7RJ

Campaign Against the Arms Trade
11 Goodwin Street
London N4 3HO

**Campaign for Homosexual
  Equality**
274 Upper Street
London N1 2VA

**Campaign for Nuclear
  Disarmament**
22/24 Underwood Street
London N1 7JG

Catholic Truth Society
38/40 Eccleston Square
London SW1P 1LT

- As many of these organizations
  rely on donations, etc., always
  send a stamped, self-addressed
  envelope.
- For local organizations use your
  telephone directory or reference
  library.

**Central American Information
  Service**
1 Amwell Street
London EC1R 1UL

**Church of England Board of
  Social Responsibility**
Church House
Dean's Yard
London SW1P 2NZ

Christian Aid
PO Box 1
London SW9 8BH

Commission for Racial Equality
10/12 Allington House
London SW1E 5EH

Compassion in World Farming
20 Lavant Street
Petersfield
Hampshire GU32 3EW

Gay Christian Movement
BM 6914
London WC1N 3XX

**Gingerbread Association for
  One Parent Families**
35 Wellington Street
London WC2 7BN

Greenpeace
36 Graham Street
London N1 2XJ

Health Education Authority
78 New Oxford Street
London WC1A 1AH

Help the Aged
St James Walk
London EC1R 0BE

**Institute for the Study of Drug
  Dependency (ISDD)**
1/4 Hatton Place
Hatton Gardens
London EC1N 8ND

LIFE Organization
118–120 Warwick Street
Royal Leamington Spa
CV32 4QY

Radical Alternatives to Prison
BMC Box 4842
London WC1N 3XX

**Royal Association for Disability
  and Rehabilitation**
25 Mortimer Street
London W1N 8AD

Marriage Guidance Council
76A New Cavendish Street
London W1M 7LB

**Martin Luther King Memorial
  Trust**
1/3 Hildreth Street
London SW12 9RQ

National Abortion Campaign
70 Great Queen Street
London WC2

Oxfam
274 Banbury Road
Oxford OX2 7D2

Pax Christi
St Francis of Assisi Centre
Pottery Lane
London W11 4NQ

Peace Pledge Union
Dick Sheppard House
6 Endsleigh Street
London WC1H 0DX

**Quakers (The Religious Order of
  Friends)**
Friends House
Euston Road
London NW1 2BJ

World Wildlife Fund
11/13 Ockford Road
Godalming
Surrey GU7 1QU

RSPCA
The Causeway
Horsham
Sussex RH12 1HG

Samaritans
17 Uxbridge Road
Slough SL1 1SN

United Nations Association
3 Whitehall Court
London SW1A 2EL

INDEX